THE DRAMAS OF
HEINRICH VON KLEIST

The University of North Carolina Press, Chapel Hill, N. C.; The Baker and Taylor Company, New York; Oxford University Press, London; Maruzen-Kabushiki-Kaisha, Tokyo; Edward Evans & Sons, Ltd., Shanghai.

THE DRAMAS OF HEINRICH VON KLEIST

A Biographical and Critical Study

BY

JOHN C. BLANKENAGEL

CHAPEL HILL
THE UNIVERSITY OF NORTH CAROLINA PRESS
1931

COPYRIGHT, 1931, BY
THE UNIVERSITY OF NORTH CAROLINA PRESS

TO MY MOTHER
LUCIE BECKER BLANKENAGEL
AND TO THE MEMORY OF
MY FATHER
AUGUST BLANKENAGEL

FOREWORD

IN THE history of German drama Heinrich von Kleist occupies a place which is just as singular as it is significant. Although influenced somewhat by earlier dramatists, he stands out ruggedly as an original, independent, individualistic writer, aligned closely with no school or movement. Unappreciated during his lifetime, he was virtually forgotten for a decade after his death. Of his eight dramas, but two—*Der zerbrochene Krug* and *Das Käthchen von Heilbronn*—were staged publicly prior to Kleist's death;* his last two dramas were not even published until ten years after his demise. A novel, to which he refers in a letter, has been lost altogether and not even its title is known. Various periods and events in Kleist's life are shrouded in mystery; they have given rise to vague suppositions, to fanciful interpretations, and even to slanderous conjectures. Distorted presentations of his character and malodorous analyses of his works have been based on untenable hypotheses. He has been pronounced an idealist and a depraved degenerate, a rationalist and an emotionalist, a man of firm, ethical purpose and a vacillating, morbid sensualist. His life was one of hardships and struggles with poverty and adverse circumstances; disappointments, loneliness, failure, and disillusionment were his lot. When various goals of his had successively crumbled into dust, he ended his life voluntarily. Fate dealt unkindly with Kleist during his lifetime; fate likewise

*See p. 262.

has dealt niggardly with those interested in the facts of his career. Only a meager volume of his letters has been preserved from destruction; yet enough of them remain to make the careful reader grieve at their dearth, for, few as they are, they illumine Kleist's personality, ideals, ambitions, fortitude, and courageous struggles.

Kleist's claim to literary fame is based primarily on his dramas, although his narrative prose is a noteworthy contribution to the literary form known as the *Novelle* which has been so highly developed in Germany. His tales, however, have never shared the popularity enjoyed by those of Keller, Heyse, and Storm. They are so compact as to give the impression of being abridged, dialogue is reduced to a minimum, events and even conversations are narrated to a large extent in indirect discourse, and the sentence structure is involved and formidable. Although there are occasional lyric passages in some of his dramas, Kleist is not a lyrist; in fact, the lyric is the one of the three fundamental literary forms which he used least as a vehicle for expression. Kleist also was a journalist of ability, although financially his journalistic ventures were decidedly unsuccessful.

Kleist's dramas have not achieved popular success and very likely never will. The number of stage adaptations of some of them, notably of *Der zerbrochene Krug* and *Das Käthchen von Heilbronn* would seem to indicate that in the minds of producers they are characterized by a certain refractoriness. Interested primarily in his characters, in their frame of mind and in their emotions, Kleist was inclined to neglect the practical requirements of the theater and the technical devices that would win plaudits on the stage. He was concerned more with unusual situations, often of a most trying kind, in which his characters are severely

FOREWORD   xi

and sorely tested. Neither as a narrator nor as a dramatist was Kleist possessed of qualities which make for wide popular success. Yet in the wake of the World War the attention of Germany was directed to Kleist as a patriotic poet who had vainly endeavored to arouse and unify his countrymen against Napoleonic aggression and domination, and who had called upon them to sacrifice everything—life and property—for the sacred ideal of liberty. In this recent period of national crisis, interest was focused upon his patriotic writings, upon *Die Hermannsschlacht*, which enjoins absolute surrender of the individual to the cause of national freedom, and upon *Prinz Friedrich von Homburg*, which sets forth noble, enlightened conceptions of the sacrificial relationship of the individual to the state.

Kleist's dramas are not easy to translate into other languages. *Der zerbrochene Krug, Das Käthchen von Heilbronn*, and *Prinz Friedrich von Homburg* have been rendered into French; *Die Familie Schroffenstein, Das Käthchen von Heilbronn*, and *Prinz Friedrich von Homburg* have appeared in English translation. Moreover, Kleist has not been given the prominence in French and English studies to which he is entitled. Although there are large volumes in English on other German dramatists such as Lessing, Goethe, Schiller, Grillparzer, Hebbel, Hauptmann, and Sudermann, one on Kleist's dramas has failed to appear. Nevertheless, he is indisputably one of the outstanding dramatists of Germany, a country which has made a notable contribution to the world's dramatic literature. Consequently this attempt has been made to acquaint the American student of drama with works of a German dramatist of power and individuality. In order to give those who do not read German a more nearly adequate approach to Kleist's dramas, somewhat detailed synopses of the plots have been given. This has seemed all the more advisable because English translations of but two of Kleist's dramas can be purchased, and even these are available only in volumes containing works by other authors.

Herewith the author takes pleasure in acknowledging his gratitude to Professor Lawrence Marsden Price for permission to quote from the translation of *Die Familie Schroffenstein* which appeared in Volume XXVII of *Poet Lore* for 1916; to Professors Carl F. Schreiber and Frederick E. Pierce and to the Oxford University Press for authorization to quote from Professor Pierce's translation of *Das Käthchen von Heilbronn* as published in 1927 in *Fiction and Fantasy of German Romance;* to the late Professor Kuno Francke for permission to quote from Mr. Hermann Hagedorn's translation of *Prinz Friedrich von Homburg* as included in Volume IV of *The German Classics*, which were published under the general editorship of Professor Francke.

The manuscript for this study was completed in the fall of 1929.

JOHN C. BLANKENAGEL.

Delaware, Ohio

TABLE OF CONTENTS

Foreword	ix
I. Heinrich von Kleist: A Biographical Sketch	1
II. Die Familie Schroffenstein	33
III. Robert Guiskard	56
IV. Amphitryon	81
V. Der zerbrochene Krug	103
VI. Penthesilea	127
VII. Das Kæthchen von Heilbronn	152
VIII. Die Hermannsschlacht	175
IX. Prinz Friedrich von Homburg	201
X. Conclusion	234
Bibliography and Notes	247

THE DRAMAS OF
HEINRICH VON KLEIST

CHAPTER ONE

HEINRICH VON KLEIST: A BIOGRAPHICAL SKETCH

BERND Heinrich Wilhelm von Kleist, known to literary history as Heinrich von Kleist, was born on October 18, 1777, in Frankfurt an der Oder. On his father's side he was a descendant of an old Prussian family of nobles which for many generations had distinguished itself in military service. In addition to numerous generals and other high officers, it had produced one well known poet, Christian Ewald von Kleist (1715-1759), the author of *Der Frühling*, a descriptive poem inspired by *The Seasons* of James Thomson. In the eyes of his family, whose cultural horizon was none too wide, such authorship was doubtless more laudable because it added literary fame to military achievement; literary renown at the sacrifice of a career as a Prussian officer was a very different matter, as Heinrich von Kleist was destined to realize. The early death of his parents left him almost without intimate family contacts, for of his brothers and sisters, only his older step-sister, Ulrike, remained his devoted, self-sacrificing friend upon whom he could count in need. After an early education at home and in Berlin under the guidance of private tutors, he entered the Prussian army as a mere boy. His military service extended over a period of seven years, from 1792 to 1799, and included participation in the campaign against the French as well as subsequent garrison service at Potsdam. Letters and other sources shed but meager light on his life until the year 1799. The peace-loving young lieutenant of the Prussian guards soon tired of the routine of garrison life, chafed under its restrictions, and longed for freedom to devote himself to study. Interested in music, literature, science, and mathematics, he felt out of place in an environment in which intellectual interests found neither understanding nor encouragement. In 1798 Kleist wrote a letter to the king applying for dismissal from the army, but he did not present his request until a year later. Upon his discharge in the spring of 1799, he was free to continue the studies which he had already begun while in garrison at Potsdam.

The most significant of Kleist's earlier letters is one written to Christian Ernst Martini, his former tutor, just prior to his discharge. In addition to setting forth his reasons for preferring the life of a civilian, it reveals his intellectual interests and outlines the educational program he has in mind. He writes that his resolve to present his resignation grows out of the desire to be happy. Happiness he regards as the pleasing contemplation of the moral beauty of one's being. Contentment with self, the consciousness of good deeds, and the maintenance of dignity in the face of a thousand trials and temptations are the foundations on which he fancies he can base a profound happiness which will not be undermined by the outward vicissitudes of life. The desire to be happy, he continues, is the foremost of our wishes and is voiced by every nerve and every fibre of our being; it accompanies us throughout the entire span of life, from the first remote thoughts of childhood to the grave. This longing for happiness, he concludes, cannot be an idle dream, for God would not have implanted an inextinguishable desire in the human soul without granting the possibility of its fulfillment. Significantly enough, the young Kleist considers happiness as quite independent of material things, as rooted in intellectual pursuits, quiet contemplation, ethical idealism and the perfection of one's higher self. Such aims, he tells Martini, have compelled him to withdraw from military life with its moral and intellectual enslavement which robbed him of all human freedom and degraded him by exacting compliance with orders regardless of their merits. Even in the Potsdam garrison Kleist was a student rather than a soldier. Although he received some instruction from a tutor, most of his studies at the time were carried on without the guidance of others. This accounts for a lack of perspective, which was, however, offset to some extent by the thoroughness with which he mastered the particular tasks he undertook.

The young man's resolve to abandon the career of an officer in the Prussian army found no favor in the eyes of his family. They insisted that his studies be of a practical turn so as to provide him with bread and butter; they questioned the feasibility of his plans, argued that he was too old to study, emphasized the slenderness of his inherited resources, dwelt upon the difficulty of earning a living, and pointed out how definitely assured his livelihood would be in the army. But all these objections were unavailing, for with characteristic determination and singleness of purpose he set out to acquire a cultural education which he could not obtain as a soldier. Disdainful of material things, he gave no thought to the practical use which he might subsequently make of his knowledge. He declared that this resolve was born of his heart and approved by his reason; with optimism and confidence he therefore counted upon a happy, successful future.

This same youthful assurance is in evidence elsewhere in Kleist's early letters. To his sister, Ulrike, he writes in May, 1799, about the possibility of definitely guiding one's own destiny. Inspired with self-confidence by the firmness with which he has persisted in his projects in the face of family opposition, he assumes that a definite plan of life will enable man to triumph over the caprices of fate. He sees thousands of people who are impelled by vague inclinations and whose actions are determined by momentary circumstance. Such people follow vague impulses wherever they happen to lead: to happiness which is enjoyed but feebly and to misfortune whose force seems doubled. The ardent young disciple of a life of reason considers such slavish yielding to the whims of tyrannical fate quite unworthy of a free, thinking human being. For such an emancipated individual, says he after the manner of Lessing, does not remain where chance happens to cast him, or, if he does remain, he has reasons for doing so and makes a deliberate choice of the better. A thinking being feels that he can rise above fate and that it is indeed possible to guide his destiny by determining what constitutes the greatest happiness, by formulating a plan of life looking toward its achievement, and by systematically striving for its attainment with all his faculties. Early formulation of a plan of this kind, says he, would have prevented the irretrievable loss of seven precious years which he spent as a soldier. The results of such a careful project are consistency, coherence, and unity. It is incomprehensible to him how man can live without carefully planning his life; to him it means security in the present and quiet confidence in the future. Without a definite goal, man is constantly buffeted back and forth by vague desires; his actions run counter to duty; he is a prey to chance and a mere puppet in the hands of fate. This unworthy state, he asserts, is so contemptible and would make him so miserable that death would be highly preferable to it. And accordingly Kleist urges subordination to the dictates of reason as a guarantee of poise and tranquillity in a world which a capricious fate seeks to dominate. He declares that he and Ulrike must hold the laws of reason all the more sacred because of their lack of veneration for conventional demands and religious ceremonial.

Kleist's ardent desire for happiness, which sounds the keynote of his early letters, is heightened by a haunting fear of the vicissitudes of human existence— a fear from which he never entirely freed himself. His formulation of a plan of life and his early worship of reason as a stabilizing force are acts of defense against uncertainty and misfortune, of whose menace he was ever aware. It is as if he already had a premonition of the dangers lurking in his tendency to extremes and as if he were quite conscious of the necessity of warding off impending disasters. For in an early essay he recommends choosing a middle path between the highest outward happiness and unhappiness. Although admitting his antipathy for middle roads of all kinds—an antipathy arising from a violent misleading impulse of his nature—he has the feeling that time and experience will convince him that they are the best. He sees another weighty reason for desiring moderate happiness in the fact that such happiness is actually most frequent; consequently moderation in desire is less likely to lead to disappointment. It is of ominous significance to read such counsels in view of Kleist's subsequent cursing of a heart that is incapable of moderation. For the present, however, he states his conviction that Homer was right in considering that man happiest to whom the gods on Mount Olympus meted out equal portions of fortune and misfortune.

From the time of his discharge from military service until August, 1800, Kleist devoted himself zealously to his studies at the University of Frankfurt an der Oder. His very zeal seems to have been a handicap in that it impelled him to plunge headlong into a subject without first acquiring a thorough knowledge of fundamentals. In his eagerness to make up for lost time, he overburdened himself with work, thereby beginning the undermining of his nervous system.

During a brief respite from his studies he writes to Ulrike that it is a real joy to abandon himself to his emotions after having been busied so long with serious abstractions, which stimulate the mind but afford the poor heart nothing. As a result of constant demonstrations and deductions his heart almost forgets how to feel, and yet happiness dwells only in the heart and not in the understanding. For happiness, he adds, cannot be demonstrated like a mathematical theorem but must be felt. Consequently, like Serlo in Goethe's *Wilhelm Meisters Lehrjahre*, he recommends that the heart be stimulated daily by the enjoyment of pleasures such as reading a good poem, seeing a beautiful painting, listening to a sweet song, or engaging in kindly converse with a friend. A sense of loneliness—and Kleist's life was a lonely one—has already come over him. For the time being, this loneliness grows out of the consciousness of being different from those about him. He observes that a thousand bonds, such as similar opinions, interests, desires, hopes, and prospects unite men. Yet his interests are so foreign to other people that they find no appreciative hearing. Unsuccessful efforts at arousing

A BIOGRAPHICAL SKETCH

the interest of others in matters so vital to him have led him to lock his ideals away in the deepest recesses of his heart. Imbued with a cultural ideal, this impractical student finds no understanding in the prosaic, superficial circles of Frankfurt. He becomes increasingly ill at ease in society and is uncomfortably conscious of seeming dull and lacking in ideas. From this sense of inferiority he reacts violently by delving deeper and deeper into his studies and by limiting his circle of associations.

One person, however, seemed to listen to the sensitive, high-strung youth with sympathetic understanding and to have an appreciation for his interests. This was Wilhelmine von Zenge, the daughter of a major general living in Kleist's native city. The prompt engagement of the two, their relations during their betrothal, and their ultimate rupture present a strange chapter in Kleist's life. Their correspondence sheds significant light on his conception of woman and her relation to man as later portrayed in his dramas. In one of his first letters to Wilhelmine he requests her to open her heart to him with the utmost frankness and confidence, for love is to ennoble them and to be the source of greatest happiness. It is but natural that his profound desire to widen his intellectual horizon in the pursuit of knowledge and truth should affect his attitude toward his fiancée. And in fact he considers it a sacred duty to direct her cultural development in accordance with his ideal. On one occasion he writes to Wilhelmine that just as he has to shape a mouthpiece for his clarinet to fit it to his lips so he prefers to mould the character and attainments of a girl rather than to find her already highly accomplished and close to perfection. Of necessity, this viewpoint introduces a somewhat pedantic element into his relations with her, and all the more so because he is convinced of the natural superiority of man to woman. He formulates formidable questions to stimulate his fiancée's powers of observation, comparison, and judgment, suggests outlines with logical sequences for written replies which he corrects, composes long didactic letters, recommends books for her to read, directs her attention to Rousseau, and endeavors to awaken an appreciation of nature in her. Extant letters contain few indications of a passionate, erotic element in their courtship, but doubtless Wilhelmine, who later married another man, destroyed epistles containing such passages. That Kleist's expectations and demands on his fiancée must have become very trying even to one endowed with her meek patience is evident from his letters. Yet all this pedantry assumes slightly different proportions when one realizes that Kleist considered wifehood, motherhood, and the education of her children the sacred duty of woman, for which she must prepare herself with the greatest of care. He admired the generous impulses, spontaneity, kindness, unselfishness, devotion, and tenderness which seemed much more strongly manifest in woman than in man. But in recognition of such qualities he demanded a greater sacrifice than Wilhelmine was able to make. Carried away by a Rousseauesque ideal, he planned to settle on a small estate in Switzerland and to live a life of rural simplicity far removed from the artificialities of urban surroundings. When she wrote her objections to this plan, pointed to her filial desire to be near her parents, pleaded physical frailties as standing in the way of so strenuous a peasant life, and claimed that exposure to sunshine gave her headaches, he was sorely disappointed but postponed a reply for two weeks so that his answer might be less impatient. Some months later, in May, 1802, he acknowledged a letter received in January, in which she had once more urged him to return home and had set forth the reasons why she could not follow him to Switzerland. Although he had meanwhile given up his project of settling there, he had become absorbed in his literary endeavors, was impoverished, had no prospects for the future, and had become estranged from her. With cruel candor he told her that a letter recently received from her awakened memories which fortunately had become somewhat obscured and he requested her to write to him no more. Wilhelmine's subsequent marriage to a professor of philosophy undoubtedly led to a calmer, less trying existence than life with a man of Kleist's harassed, violent, high-strung, sensitive nature would have been. Although he had close friendships with other women, his relationships with them represent less significant incidents in his development.

During his engagement to Wilhelmine, Kleist's life was marked by a number of important events. The desire to marry had brought home to him his responsibility toward his fiancée and the practical necessity of qualifying himself to earn a living. Moreover, his relatives were constantly urging him to seek a civil appointment, but he rebelled against the enslavement of such service which would deprive him of freedom of thought and action, rob him of opportunity for study, and be scarcely preferable to the tyranny of military life. He repeatedly cursed the prejudices and conventions of the titled aristocracy, which seemed determined to force him into a strait-jacket existence. Unable to make a choice, he one day decided to lock himself up in his room until he had made up his mind as to his future. But a week elapsed, and he left his self-imposed solitary confinement as undecided as before. In August, 1800, he journeyed to Berlin, presumably to give his ever insistent family the impression that he was about to apply for a position in government service. But instead of remaining in Berlin, he soon set out on a journey to Würzburg, concerning the purpose of which he wrote in exalted, mystifying terms. Various conjectures have been made as to the unknown aim or aims of this journey, but the most satisfactory one seems to be that he underwent treatment intended to cure him of real or fancied impotence. Apart from the psychological effect of this quest and his beneficial association with a most unselfish, sympathetic friend named Ludwig Brockes, Kleist profited signally by coming to an intimate appreciation of nature on his travels by coach through regions of rare charm and beauty. His letters written on this journey abound in picturesque descriptions of landscapes and in vivid personifications of nature. It is as if his eyes had suddenly been opened to things which had hitherto been hidden from view. Instead of dealing in cold, rationalistic abstractions, his letters now are full of feeling, of joy in life, enthusiasm, and hope. Labored logic, stilted pedantry, and carefully thought out comparisons give way to poetic spontaneity. Although certain passages in his letters seem somewhat studied, others are born of inspiration; this is particularly true of those in which animate nature is portrayed with a strong sense of the dramatic. Brockes' influence on his young friend during this trip was a profound one. Although temperamental, emotional, passionate, and unstable, Kleist had developed a genuine admiration for a rationalistic view of life as a safeguard against the instability of his nature. Brockes' severe criticism of dry rationalistic scholarship was all the more impressive because of his remarkable freedom from general prejudice and his wide range of knowledge. Kleist was therefore greatly impressed by his friend's insistence that deeds are better than knowledge and by his characterization of reason as cold and the heart as creative and active. Moreover, Kleist observed that Brockes, though endowed with a penetrating mind, was exceedingly skeptical of reason and always yielded to his first impulse without being misled. Such challenging distinctions and the conflict they opened up between the merits of rational and intuitive judgments as guides to action exerted an influence on Kleist which is subsequently reflected in a number of his characters and in the situations confronting them.

Early in the year 1801, Kleist, who had returned from Würzburg to Berlin in an optimistic mood, became more and more morose. He rebelled at the servitude which seemed inevitable if he accepted a government appointment; at the same time, he found the trivialities with which scholars occupied themselves unspeakably boresome. These people seemed to him like caterpillars seated on leaves; each one fancied that his was the best and was unconcerned with the tree itself. He was, in fact, approaching a crisis in which his whole conception of life and its values was destined to be rudely undermined. The struggle which he was undergoing, the uncertainty of the future, and the consciousness of being different from other people gradually overwhelmed him. At this time he again writes to Ulrike that he does not feel at home in society and that he can be cheerful only when alone; in society he is compelled to dissemble, but in his own company he can be himself. Unfortunately, says he, nature has endowed him with the sad capacity of penetrating outward shams. This gives him insight into the thoughts and motives which underlie every look, word, and act; as a result, everything stands out in miserable, loathesome nakedness. At the same time, he is overcome by an inexplicable embarrassment and self-consciousness; although outwardly strong and vigorous, inwardly he is as weak as a child and as paralyzed as if bound hand and foot. Consequently he is dependent on outward impressions and can be fairly annihilated by the silliest of girls or the most empty-headed fop. Life seems like a difficult game in which he is constantly called upon to draw another card without knowing what is trump. He has begun to doubt the value of knowledge and repeats Brockes' statement that action is better than knowledge. Kleist, who has striven to acquire truth because it is truth, now admits that it is very sad to be nothing but learned. All his friends advise him to specialize in some one field of knowledge, but, having no preference for any one science, he seems condemned to go from one to another, ever to float on the surface and never to penetrate beneath. For some weeks Kleist has the feeling that some decisive development in his life is imminent; in the meantime he broods morosely over the future. His head, says he, is like a lottery bag which contains but one good lot among a thousand blanks. Repeatedly he has been on the point of submitting to the enslavement of government service and has comforted himself with the thought that Apollo, too, was condemned to menial service on earth. Nevertheless, his former high purpose still tempts him and he cannot discard it without a sense of shame.

What was the nature of this exalted goal which Kleist had been worshiping? Although realizing that human intelligence is unable to comprehend nature's plan for eternity and convinced that man's primary concern consequently must be with life here below, Kleist regarded terrestrial existence as merely a significant stage in man's progress toward a higher goal. In an important letter of March 22, 1801, he wrote to his fiancée that as a mere boy he had become imbued with the thought that the attainment of perfection is the end and aim of creation. He had believed that after death man continued this development on another planet by adding further truths to those already acquired. These thoughts had become the foundations of a personal religion motivated by the single desire never to rest content but ever to strive toward a higher stage of development. Consequently, culture had seemed the one goal worth striving for and truth the only possession of any value. These aims had been most sacred to him, and for them he had made the greatest sacrifices. The above statement serves to explain Kleist's indifference to material things and his search for truth solely because it is truth. Although Kleist was under the impression that he had become acquainted with this conception of the aim of life through a treatise by Wieland, it is quite possible that he may have derived some of the ideas directly from Leibniz. At any rate, the idea of human perfectibility as developed by Leibniz was part and parcel of the rationalistic conceptions of the eighteenth century. Lessing, too, was inspired by this stimulating view of life when in his treatise, *Über die Erziehung des Menschengeschlechts*, he suggested the necessity of continued personal existence as a means of arriving at the perfection which God intends humanity to achieve.

To the youthful, ardent Kleist, the idea of human perfectibility became, indeed, a religion which he embraced with the fervor born of his impetuous nature. Strangely enough, so rationalistic a view of life stirred his emotions to high enthusiasm. He regarded the deity as divine by virtue of its absolute perfection. For Kleist, absolute perfection involved absolute truth; consequently the acquiring of truths meant an approach to perfection and to divinity. And since human life on this earth is too short to attain ultimate perfection, he believed firmly in personal immortality which alone could make such achievement possible. Moreover, since constant striving after truth hastens the attainment of the divine goal, Kleist feverishly pursued his quest for a store of truths on the basis of which he might grow more rapidly in a continued personal existence on another star. God, divinity, truth, perfection, virtue, immortality, and constant striving were thus united in his rationalistic but stimulating religion. Having become aware through his friend Brockes, through Rousseau, and through his own experiences of the contradiction and conflict between reason and emotion, he might have changed his conceptions of life gradually and painlessly if Kant's *Critique of Pure Reason* had not rudely undermined his faith. As it was, he received a rude jolt which dashed his youthful hopes and ambitions with cataclysmic violence. His account of the catastrophe is graphic. If all human beings, writes he, had green glasses instead of eyes, they would have to judge that objects they behold therewith are green, and never would they be able to determine whether the eye shows them things as they are, or whether that which we call truth is really truth or merely seems so to us. If the latter is the case, then the truths we gather here no longer exist after death, and all our endeavor to acquire a possession which will accompany us to the grave is in vain. He declares that he has been wounded in that which he has held most sacred; his sole goal, his highest goal has vanished, leaving him devoid of any aim.

Kleist, who has been afraid to face life without a definite plan, now sees the rationalistic foundations of his existence tumbled into the dust like a house of cards. Steadfast devotion to his search for eternal verities has fortified him by giving direction and stability to his efforts; consciousness of the pursuit of an ideal has lifted him out of his depressing sense of inferiority. Now, overwhelmed by his loss, he leaves his books untouched, paces up and down his room in disquieting inactivity, seats himself at his window, rushes out into the open, goes from one café to another, attends theaters and concerts to distract himself, and commits deeds of folly which he is ashamed to relate. He tries to drive himself to work but his will power is paralyzed by a feeling of loathing. In wind and rain he wanders to Potsdam to find relief in the company of his friends. Unable to work, he is a prey to morose brooding over the miserable aimlessness of his existence. He decides to seek relief in travel, for he is unable to endure idleness and the violent impulse to activity without a definite aim. It happens that he is compelled to take Ulrike with him on his journey to France, for he has previously promised not to leave the country without her. In his troubled state of mind he would prefer to travel alone. And since he has to give some reason for his journey in order to obtain a passport, he can think of none other than that of studying mathematics and natural science in Paris. Consequently his friends force letters to French scholars upon him, thereby making it necessary for him to frequent the very circles which he is desirous of avoiding. Such combinations of circumstances which force his hand make him feel more than ever that he is a mere puppet in the hands of a capricious fate. His eternally agitated heart affords him nothing but grief; he would prefer to give up all travels, all knowledge, and all former ambitions.

On his journey to Paris in the spring of the year 1801 he sees nature lavishing beauty and joy on all creation, but he goes empty handed. He writes that on his travels from Berlin to Dresden he has not spent a single happy hour; his most cheerful moments are those in which his thoughts are diverted to other things. He has neglected even his diary because all writing fills him with loathing and because he is unable to think of his condition without shuddering. Nevertheless his letters indicate that he is gaining a deeper appreciation of nature and of art. He would fain live for the moment, but he is unable to find anything of value in the present. Everything is confused within him and his fleeting desires are all at variance with one another. Yet, he is already considering the plan of settling down in Switzerland to a life of rural simplicity and seems to be thinking of himself as a budding poet. His future, however, lies dark before him and he wonders whether there will be happiness for him anywhere. The manifold new impressions which surge in upon him leave him apathetic and grant him no satisfaction. Thoughts of death come to him, and the fear of death seems nauseating as he thinks of the contradictions of life. And although he would like to throw his life away, he trembles at the thought of annihilation. Overwhelmed at the impossibility of comprehending the purpose of existence, and sorely impressed with the limitations of human understanding, he asks whether God has any right to hold frail beings responsible for their acts. He distrusts reason as well as the promptings of the heart and momentarily flirts with a hedonistic view of life. His letter to Wilhelmine of August 15, 1801, refers vaguely to a resolve which may determine his whole future. Yet, characteristically enough, he shrouds it in mystery, asserts that he is not going to make a hasty decision, and threatens to end his life if he commits another rash error. About two months later, he alludes to busying himself with writing books but expresses his feeling of horror at the thought of writing them for money.

Since he viewed Paris and human civilization with the eyes of Rousseau, Kleist developed a bilious dislike of the metropolis and its seemingly depraved citizens. His desire to acquire land in Switzerland, where he might live close to nature, took him to Bern late in December, 1801. He had found his adventurous sister Ulrike a burdensome traveling companion and looked forward with a sense of relief to parting from her at Frankfurt am Main. Nevertheless, he was no less devoted to her now than when, out of a desire to be near her, he had previously made his decision to study in his native city rather than at some more prominent university. But having gained confidence in his poetic talents, he was desirous of working in quiet seclusion and of returning home only with tokens of success.

In Bern, Kleist found friends who had literary interests, among them Heinrich Zschokke, Ludwig Wieland, and the publisher, Heinrich Gessner. Wieland wrote to his father at Weimar that he had discovered a young man of unusual talent from whom something greater might be expected than Germany had hitherto produced. Gessner offered to publish Kleist's first drama, which was now recast under the title of *Die Familie Schroffenstein*. Stimulated by his friends and their confidence in his ability, the young dramatist busied himself with a variety of themes. Owing to the troubled political conditions in Bern and to his desire of purchasing an estate, Kleist spent some time in Thun and eventually rented a small house on an island of the Aar River at Lake Thun. Here he lived in seclusion, reading no books or newspapers, seeing no one except his friends from Bern, who occasionally visited him, and working on dramatic projects. Under such conditions he might have been fairly content if only he had not acquired the habit of brooding over unpleasant things. He was haunted by a strange fear that he might die before completing his work. Life, momentarily, had become simplified in that he had but one desire, namely to die after having become the father of a child, written a beautiful poem, and accomplished a great deed. For there seemed to be nothing more exalted about life than to be able to cast it away nobly. Although the uncertainty of the times induced Kleist to give up his plans of buying property and settling in Switzerland, he dismissed all thoughts of marrying Wilhelmine who, as shown above, had not desired to share rural life with him. As a result of overtaxing his sensitive, shattered nerves with work on a drama entitled *Robert Guiskard,* Kleist was taken seriously ill and went to Bern for treatment. After an illness of some weeks he wrote to his brother-in-law, saying that he was praying to God for death. His self-sacrificing sister, Ulrike, hastened to his aid, nursed him, and succeeded in persuading him to leave Switzerland.

On arriving at Weimar on their return to Germany, Ulrike parted from her brother, who subsequently accepted an invitation from the poet, Christoph Martin Wieland, to sojourn at his estate in Ossmannstedt near Weimar. Wieland's fatherly interest, encouragement, and approval were a great stimulus to the young man who was wrestling with the refractory drama, *Robert Guiskard.* For a time he had high hopes of being able to complete a masterpiece and begged his relatives to grant him a few months of peace and refrain from driving him mad with their fears about his future. In March, 1803, he suddenly went to Leipzig but gave no explanation for his precipitate departure other than that he had left Wieland's home, where he had found more love than the whole world, with Ulrike's exception, could bestow. Wieland's young daughter, Luise, had fallen madly in love with Kleist, who, though doubtless attracted by her, sacrificed everything to the success of his drama.

In Leipzig and Dresden Kleist continued his fruitless efforts to complete *Robert Guiskard*, until a friend of his, Ernst von Pfuel, persuaded him to take a journey in the hope of distracting him. Kleist declined his friend's offer to provide him with funds, borrowed money from Ulrike, who constantly had to finance him, and the two men set out on their trip through Switzerland, to Italy, back to Switzerland, and through France to Paris. A letter to Wilhelmine written from Geneva in October tells her of the failure of his efforts to conclude his drama and is indicative of impending disaster. In Paris, in a fit of despair, Kleist burned the fragmentary manuscript and suddenly disappeared. Pfuel, whom Kleist, as is alleged, had, on a previous occasion, urged to commit suicide with him, feared the worst and sought him among the dead at the Paris morgue. But, although desiring to die, Kleist had not attempted to take his own life, but had set out for Boulogne-sur-Mer to join the Napoleonic expedition which was supposedly planning to attack England. In this hazardous undertaking he hoped to find death and release from his tragic existence. But the expedition did not materialize, he returned to Paris, set out for Germany, and collapsed on his arrival in Mainz. His overwrought nerves had given way and demanded rest. After being confined to his bed and to his room for months, he finally turned up in Frankfurt and in Berlin in June, 1804.

In the Prussian capital Kleist applied for a civil appointment. His request did not find immediate favor in the eyes of the king's adjutant general, who heaped reproaches upon him which called forth numerous explanations of past conduct. The young man stated that no political motive had underlain his desire to enlist under Napoleon against England. In a letter of July 29, Kleist declared that he was unable to give sensible minded people any explanation of this strange journey which took him to Boulogne-sur-Mer. Since his illness, he himself had lost all insight into its motives and was unable to comprehend the succession of events. To the adjutant general he explained this act of madness by stating that it grew out of a morbid state which impelled him to seek change and distraction; moreover, he maintained that it would be cruel to hold him responsible for acts prompted by attacks of excruciating pain.

Meanwhile, his hopes of accompanying the Prussian ambassador to Spain as an attaché of the legation failed to materialize. In May, 1805, Kleist went to Königsberg on a special appointment to the board of domains. Having failed in his ambitious plans to achieve success as a dramatist at a single bound, and still feeling somewhat enfeebled by his severe illness, he swallowed his pride and yielded to pressure exerted by Ulrike and his family. He seems to have resigned himself with considerable grace to bowing under the yoke which had seemed so hateful to him and to have worked diligently and faithfully in his enforced employment. His devoted but practical sister, who had no appreciation of his literary bent, breathed a sigh of relief on seeing him established in a government position with the opportunity of receiving instruction which would lead to a definite career. In addition to studying political economy under a disciple of Adam Smith, Kleist frequented the homes of distinguished citizens of Königsberg, studied mathematics, read widely in French literature,

A BIOGRAPHICAL SKETCH 21

wrote a brilliant essay, *Über die allmähliche Verfertigung der Gedanken beim Reden*, and devoted himself to a number of other literary projects. Impelled to poetic effort, he first contented himself with two adaptations from the French: *Die beiden Tauben* based on Lafontaine's *Les deux pigeons*, and his version of Molière's *Amphitryon*. In addition, he seems here to have completed the comedy *Der zerbrochene Krug* and to have begun the tragedy *Penthesilea;* he likewise busied himself with prose narratives. This tremendous activity seems all the more remarkable in view of his impaired health, which compelled him to take to his bed for weeks. During his sojourn at Königsberg, Kleist became more calm and viewed life with greater equanimity than in the preceding hectic years of doubt and unsatisfied ambition. The struggle of his country against the aggressions of Napoleon aroused his interest, and the distress of Prussia impressed him with the necessity of thinking in terms of the fatherland as a whole. The desire to devote himself more and more to poetic productivity rendered his employment irksome and induced him to request in July, 1806, that he be relieved of his duties on the ground that ill health incapacitated him. He had overcome his former aversion to the thought of writing books for money and now estimated that, in view of his ability to write a drama in three to four months, he could live on the proceeds from the sale of his writings.

After receiving leave he was later released from his position. In company with several friends he set out on foot from Königsberg to Berlin in January, 1807. On their arrival at their destination they were arrested by the French on the charge of espionage and transported to Fort de Joux near Pontarlier. Here Kleist was incarcerated in the same prison, though not in the same cell, in which Toussaint L'Ouverture had died. He bore up courageously under solitary confinement in his dungeon and in time was able to secure better quarters for himself and his two friends. In April they were transferred to Châlons-sur-Marne, where they were treated as ordinary prisoners of war and accorded greater freedom. As usual, Kleist was in financial straits. On hearing of his imprisonment, Ulrike hastened to Berlin to take steps leading to her brother's liberation, and on July 13 he was finally given his freedom and commanded to report to the French General Clarke, who was in command of the Berlin area.

Kleist's next sojourn of any length was in Dresden, where he remained from the end of August, 1807, until the latter part of April, 1809. In spite of his overwrought nerves he embarked on a period of intense literary activity with high hopes of success. In the months of September and October he wrote to Ulrike of his enjoyable social contacts with distinguished families, of the enthusiastic reception accorded the readings of his two comedies, and told her that, without exception, all his hopes were being fulfilled. In Dresden he found his old friends, Pfuel and Rühle von Lilienstern, as well as Adam Heinrich Müller, an influential young writer and lecturer, who, during Kleist's imprisonment, had interested himself in the publication of the dramatist's adaptation of *Amphitryon*. Through these friends Kleist made the acquaintance of literary groups in which his works were circulated, read, and received with favor. Such recognition and appreciation filled him with optimistic hopes for the future. In order to realize greater profits from the sale of his works, he planned to associate himself with several friends in the establishment of a publishing house. Moreover, he hoped to be authorized to print the *Code Napoléon* and to serve as the distributor for publications of the French government in Germany. But lack of funds and other difficulties prevented the realization of this project, over which Kleist had been most enthusiastic. Two months later he was organizing another undertaking, namely the publication of a literary journal, *Phöbus*, in which he and Adam Müller intended to print their own and other writings. Although sanguine hopes of securing the collaboration of distinguished authors like Goethe and Wieland were unfulfilled, the journal was established, and the first number appeared in January, 1808. But without the support of illustrious contributors the *Phöbus* was but short-lived. In addition to articles by Adam Müller and selections from his lectures on literature, art, and esthetics, the *Phöbus* contained excerpts from Kleist's dramas *Penthesilea, Der zerbrochene Krug, Robert Guiskard, Das Käthchen von Heilbronn,* a prose narrative entitled *Die Marquise von O . . .*, part of his narrative, *Michael Kohlhaas,* and some of his minor writings. After four months the dearth of subscribers and scarcity of funds brought Kleist to a realization of the necessity of disposing of the journal. Efforts to persuade Göschen and Cotta to take it over failed, but beginning with July another publisher continued the publication until the end of the year. After its transfer Kleist contributed comparatively little to the remaining numbers. In addition to these labors Kleist wrote the dramas, *Das Käthchen von Heilbronn* and *Die Hermannsschlacht,* as well as patriotic lyrics during a sojourn of about twenty months in Dresden— a truly astounding activity for one with his undermined consitution. Yet Goethe's unsympathetic attitude, the failure of *Der zerbrochene Krug* on the Weimar stage, the lack of success of the *Phöbus,* the estrangement from Julie Kunze, a friend of the Körner family with whom Kleist had fallen in love, and the oppression of Prussia by Napoleon eventually cast a cloud over the Dresden period which had begun so auspiciously.

Near the end of April, 1809, Kleist left Dresden, accompanied by a friend, Friedrich Dahlmann, to go to Vienna by way of Prague. He apparently had no definite plans in mind and was depending upon time and chance to determine his future course. His desire was to play a part in the events of the day and to aid in one way or another in throwing off the hated domination of Germany by Napoleon. After spending two weeks in Prague, the two men set out for Vienna without knowing that the war between Prussia and France, on which Kleist had set such high hopes for Germany's liberation under the leadership of Archduke Charles, was doomed to disastrous failure. On arriving on the battlefields at Aspern they were in danger of being treated as spies by the Austrians but were finally released. On his return to Prague Kleist again contemplated founding a journal; this publication, entitled *Germania*, was to be a patriotic weekly, issued for the purpose of arousing all the German states to united struggle against Napoleon. But once more his hopes were dashed. To Ulrike he wrote from Prague on July 17, 1809, that he had never before been so perturbed. He had left Dresden with the intention of throwing himself without reserve into the movement of the day, but, strangely thwarted at every turn, he had been forced to take up his abode in Prague quite contrary to his wishes. Nevertheless, for the moment it seemed as if a sphere of activity were opening up for him there. It was just after the battle of Aspern, and at a social gathering he had read some of his articles which were intended for a patriotic weekly. These were greeted with such enthusiasm that others agreed to find a publisher for his journal. Never before, writes he, has his future seemed so auspicious. But the battle of Wagram with its decisive defeat of Austria put an end to this project and destroyed Kleist's hopes.

For several months after, Kleist seems to have dropped out of existence. In all probability his shattered nerves again exacted their toll and threw him into physical collapse. His friends and relatives heard nothing from him, and rumors of his death were spread. In November he journeyed to Frankfurt an der Oder but did not find Ulrike at home. After subsequent wanderings, which took him to Frankfurt am Main and Gotha, he eventually went to Berlin in February, 1810, where the final period of his activity began. He renewed old acquaintances and made new ones, associating in a literary circle with Adam Müller, Achim von Arnim, Clemens Brentano, and others. His sonnet presented to Queen Luise of Prussia on her birthday in March, 1810, found favor, but the queen, who might have been a great aid to him, died only a few months later. Always in financial difficulties, Kleist hoped for relief from the sale of his writings. But he was unable to find a publisher for his last two dramas, *Die Hermannsschlacht* and *Prinz Friedrich von Homburg*. In addition to completing the latter and *Michael Kohlhaas*, he wrote several further prose narratives and busied himself with a novel, which has been lost. Carefully revised, his eight narratives were published in two volumes. In view of the interruptions and the difficulties occasioned by his journalistic undertaking, his creative productivity is nothing short of amazing. Since his dramas and narratives yielded very scant returns, Kleist once more decided upon a journalistic venture as a means of augmenting his income. Needless to say, he was also actuated by the hope of exerting patriotic political influence in spite of the restrictions imposed by rigorous censorship. His aims were designated as the entertainment of all classes of people and the furthering of the national cause. From a practical standpoint the journal represented very desirable innovations. In contrast with the two older Berlin morning newspapers, which were published but three times a week, Kleist's organ was an evening paper appearing six times a week. The first copy of the *Berliner Abendblätter* was issued October 1, 1810. Because of opposition to the financial policy of Chancellor von Hardenberg, Kleist soon encountered difficulties with the censorship, which extended even to non-political columns of his journal. Kleist seems finally to have been offered financial support through the chancellor's office on condition that he publish a "suitable" journal, that is, one which would refrain from criticism of the government's reform policy. Although Kleist declined to barter away the independence of his publication, an understanding of some kind was reached after the harassing censorship had made it impossible for him to carry on his original editorial policy. He did not accept a financial subvention but contented himself with a promise of official communications, interest in which would offset the loss of those readers who had been attracted by the former critical independence of the paper. But although he made these enforced concessions, the journal's original popularity waned, and for financial reasons Kleist was compelled to discontinue its publication on March 30, 1811. His letters of the time present a graphic picture of his tenacious struggle to carry on his undertaking against insurmountable obstacles and reveal the courage with which he combated intrigue and misrepresentation.

But in spite of unceasing toil and heroic effort, his final journalistic venture failed, and he was financially ruined.

In vain Kleist requested Hardenberg for an indemnity to offset the losses incurred through the failure of the chancellor's office to live up to the promises held out to him. Since his appeal was not granted, he bowed to the inevitable and applied first to Hardenberg and later to the king of Prussia for a civil appointment which might save him from starvation. Pending such appointment he requested an advance of money which he was ready to accept in lieu of an indemnity. Harassed by poverty, helpless and destitute, he then petitioned the king to grant him a commission in the army, but Frederick William III merely gave him hopes of a commission in the event of a renewal of war. Meanwhile Kleist requested Reimer in vain to print his drama, *Prinz Friedrich von Homburg*, or to agree to publish a novel of his which he stated was fairly well advanced.

Distress and failure render his letters increasingly sombre. In August, 1811, he writes of the lonely, sad life he is leading; he no longer visits even the two or three homes he has frequented, but spends practically all his time in the seclusion of his room without seeing anyone who might tell him what is going on in the world. In this solitary existence even his imagination refuses to function. The political situation adds to his unhappiness, his soul is as if blunted, and there is not a single ray of light in the future which he can contemplate with joy and hope. It is most strange, writes he, how all his undertakings fail and how the very ground seems to recede whenever he is able to make up his mind to take a definite step. And yet, notwithstanding the growing disconsolateness of his moods, he has an occasional hopeful moment in which he feels that a bit of real enjoyment of life might resolve everything into harmony for him in spite of the disagreeable circumstances in which he lives. In that event he would give up literature entirely for a year or more and, apart from some study of the sciences, he would devote himself to music because of its intimate relation to poetry. And in this same month of August he writes that life, which had seemed so desolate, is suddenly looming up with rare splendor, and that energies which he had thought extinct, are stirring anew within him. This warrants the conclusion that friendly encouragement and timely relief from the uncertainties of existence would have enabled Kleist once more to rise above the difficulties besetting him. Unfortunately no such aid was in sight. In October he went to Frankfurt to secure a loan from Ulrike or through her aid. But, emaciated and hollow-eyed as he must have looked, his appearance upset her so that he was quite overcome with terror at her agitation. Consequently he gave up his plan of borrowing money and requested her but once more to allow him to spend a few hours with her.

With all opportunity blocked, Kleist, who at various times in his tragic life had thought of death as the only escape from an unbearable existence, now yielded to the pressure of ever mounting misfortune. His last letters to Marie von Kleist, a cousin by marriage, contain a strange admixture of woe and exaltation at the thought of ending his life. It is not surprising that he bared his soul thus to her, for she had long been a devoted friend and was doubtless the woman who understood him best. She had been instrumental in winning the queen's favor for him; in fact the idea has been advanced by Professor Georg Minde-Pouet, the editor of Kleist's letters, that she herself paid the pension which the queen was supposed to have conferred upon him at her solicitation. In his letters to her of the ninth, tenth, and twelfth of November Kleist feels the need of explaining to her why he is making his reckoning with life. He tells her that she is the only person whose feelings and opinions mean anything to him, and that she is the one being on earth whom he desires to meet again beyond the grave. His last meeting with Ulrike evidently has left a sting within him, for he states that she does not know how to sacrifice herself completely and how to immolate herself for the object of her affections. He is going to die because there is nothing more to learn and to acquire on earth. His cousin's letters, says he, have pierced his heart, and if it were in his power to give up his resolve to die, he would do so. But it has become utterly impossible for him to live any longer; his soul has become so sensitive that the very daylight causes him pain. As a result of constant contemplation of beauty and ethics he has become so sensitive that even the slightest attacks, to which the feelings of all human beings are exposed here below, hurt him two- and threefold. He assures her that he would rather suffer death ten times over than again to be subjected to the reproaches of his family circle as he was on his last visit to Frankfurt. Though he has remarked but little on the subject, one of his profound desires has been to bring joy and honor to his family through his literary achievements. He admits that of late it has been difficult to get along with him and that he is all the less inclined to accuse his relatives of having abandoned him, since he is aware that the general distress of their country has weighed heavily upon them, too. Nevertheless, he grieves profoundly at the thought that his merits, be they great or small, are entirely unrecognized, and that he is regarded by his family as an utterly useless member of society. This thought robs him not only of the joys for which he has hoped from the future, but it poisons the past for him, as well. Moreover, the alliance which the king is contemplating with the French is not such as to make him cling to life. The times, says he, are out of joint and, like others, he lacks the strength to right them. Why serve the king after such an alliance? For the time has come when loyalty to the king, sacrifices, fortitude, and all civic virtues are rewarded on the gallows. Having found a friend who is ready to die with him, he has but one concern, namely to find an abyss deep enough to plunge into with her. In his last letter to his cousin, Kleist assures her that he is quite blissful at the thought of death. Night and morning he thanks God for a life fuller of torment than any other man has ever led, since this is now being rewarded by the most joyful of deaths. He has been seized by a vortex of bliss such as he has never felt before. The letter ends with the wish that God may soon call her, too, to a better world.

On the morning of his death, Kleist wrote a farewell note to Ulrike declaring that, happy and content as he was with the entire world, he could not die without having made his peace with her. He begs to be allowed to retract the severe statement about her in his letter to his cousin Marie, and assures her that she has done for him everything in the power of a sister, everything that was humanly possible. The truth is, he adds, that it was quite impossible to help him on earth. He concludes with the hope that heaven may grant her a death but half as joyful and unspeakably cheerful as his; this is the most profound and heartfelt wish he can utter.

On the twenty-first of November, 1811, Kleist and Henriette Vogel, the friend who desired to die with him, went to their death near the shore of a small lake, Wannsee, in the vicinity of Potsdam. Henriette Vogel, with whom Kleist had become acquainted through Adam Müller, was of his age. Afflicted with cancer of the uterus, she had repeatedly expressed the desire to die in order to find release from suffering. Kleist seems to have been drawn to her by their mutual fondness for music and because she shared his old conception of immortality which had not lost its fascination for him in spite of the undermining effect of Kantian philosophy on his early beliefs. According to rumor, she once exacted a promise from him to fulfill a wish of hers, and subsequently demanded that he shoot her. Like numerous other tales about Kleist, this, too, may have been but idle gossip. But be that as it may, it chanced that she was ready to die with him just at the moment when he found life intolerable. The nature of her malady and her reported devotion to her husband and daughter seem to exclude the probability of an erotically passionate relation to Kleist. His great concern, as expressed in his last letters to Marie von Kleist, was that his cousin should not misunderstand his dying with Henriette: he assured her that he never would have chosen to live with the woman with whom he went to his voluntary death. After writing letters setting forth their last wishes, Kleist and Henriette Vogel faced death with strange exaltation and in the spirit of a voyage of discovery. After shooting his companion, he ended his own life. In view of the unhappiness, the trials, failures, loneliness, and misery of his existence, in view of his emotional instability which was heightened by sensitive, overwrought nerves, it is astounding that Kleist did not yield earlier to the recurring temptation to self-destruction. One cannot help but be impressed by the courageous, tenacious struggle he waged against overwhelming odds and by the greatness of his achievements in the face of handicaps and adversity. Kleist's tragic life and death moved the dramatist, Friedrich Hebbel, to characterize him as a poet and a man who need yield to none, not even to the highest; few, declared Hebbel, can be compared with him in power and probably none in misfortune.

CHAPTER TWO

DIE FAMILIE SCHROFFENSTEIN

DIE FAMILIE SCHROFFENSTEIN, Heinrich von Kleist's first drama, is a gloomy tragedy of suspicion, distrust, and infuriated passion which has aptly been named a tragedy of errors. Though not a great, finished literary product, it nevertheless merits careful study because in it is manifest much that is characteristic of Kleist's later dramas. Certain critics have regarded *Die Familie Schroffenstein* as a tragedy of fate in which an unintelligible, capricious destiny either allows chance circumstance to play the decisive rôle or wilfully and malignantly plunges man into dire misfortune. Others have maintained that in the wake of his disillusionment through Kant's *Critique of Pure Reason* Kleist wished herein to set forth the inadequacy of reason as the discriminating and guiding force in human existence. Another interpretation seems quite as valid as either of these. Since the action is determined largely by character as it manifests itself under specific conditions, the drama can scarcely be termed a tragedy of fate. And although reason is temporarily clouded and paralyzed by uncontrollable passion, Kleist cannot be said to have intended to present reason as eternally doomed to failure. For, in this violent tragedy, rage and fitful emotions temporarily convert the mind into a veritable blank, thereby depriving calm reason of any opportunity to assert itself and to clarify a comparatively simple situation. It is quite conceivable that Kleist wrote his first tragedy in order to free himself from the haunting conception of a cruel, unintelligible fate which draws man on to an unfortunate end. For, in the wake of the catastrophe induced in his thinking by Kantian philosophy, he had come to regard life as meaningless and to view man as a plaything in the hands of a capricious, inexorable destiny. This tendency had to be undermined before he could gain any new constructive, positive view of life. And, obsessed by a nervous fear of disaster, Kleist found it impossible to live without some positive conception of life. Indeed, his career presents a search—at times a frantic, desperate search—for some anchor in a hostile or at best a dangerously indifferent world. Aware of the fundamental instability of his nature, he early sought a definite plan of life and an orderly interpretation of the universe which might enable him to triumph over the waywardness of chance and caprice. In *Die Familie Schroffenstein* Kleist evidently endeavored to resolve the conception of an outward hostile fate into a series of intelligible interrelated happenings, which though leading to an unfortunate end, had their source largely in the turbulent passions growing out of a given situation.

The drama presents two branches of the Schroffenstein family; the one living at Rossitz consists of Count Rupert, his wife Eustache, their son Ottokar, and a natural son of Rupert named Johann. The other line has its seat at Warwand, and includes the old blind Count Sylvius, his son Sylvester, the latter's wife Gertrude and their daughter Agnes. A youth by the name of Jeronimus belongs to a third branch of the family. A brief exposition discloses the origin of the suspicion which exists between the two groups. An hereditary pact provides that, at the extinction of either line, all its possessions shall revert to the other. Obviously enough, neither family can believe that the other is viewing its extinction with disinterestedness. In fact, jealousy and distrust have assumed such proportions that members of each household believe the other is intent upon exterminating it by murder. Each branch fancies that accidents, illness, and death bring joy to the hearts of the other. These are the sinister presuppositions which to a greater or lesser degree have poisoned the minds of the two families and upon which the tragedy of misunderstanding is based.

The opening scene is staged in the chapel at Rossitz, where Rupert, Eustache, Ottokar, Jeronimus, knights, members of the household, and a chorus of youths and maidens are grouped around a coffin. Chanting solemnly to the accompaniment of music, the chorus of maidens proclaims the murder of a child of angelic charm. In sonorous accents the chorus of youths responds and swears vengeance in the name of the Lord; vengeance, they declare, is the will of the Lord, and His will is to be fulfilled. Each of the three chants by the maidens is followed by the vow of vengeance, which gains in solemnity by repetition; the chant of the youths contains no exposition as does that of the maidens but sounds the keynote of the tragedy with dramatic, impressive, vengeful insistence.

As the chant draws to a close, Rupert, Ottokar, and Eustache, in turn partake of the sacrament and swear upon the consecrated host that they will avenge the death of Rupert's little son Peter upon Sylvester, whom they accuse of having instigated the murder of the child. At his father's insistent demand, Ottokar vows vengeance not merely upon Sylvester

Schroffenstein but upon his whole murderous family as well. With utter ruthlessness Rupert has resolved upon a wild orgy of revenge and annihilation, whose goal is to be the extermination of the accursed foe. Although his anger does not render him inarticulate, his speech is broken, halting, and intense as he commands Aldöbern, a vassal, to bear a declaration of war to Sylvester.

Jeronimus, who has been away for some time in distant lands, subsequently interrogates a church warden about the situation, for he considers the charges against Sylvester incredible and desires to know the facts. Various details attendant upon the death of little Peter are thus revealed. One evening, while walking in the mountains, Rupert had found his son slain, and two men from Warwand standing beside him with bloody knives in their hands. They were captured and tortured on the rack without, however, making any confession. But it was claimed that one of them, amid the confusion and turmoil on the market place, uttered the name of Sylvester just before dying. This one word and no more. Yet in the suspicious, morbid minds of the Rossitz household this single word sufficed to establish the conviction of Sylvester's guilt. The warden exposes this situation with a firm belief in its validity. Jeronimus' attitude toward the narrative robs it entirely of the appearance of exposition as such. For his rather challenging, insistent interrogation elicits this information much as if he were cross-questioning a witness whom he desires to involve in contradictions. In view of this apparently skeptical attitude toward the details as narrated, it is surprising to find Jeronimus convinced of the truth of such rumor and hearsay, and, in the turn of a hand, siding against Sylvester. The scene draws to a close with the added discovery that

DIE FAMILIE SCHROFFENSTEIN

Ottokar and his half-brother Johann are in love with the same girl, Sylvester's daughter Agnes, whom they have encountered from time to time in the mountains.

In characterizing the attitude of the Warwand household toward Rossitz, Kleist amplifies the general expository facts presented in the opening scene. Here, as at Rossitz, rumors are repeated; as they are passed on and on, they lose the character of mere hearsay until unfounded supposition is finally regarded as established fact. At Rossitz, Eustache made a feeble effort at restraining the violence of Rupert. Here, on the contrary, the women are the accusers; they regard the sudden death of Sylvester's son Philipp as a murder instigated by Rossitz. Sylvester cannot tolerate such nonsensical gossip in his home and blames Gertrude for sowing the seeds of suspicion, saying:

> Thou
> Alone Gertrude, art to blame for this.
> Distrust is like a plague spot on the soul
> That makes all things, however pure and clean,
> Seem to the eye to wear the garb of hell.
> The meaningless, the common things of life,
> Are shrewdly sorted out like tangled yarn
> And knit into a pattern which affrights
> The soul with fearful forms.

Aldöbern now delivers Rupert's declaration of a cruel war of vengeance upon the entire Warwand family. Peace-loving, kind, and gentle as he is, Sylvester still combats the tendency to believe evil of Rupert, and insists upon going to Rossitz in the hope of propitiating his relative. The end of this scene is linked up with the close of the first scene by the arrival of Jeronimus who denounces Sylvester as an assassin; Sylvester is so overwhelmed at being branded as a murderer that he falls into a deep swoon.

On the whole, this act is a tribute to the dramatic talent of a young author essaying his first tragedy. A most sinister conflict is foreshadowed between two branches of a family. Although related by the ties of kinship, they are blinded by a suspicion of long standing which has flared up into a consuming flame because of sudden deaths in each household. The tragic character of this conflict is deepened by differences in viewpoint between husband and wife in both homes and by the love between members of the younger generation. Kleist has succeeded in creating an atmosphere of hopelessness and helplessness on the part of innocent persons who apparently are being rushed irresistibly to their doom because of their inability to effect an understanding. One aspect of this first act, however, is anything but convincing. It is surprising to find Jeronimus, who had been assured of the innate nobility of Sylvester's character, so promptly converted to the opposite belief by the unfounded accusations of the church warden, whose every word he seemed to challenge. Yet the very weakness and instability of Jeronimus, who later acts as a mediator between the hostile camps, renders the outlook all the more hopeless.

The first scene of the second act is staged in the open, in a mountainous region with a cave in the foreground. Ottokar and Agnes meet for the first time since he has been apprised of her identity by Johann. Ottokar, who seems to require confirmation of his brother's revelation, insists upon hearing from her who she really is. In truly Kleistian fashion he demands that she take him completely into her confidence and conceal nothing whatsoever from him. The arrival of Johann prevents an exchange of confidences and arouses her fears to such a pitch that she flees. Johann follows her, overtakes her before the gates of Warwand castle, and begs her to slay him with his own dagger; since she does not love him, he prefers to die. Alarmed by his pursuit of her, she fancies that he is an enemy from Rossitz intent upon slaying her. This misunderstanding is plausible enough because of her state of mind and because Johann has madly seized and embraced her. She cries for help and swoons just as Jeronimus appears. Seeing her lying unconscious, he concludes that Johann has attacked her with the dagger; he, therefore, strikes down and slightly wounds the supposed assassin. On regaining consciousness, Agnes learns from Jeronimus that Ottokar has sworn to take her life.

The third act opens at the cave in the mountains. Agnes, who has been called hither by Ottokar, tells him she knows now that he is Ottokar and that he has sworn to slay her. In spite of her fears, she reveals her identity, for life without his love would be valueless to her. At last, the hide-and-seek game which characterizes their supposed ignorance of each other's identity is ended. Kleist's manipulation of this episode has not been devoid of contradiction and awkward repetition. The lovers gradually succeed in banishing all suspicion from each other's minds and become convinced that the charges of murder are unfounded. Having gained complete confidence in each other, they desire to clarify the situation for their families as well, although, significantly enough, Ottokar holds out but little hope of pacifying the blind, unreasoning rage of his father.

The second scene of the third act takes place at Rossitz. Here Rupert hears of the murder of his emissary, Aldöbern, by Sylvester's over-zealous vassals, and is told that Johann, too, has been slain at Warwand by Jeronimus. A meeting between Jeronimus and Rupert is unproductive of good results, since Rupert merely exhibits a cynical skepticism when Jeronimus attempts to convince him of Sylvester's goodness and innocence. As Jeronimus leaves, he is attacked and slain by Rupert's followers, who manifest the same vicious partisanship as that which had actuated Sylvester's vassals in their murder of Aldöbern. Here again are situations with certain outward parallels. Yet there is a difference. Sylvester lay unconscious while Aldöbern was stoned to death, whereas by word and look Rupert commanded Santing to slay Jeronimus. Although Eustache pleads with her husband to take but a single step to the window and save the youth, he coldly and cynically refuses. In this tensely dramatic scene Kleist employs a device which figures very prominently in others of his dramas, notably in *Penthesilea*. It is that of having an eyewitness report and describe in highly graphic fashion what is at the moment occurring off-stage. Eustache here combines entreaty with description:

> For God's sake, save him, save him! See, they are
> Attacking him—Jeronimus!—the mob
> With clubs—O, save him! See, they drag him
>   down—
> He's on the ground—O, do come to the window!
> They're killing him—No, now he's up again—
> He draws his sword—he fights—they're giving
>   way.
> O Rupert, I implore thee, now's the time—
> They hem him in again and he defends
> Himself with fury. Shout one word, by all
> The saints I beg thee, just one word from out
> This window! Ah! a blow struck home, he reels—
> O, there's another! Now 'tis over—now
> He falls and dies—

DIE FAMILIE SCHROFFENSTEIN

Finally, Eustache implores Rupert to spare Agnes so that his own son Ottokar, who is in love with her, may not curse him. But this disclosure only serves to precipitate disaster, for, on hearing that the lovers have a trysting place in the mountains, Rupert abruptly leaves in a mood that augurs evil.

The following scene takes place at Warwand, where the news of Jeronimus' death fills Sylvester with presentiments of misfortune. Nature, says he, appears to reflect the disaster that impends:

> It is a dismal day,
> With rain and storm and ominous commotion.
> An unseen spirit carries all along
> In its fell course,—the dust and clouds and waves.

At first sight, these lines may seem to represent a conception of the irresistible power of fate. Yet, at bottom, this invisible spirit, which powerfully draws everything in its wake, is but the spirit of distrust, hatred, and vengeance that prompts the action. Now that it is too late, Sylvester realizes that Jeronimus was courting the same danger that he himself would have faced in going to Rossitz. Sylvester's forebearance is now at an end; henceforth he, too, will be animated by but one feeling, by the desire for revenge. Rossitz shall become Jeronimus' funeral pyre.

The scene changes to a peasant kitchen. Barnabe, a young girl, is chanting incantations as she stirs a kettle over a fire. On entering, Ottokar, who is searching for some clue as to the cause of little Peter's death, learns that Barnabe is stewing a child's finger. She narrates that, while gathering herbs, she and her mother discovered a drowned child floating down a forest stream and that her mother Ursula cut off the little finger from the dead child's left hand in order to use it as a charm. Immediately after Ursula had done so, two men came along from Warwand and cut off the other little finger. For Ottokar this disclosure has the character of a divine revelation. He hastens home to acquaint Rupert with the information obtained from Barnabe: after that, his intention is to hurry to Agnes with the same news so that it may be conveyed to Sylvester. Consequently it is unintelligible why he, burning as he is with the desire to impart this knowledge to his father and to clarify the whole situation, willingly walks into prison at the invitation of one of Rupert's vassals. Eustache comes to the prison to tell him that Rupert is seeking Agnes in the mountains with murderous intent. In order to escape, Ottokar is compelled to leap fifty feet to hard pavement. He does this with the same alacrity, however, with which he had walked into the tower. In doing so, he delivers himself of the Kleistian sentiment that life has value only for him who scorns it.

The entire fifth act consists of a single scene staged in the mountain cave to which Agnes has been summoned by Ottokar. By exchanging garments with Agnes, Ottokar hopes to protect her from the murderous wrath of his father, who is bent upon slaying her. He is forced to employ a ruse in order to effect this exchange without letting her know that he is incurring danger of being killed in her place. In a lyric scene of insinuating charm he pictures to her the incidents of their bridal night as with warm sensuous imagination he conceives them:

Ottokar.—

O Agnes,
When once the word is said that sanctifies
What fills thy heart—Amidst the throng of guests
Whose glances follow us like wasps I will

Draw near to thee, and thou wilt speak a few
Embarrassed words and thou wilt turn and chat
A little with a guest. It will not vex me,
For well I know that every time a guest
Takes leave, scarce will the door be closed·behind
His back, before thy glance, where'er thou art,
Will find me and encourage me, and when
The last has taken his departure, when
At length we are alone, our fathers and
Our mothers smile, kiss thee, then me, and say
"Good night, dear children," and we turn to
　　leave,
And all the servants want to light our way
With candles, I exclaim, "One light will do."
I seize it, seize thy hand, this hand (*kisses it*), and
　　we
Ascend the stair in silence just as if
Our hearts were unperturbed and naught is heard
Except the rustle of thy skirts adown
The empty halls. Then—Agnes, dost thou sleep?
Agnes.—
　　　　　　I sleep?
Ottokar.—
　　　　　Because thou art so still. Let us
Go on. The door I softly open now.
I softly close it then behind us just
As if it were forbidden, for man fears,
Wherever as a child he has been taught
To fear. We find a bench. I draw thee down
To me and grasp thee with my arms and with
A single kiss I tell thee all my love.
(*Goes quickly to back and speaks softly to Barnabe.*)
Hast thou seen no one yet?
Barnabe.—
　　　　　　　I almost thought
Just now I saw two forms creep up the hill.

(*Ottokar returns quickly.*)
Agnes.—
  Why art thou always whispering to that maid?
Ottokar (*sitting down again*).—
Where did I stop? O yes, 'twas at the kiss.—
For bolder grows my love. Since thou art mine
And I am thine I will remove thy hat (*he does*).
Disturb thy primly ordered curls (*he does*) and boldly
Remove thy neckerchief. Thou dost entreat
Me softly to put out the light. Forthwith
The night doth cast its deepest veil about
Our sacred love, as now.
Barnabe (*from the back*).—
  O Knight, sir Knight!
(*Agnes looks around affrighted.*)
Ottokar (*interrupting, as she is about to speak*).—
Now like the swollen streams of early spring
My passion breaks all bounds. I loose this knot
And this (*he does*) and strip the vexing cloak from thee.
Agnes.—
O Ottokar, what wilt thou do to me? (*Falls upon his neck.*)
Ottokar (*busy with the second dress*).—
As Nature's handmaid I restore her to
Herself. Why this impenetrable veil
Of mystery? O Agnes, beauty needs
No other veil except its own and that
Is beauty's self.

In obedience to her lover's command, Agnes leaves the cave, and Ottokar, who impersonates Agnes, is stabbed by his own father. Immediately after the murder, Rupert endeavors to recollect why he committed the bloody crime. Kleist could scarcely have portrayed more impressively how completely reason has succumbed to a blind wave of irresponsible, choleric passion. For when told by Santing that Agnes has done him no harm, Rupert replies in a manner which indicates how closely he verges upon madness:

> No harm at all? Then why have I harmed her?
> Stare not that way at me, thou basilisk!
> But bluntly tell me why, thou devil! If
> Thou knowest not, then tell me lies!

On being reminded that Agnes is Sylvester's daughter, Rupert recalls that Sylvester has slain Peter. His brief fit of remorse gives way to a transport of rage as he stabs the body anew and kicks it. This inability of Rupert to comprehend the reasons for his mad deed of violence emphasizes his eruptive, uncontrollable temper most significantly. Such an act is quite in keeping with Kleist's conception of a tremendous, overpowering emotion that leaps irresistibly to a wild discharge. Rage stifles all possibility of reflection, and passion becomes so turbulent as to be beyond the restraint of reason and will. Rupert and Santing hurriedly leave, just before Agnes returns and finds her lover dying. Sylvester enters the cave, sees Agnes disguised and lying on the dead body of her lover, fancies she is Ottokar, the assassin of his daughter, and stabs her. As Sylvester is about to leave, Rupert and Santing are brought in as prisoners, followed by Gertrude, Eustache, Sylvius, and Johann, all of whom, for some strange reason or other, have found their way hither in the dead of night. Amid the lamentations of the bereaved parents, the blind grandfather recognizes that Rupert's victim is not Agnes but Ottokar. While Rupert is rending his hair in horror and Sylvester is lamenting his misdeed, Ursula enters, tosses a child's finger on the stage and vanishes. By a pockmark, the only one on the child's body, Eustache recognizes the finger as Peter's—truly a remarkable feat after the member had been thoroughly stewed by Barnabe. When captured and brought into the cave, Ursula confesses what Ottokar has previously ascertained about the origin of the finger; she adds that she intended to place it under her threshold in order to ward off the devil, and that two men from Warwand cut off the other little finger. Rupert and Sylvester effect a somewhat incongruous reconciliation over the dead bodies of their children, the stepsisters, Eustache and Gertrude, embrace each other, and Johann, whose reason has strangely snapped during the course of the tragedy, contributes a singular bit of buffoonery by uttering idiotic nonsense. This jangling, discordant note at the close is false and out of keeping with the general tone of the drama. It marks the failure of Kleist to resolve the warring motifs into that final harmony which is the mark of genuine, refined tragedy.

There has been a tendency on the part of various critics to pronounce *Die Familie Schroffenstein* a tragedy of fate and regard Ursula as the personification of fate. But why not take her at her own word? She tosses Peter's finger on the stage, saying: "If you have killed each other it was your own mistake." This can mean only that errors in judgment have led to the unfortunate outcome rather than that a malevolent fate inexorably guides events to a disastrous end. What has been the source of these errors in judgment? Kleist has given a definite enough answer to this question by his repeated reference to the situation arising out of the hereditary pact and by his emphasis upon the tempestuous character of Rupert as the wellspring from which disaster emanates in view of this pact. That his temper is beyond restraint is emphasized in every scene in which he appears. Ottokar's characterization of his father bears out thoroughly well Kleist's conception of Rupert's nature as the source of tragic disasters:

Ottokar.—
                                    I calm
His wrath? My father's wrath? He sways us like
The sea a ship. We ride upon the waves,
They mock at our control.

Nor is it fate which impels Sylvester, against his better nature, to commit murder. His hand is forced by Rupert, for with the death of Jeronimus Sylvester realizes that all prospects of conciliation are at an end. He must either strike at his enemy or allow himself and his family to be killed by Rupert, who has sworn to annihilate them all. Rupert's declaration of a war of extermination and the slaying of Jeronimus at his orders have changed the whole situation from one of vague rumor to one of certainty and imminent peril. Sylvester is convinced that Ottokar is just as implacable a foe as his father, for he has learned that both father and son have sworn the same oath of vengeance. Hence it is not surprising to see him attempt to slay Ottokar, whom in the darkness of the cave he takes for the murderer of Agnes. Minds which are clouded by rage, hatred, and fear are undeceived only by the terrible catastrophe of child murder. Ursula's jarring revelation of the mode of Peter's death comes when the spirit of violence that obscures reason has been deflated.

Kleist's introduction of buffoonery on the part of Johann is clearly in bad taste and may be attributed to a youthful, unsuccessful endeavor to heighten tragic effect by introducing the grotesque. This attempt grows out of a total misconception of the blending of serious and comic elements in Shakespearean drama. That Kleist himself judged this an unsuccessful expedient may be inferred from the fact that henceforth he refrained from presenting the grotesque in tragedy. Although he portrayed violent, extreme manifestations of human conduct unshrinkingly, he subsequently avoided tragic-comic effects such as those provided by Ursula and Johann. What outwardly appears as grotesque buffoonery may, however, represent Kleist's desire not merely to unmask but also to caricature the conception of fate, and thereby to rid himself all the more thoroughly of the torturing obsession that malevolent destiny and chance enslave man in this seemingly unintelligible universe.

The explanation frequently given for the unsatisfactory ending is that Kleist had become quite indifferent to *Die Familie Schroffenstein* because of the feverish intensity with which he was working on a second tragedy. If this is the explanation, it must be supplemented by the statement that he had outgrown not merely the tragedy itself, but also the period of life which had given rise to it. His new drama, *Robert Guiskard*, represents not merely a different theme and new esthetic problems but also a step forward to a changed positive view of life which was made possible by overcoming the tendency to regard human existence as determined by an inexorable, unintelligible fate. *Die Familie Schoffenstein* is an act of liberation from the fear of the caprice of chance and circumstance.[1] Having come to the realization that man's character determines his acts, Kleist was henceforth ready to portray personages who no longer grope blindly and hesitatingly but who actively

DIE FAMILIE SCHROFFENSTEIN

endeavor to carve out their own destiny. That the drama outwardly gives the impression of a tragedy of fate is not to be denied. But this seems to have been in keeping with the intention of the author who aimed to convince himself that what seems to be the result of a fatefully determining power is at bottom the outcome of a series of interrelated events whose origin can be found in the reactions of character under specific conditions. In *Die Familie Schroffenstein* misfortune is not precipitated by fate or by mere caprice. Disastrous error arises out of human passions of the basest kind, such as covetousness, jealousy, suspicion, distrust, and hatred, which obscure reason and warp the human soul. When reason is blinded by rage, the rational continuity of things may be broken; the sudden rupture manifests itself in an explosive act committed by a being who has momentarily lost all control over his deeds and who subsequently fails to grasp the motives underlying them. These indefinable acts are incommensurable with the ordinary tenor of human existence; they result when feeling is under too high a tension. Such tension in Sylvester was relieved by a swoon, but in the case of Rupert it led to bloodshed that involved others in disaster. Kleist has carefully portrayed intense passions as the mainspring of the action by linking them up with the situation arising from the hereditary pact. Moreover, he has been at great pains to demonstrate that, in view of poisoned hearts and minds, one misdeed inevitably leads to another, the germs of each succeeding act of violence lying in the preceding one. By dint of this analysis Kleist freed himself from a fatalistic conception of life which was contrary to his nature and hence intolerable. He no longer regarded this world as a madhouse in which blind caprice and a mysterious, malevolent destiny lure men on to ruin by inciting them to acts foreign to their nature. The hero of his next tragedy has a dauntless assertive will that grapples with adversity in an endeavor to maintain life and to triumph over vicissitudes.

Various weaknesses, crudities in motivation, incongruities, and inconsistencies have already been pointed out in the survey of the action. Others might be enumerated, but inasmuch as most of them involve matters of outward technique they are of secondary importance in a criticism of an author's first drama. Although there are obvious defects, the work as a whole reveals a youthful dramatic talent of power and individuality. And in spite of certain influences of Shakespeare and Schiller, Kleist's first work is marked by relatively little dependence. Ottokar and Agnes suggest general parallels to *Romeo and Juliet*, the incantations and superstitions of Barnabe and Ursula call to mind the witches' cauldron in *Macbeth*, and the free manipulation of plot and incident is akin to Shakespearean drama. Rhetorical effects and sententiousness, which Kleist subsequently tended rather generally to avoid as undramatic, are a legacy from Schiller. Of the numerous sententious statements, some are trivial and some seem forced or out of place. Others reflect the subjectivity of the young author and are occasioned by the disillusionment, pessimism, and doubt induced by his contact with Kantian philosophy. His fondness for parallels, striking contrasts, and sudden developments, and his tendency to defer to intuitive judgments based upon feeling are already sharply in evidence. Kleist's predilection for the unshrinking portrayal of violent emotions which leap to a sudden, eruptive discharge of cataclysmic violence is manifest in his very first drama. In fact, from the outset, much of the individuality of Kleist's character-drawing lies in his emphasis upon powerful emotions as distinguishing traits and in his unsparing presentation of extremes of human conduct. In *Die Familie Schroffenstein* are depicted the most heated intensity of feeling, a preoccupation bordering on aberration, and the readiness to toss away life as valueless if the one desire that lends meaning to existence cannot be fulfilled. Thus Rupert is as one obsessed when under the domination of a fit of anger, and Ottokar is deaf to everything but his grief on hearing that the girl he has loved in secret is of the family he has sworn to exterminate. And Agnes drinks water drawn for her by Ottokar, although she fears he may desire to poison her. But what is life to her, if the man she loves can be striving to murder her! She will have a whole loaf or none at all. All these tendencies are thoroughly Kleistian, have their counterpart in the dramatist's experiences, and are characteristic of his works.

In other particulars, as well, Kleist's first tragedy bears the impress of his own individuality. Like his later dramas, it is marked by sparing use of monologue. Ottokar and Agnes each pronounce two monologues. Yet one of these, at the beginning of the second act, is not a genuine monologue, for although Agnes pretends not to see her lover, she nevertheless desires him to hear her words. In the remaining three, emotions are portrayed. In none of the four do characters address themselves across the footlights to the spectator in order to acquaint him with facts which the dramatist has been unable to make known otherwise. Kleist employs monologue sparingly because he is but little interested in prolonged analyses of states of mind and in weighing the reasons for and against a course of action. Monologues do not precede significant action largely because deeds are often too spasmodic, eruptive, and precipitate to admit of previous reflection. Consequently one cannot expect from Kleist monologues in which the entire course of events is reviewed and in which the resulting situation is analyzed with a view to its effects upon the characters involved. He held that reflection before action was inclined to produce hesitancy, indecision, and temporary paralysis. His interest lay in the dramatic portrayal of sudden, violent, unpremeditated acts rather than of calm, deliberate, reasoned deeds.

Much of the dialogue in *Die Familie Schroffenstein* likewise reflects Kleist's restless, nervous temperament. It is broken, choppy, hacked, jerky, and abrupt, designed to reproduce agitation, excitability, impatience, challenge, incredulousness, surprise, and conflicting emotions. He already displays a fondness for a dialogue akin to inquisitorial cross-questioning based upon the insistent repetition of a word or phrase in such a manner as to give a violent impulsion to the exchange of words. A characteristic example of this kind has already been pointed out in Jeronimus' skeptical questioning of the church warden from whom he endeavors to ascertain the facts underlying Peter's death.

The basic meter is iambic pentameter, with which Kleist took great liberties in order to make it conform to violent outbursts and to the characteristic qualities of the dialogue. Lines of one, two, three, four, six, and even seven feet occur, and trochees as well as anapests are to be found. In fact, many lines give the impression of rhythmic prose rather than of verse; some lines can scarcely be scanned at all. Obviously, a tragedy of such turbulent emotions would be hampered by conforming to metrical regularity. The meter of the choruses in the opening scene and of Barnabe's incantation adds further variety. That of the maidens' chorus is trochaic with an occasional dactyl, whereas

DIE FAMILIE SCHROFFENSTEIN

the chant of the male chorus gains in solemnity by being uniformly trochaic. Barnabe's incantation is decidedly irregular with a predominance of dactylic and trochaic feet. Such lack of uniform cadence is quite in keeping with Kleist's avowed indifference to metrical regularity as stated in his *Letter from One Poet to Another*.[2] Although this letter appeared in Kleist's journal, the *Berliner Abendblätter*, about eight years after the publication of *Die Familie Schroffenstein*, it states a point of view which is already reflected in his attitude toward meter in his first drama. He regarded diction, rhythm, and euphony as necessary evils, as the hampering, corporeal elements of which, unfortunately, a thought cannot divest itself if it is to be transmitted. Consequently he held that all formal elements should be as inconspicuous as possible, for when outward form is thoroughly in harmony with content it ceases to be noticed. Hence, concludes Kleist, iambs, rhymes, and assonance, as such, are of no significance.

The speech of characters in *Die Familie Schroffenstein* is but slightly differentiated with a view to reflecting temperamental differences. Sylvester, for example, who is more dispassionate than Rupert, is more inclined to lengthy discourse and to sententiousness. Kleist subsequently emancipated himself from this early tendency to insert generalizations and abstractions. They are undramatic, present an obstacle to the uninterrupted development of action, and are not in harmony with the realistic, individualistic, and strongly emotional quality of much of Kleist's drama. His vocabulary is of wide range and is not limited to refined, elevated, elegant diction. Though occasional far-fetched and unesthetic figures of speech occur, the youthful author has exercised remarkable restraint in avoiding coarseness of diction while dealing with such violent passions. Kleist's fondness for amplifying and developing similes and metaphors is already in evidence. His figures of speech often give the impression of having been shot forth from a surcharged imagination; yet their semblance of vigor and power tends to offset an occasional lack of logic. Emphasis is frequently gained, as suggested above, by the repetition of a word or phrase by the same person or by two characters engaged in rapid dialogue. The very rapidity of tempo in dialogue, its breathless restlessness, adds to the incisiveness of Kleist's diction. Interjections, interruptions, and short periods serve to hasten this tempo.

Three versions of Kleist's first tragedy have been preserved. The first one is a brief scenario in skeleton form entitled *Die Familie Thierrez;* the second is a five-act tragedy bearing the name, *Die Familie Ghonorez;* and the final one is *Die Familie Schroffenstein.* Theophil Zolling, who discovered the manuscripts of the first two versions in the Royal Library of Berlin, first published them in the year 1885 in Kürschner's *Deutsche National-Literatur.* The most recent edition of *Die Familie Ghonorez* was prepared by Paul Hoffmann; it appeared as a publication of the Kleist-Gesellschaft in 1927 and includes the entire tragedy in facsimile reproduction as well as in type. *Die Familie Schroffenstein* was first published anonymously in Bern in 1803 by Kleist's friend, Heinrich Gessner, son of the poet, Ludwig Gessner. Just when the author began work on this theme is a matter of speculation, owing to the absence of definite documentation. Paul Hoffmann sets a very early date in affirming that the beginnings date back to Kleist's sojourn in Würzburg in the year 1800.[3] This is not the place to enter upon a comparison of the three versions nor to attempt to determine the authenticity of the tragedy as published in 1803. How much of the final revision of *Die Familie Schroffenstein* as published by Gessner is to be attributed to Kleist and what part of it, notably in the last act, represents tampering by other hands is again a matter of conjecture on which the final word remains to be said. Since the manuscript used by Gessner has been lost, positive evidence is lacking as to the extent of Kleist's final revision. Suffice it to say that this revision transfers the scene of the action from Spain to Swabia, substitutes German names for the Spanish names of characters, converts the prose speeches of persons mostly of humbler rank into verse, and includes other changes largely of a formal nature. Because of the lack of local color and of individualization of background, the transfer of the action from Spain to Swabia necessitated nothing more than a substitution of names.

Kleist's first tragedy aroused but little interest at the time of its publication and, like most of his dramas, was not staged during his lifetime. Ludwig Tieck, who published a number of Kleist's works posthumously in 1821, devoted considerable space in his introduction to a discussion of *Die Familie Schroffenstein*, bestowing high praise on its general structure, characterization, and diction, but roundly condemning the ending as disharmonious. Kleist himself, who was soon absorbed in writing a second tragedy entitled *Robert Guiskard*, wrote to his sister Ulrike on March 14, 1803, requesting her to do him a favor by not reading *Die Familie Schroffenstein*.

CHAPTER THREE

ROBERT GUISKARD

DURING his sojourn in Switzerland in 1802 Kleist was interested in a number of dramatic projects. In addition to revising *Die Familie Schroffenstein* for publication he began a comedy entitled *Der zerbrochene Krug*, became more and more absorbed in the tragedy *Robert Guiskard*, and, according to a report, was at work on another dramatic theme entitled *Leopold von Oesterreich*. Of the latter no trace remains. The only information about it came from Pfuel, a friend of Kleist's, who gave the following summary of the principal scene of the one act which he claimed had been completed.

On the eve of the battle of Sempach, according to Pfuel, Leopold's knights are gayly carousing, engaged in a game of dice to determine in a sportive mood who will survive the battle on the morrow and who will lose his life in the conflict. The proud knights begin their game in a boisterous humor. The dice have one black face and three white ones, the black one signifying death. The first few knights draw death as their lot and are greeted with laughter and jest, but, as the game continues, one knight after another draws the same fateful color. Gradually, the loud merriment ceases and the company becomes reflective and sober. Finally, everyone has been apprised of the same fate. Pfuel reported that this gradual transition from hilarity and mirth to uncanny fear and gruesomeness was portrayed with overwhelming impressiveness. This scene represents a striking prelude to the disastrous battle of Sempach of July 9, 1386, in which Leopold and most of his bold knights were killed. Work on this sombre tragedy had to make way for Kleist's struggle with another theme, that of *Robert Guiskard*, which absorbed him completely.

Robert Guiskard's spectacular rise to prominence and power and the sudden frustration of his ambitious plans appealed to Kleist for more than one reason. A life of study and contemplation had lost its former charm for him since he had come to the conclusion that it could not lead to knowledge that is certain and absolute; activity, manifesting itself in great deeds and achievements, now seemed far more significant. Consequently, at this time, a man of action had a decided fascination for him. Moreover, the spectacle of a great adventurer, seemingly thwarted in his plans, but summoning all his will power to triumph over a sick body and over hostile intrigue, aroused his admiration at a time when he had overcome the dread fear of a menacing fate which appeared to control human destiny by allowing chance and error to lead man to disaster.

The career of Robert Guiskard was, indeed, a dramatic one. His father, Tancrède de Hauteville, was a Norman knight blessed with children rather than with wealth. By dint of clever strategy, dauntless courage, and dominant personality Robert was able to attain to great power in the anarchy that marked the eleventh century. He was a great warrior but not discriminating in the means he employed to satisfy his ambitions. After the death of his brother Humphred, he was proclaimed count and leader by his warriors, whose enthusiastic loyalty he had gained through his valor and who preferred him to Humphred's son, Abélard. He became duke of Apulia and Calabria, conquered Sicily, vanquished the Saracens and Greeks, married his daughter Helena to Crown Prince Constantine of Greece, and was planning a campaign to seize Constantinople when he succumbed to an epidemic in the year 1085. In the tragedy, Kleist concerned himself merely with the closing events in the life of the hero and portrayed him as already encamped before Constantinople with the goal of his tremendous ambitions within sight and almost within reach.

Of this tragedy, *Robert Guiskard, Herzog der Normänner*, there is extant but a torso of 524 lines which the author published some years after a bitter struggle for the completion of his project had failed. How far his work had progressed when, in a fit of despair, Kleist burned it in Paris in 1803 is unknown. In 1808, ten scenes were published in Kleist's journal, *Phöbus*, but plans for completion were never carried out. No definite information is available as to the manner in which these few scenes were reproduced. Some have surmised that a copy of the original manuscript may have been lent to a friend and escaped the conflagration; yet the more plausible conclusion seems to be that the author rewrote these scenes largely from memory. This conjecture is based upon Kleist's prodigious memory as it manifested itself in the repetition of expressions and incidents in his writings and upon the fact that he recited parts of his drama to his fatherly friend, Christoph Martin Wieland. Kleist, whose speech was rather halting, had gone so far as to study declamation in order to be able to recite this tragedy to better advantage. The sole manuscript of *Robert Guiskard* is in the Prussian State Library at Berlin; it contains only lines 44 to 425 and is not an original manuscript but merely an incomplete copy made from the *Phöbus* publication.

Kleist's active work on this tragedy dates back to the spring of 1802. His source seems to have been a lengthy, detailed, and somewhat rambling article by Major Karl Wilhelm Ferdinand von Funk, published in Schiller's journal, *Die Horen*, in 1797 under the title *Robert Guiskard, Herzog von Apulien und Calabrien.* It is possible that Kleist was familiar also with the memoires of the Byzantine princess, Anna Kommena, as published by Schiller in 1790 in his *Allgemeine Sammlung historischer Memoires.*[1] Funk's article, which depicts various episodes of Guiskard's life with tensely dramatic interest, gives a much better characterization of the valorous Norman adventurer than do the memoires of Anna Kommena, in which Guiskard does not occupy a place of primary interest. Of the two accounts, Funk's sheds far more significant light on the person, character, career, and exploits of Guiskard, although similar traits are assigned to the dauntless hero by both writers. As usual, Kleist took great liberties with historic materials, selecting whatever served his dramatic and poetic ends, rejecting and changing whatever did not conform to them. For this reason his sources shed little, if any, light on the probable development and conclusion of this tragedy, though there has been much futile speculation as to the outcome of the plot.

The *dramatis personae* include Robert Guiskard, his son Robert, his nephew Abälard, his wife Cäcilia, his daughter Helena—the widowed empress of Greece who is affianced to Abälard—an old man, a delegation of Norman warriors, and the Norman people. The ten scenes are staged in the same locality. Kleist has indicated the setting with some care, departing therein from the indifference to scenic background manifest in his first tragedy. Here a number of details indicate a varied and picturesque setting which is in keeping with the colorfulness introduced by so vast a gathering of people. Cypresses grow at the foot of a hill on whose crest is pitched Guiskard's tent in the Norman camp before Constantinople. In the foreground fires are fed from time to time with incense and strongly fragrant herbs. The fleet is seen in the background. In *Die Familie Schroffenstein* each new scene represents an actual change of locality, but here change of scene is determined by the entrance or exit of characters rather than by transfer of the action to another place.

In the opening scene a delegation of Normans in military attire appears, accompanied by people of both sexes and of every age. A note of uneasiness is introduced at once by the restlessness of the people. In unison they address their representatives, whom they are accompanying to Guiskard's tent and whom they are instructing as to the importance of their mission. With a master hand Kleist has portrayed the desperate situation in the Norman camp, which is ravaged by pestilence. All are obsessed by the haunting fear of death; they are actuated by but one desire, that of being led from the pest-ridden camp before they all fall victim to the dread plague. Their anxiety is heightened by their knowledge of the determination and firmness of Guiskard, whom they are entreating to forsake his plans of conquest lest death by pestilence claim them all. As the waves of the sea dash upon a rock in vain endeavor to move it, so this army surges down upon Guiskard. The twelve representatives are implored to send a thunderbolt down upon him so that he may lead them away from the horrors of the camp. The persuasive efforts made by the people to convince their spokesmen of the necessity of moving

Guiskard indicate that their hopes are none too high. Their chieftain, one may infer, is not the man to yield to exhortations and to turn his back upon Constantinople, whose very walls he has reached. By stressing the necessity of a powerful appeal, the people at the same time reveal the situation in all its horror. If Guiskard does not snatch them from this devouring pestilence, there will be nothing left of his army save one great funeral mound by the sea. Grimly personified, the plague stalks with long terrifying strides through the fear-stricken hosts; from swollen lips it breathes the venomous fumes of its bosom into their faces. Sudden death sweeps away both horseman and steed; the fear of contagion drives friend from friend, bride from bridegroom, and mother from child. Those attainted by the disease have been isolated on a hill, from whose distant, desolate crest their wails are heard. Hideous vultures, in such numbers that cloudlike they darken the sky, surge down upon the helpless even before death releases them from their horrible sufferings. To this terrifying picture the people add a warning which contains a sinister premonition. If Guiskard, their fearless, defiant leader, does not yield to their entreaties, he himself may be stricken by the malady and, rather than conquer the imperial city, he may come to an untimely death. Instead of blessing him, their children may curse him for the annihilation of their fathers as in wrath they eject his bones from his grave. This opening scene, spoken in its entirety by the people, is of rare power and impressiveness, and clearly sets forth the general situation without the slightest trace of conventional exposition. A nameless dread of contagion haunts Guiskard's forces, impelling them to make a request of their chieftain which they fear will not be granted, since such compliance would be altogether out of keeping with his nature. Their admiration for his dauntless courage and indomitable will is mingled with a feeling of resentment at the thought that he may not yield to their entreaties and that inglorious horrible death from the hideous plague is threatening them all. Consequently, one wonders at once what effect a refusal, which seems imminent, may have upon this agitated throng. The regularity of meter, striking compounding of words, sonority of diction, individuality of imagery, and a sense of impending doom combine to make this scene one of sombre portent. Speaking in unison as they do, the people produce the effect of tremendous power and of being of one accord in their insistent demand.

In the second scene, Armin, an old man, endeavors to disperse the terrified mob, whose agitation is becoming more and more violent. The growing perturbation manifests itself in the dissolution of the chorus into individual voices. Armin rebukes them for their unruliness, which smacks of rebellion, and offers to carry their entreaty to Guiskard. His offer is accepted with the instruction that he is to press their case before Guiskard, the inexorable; if the latter turns a deaf ear, Armin is to remind him with a voice like thunder of his duty toward his people. At this, the tent opens and Helena appears. The old man warns the people to be quiet, reminding them that he is the spokesman of supplication and not of rebellion.

Helena endeavors to calm the people, who have been growing more and more turbulent, by an appeal to their long devotion to Guiskard; then she reminds them that at the first dawn of day they are disturbing the brief slumber of their chieftain, who has spent the past three nights arduously combating the plague and destruction which are closing in on all sides. To this, Armin replies that the sun is high in the heavens and that, as long as he can recall, Guiskard has always risen much earlier than they; he promises, however, that they will wait quietly until he awakens. Ill at ease, Helena obviously desires them to leave but dares not press her request that they go. She reënters the tent, alleging that she seems to hear Guiskard's footsteps within. Her words have carried no conviction; indeed, various individuals have sensed her uneasiness and have observed the contradiction in which she involved herself by stating in almost the same breath that her father was both sound asleep and walking about in the tent. On other occasions she has seemed glad to see the people approach, but today she clearly wishes to be rid of them.

Immediately after these manifestations of uneasiness a Norman enters, beckoning to Armin and to a warrior. The newcomer's countenance is troubled, his lips are pale; though struggling to appear calm, he gives every visible sign of being deeply agitated. Having looked about anxiously to see whether he is being observed, he exhorts the two men to manifest no signs of amazement, and to betray emotion neither by exclamation nor by change of facial expression. He leads them forward and mysteriously narrates his story. While standing guard at midnight before the entrance to Guiskard's tent, he suddenly heard pitiful moans and groans which sounded as if a sick lion were breathing his last. Thereupon, anxious, feverish activity followed within, and the duchess herself awakened a servant, who rushed forth to summon the entire family. One by one they hurried in, troubled and in scanty attire; finally the servant returned with a weird mummy clad in mantle, boots, and helmet, whose attire hung on him as if suspended from a nail. Seized by strange forebodings, the sentry laid hold of this mysterious being, turned its face to the moonlight, and recognized—the duke's physician. The sentry ends his account but does not dare to formulate in words his suspicion that Guiskard has fallen a victim to the contagion.

At this tense moment the tent opens and young Robert emerges with Abälard. The former abruptly summons the spokesman of the throng to step forward and rebukes the old man roundly for having consented to become the mouthpiece of mutiny and for having dared to call the chieftain from his tent. Armin remonstrates gently, protesting his humble devotion to Guiskard. He refers to the old custom in the Norman army of requesting the leader to appear, pointing out that Guiskard has graciously complied with such requests in the past, whereas Robert has repeatedly denied them. Robert's angry, arrogant retort is characterized neither by moderation nor by sound judgment; he orders Armin to leave at once. This affords Abälard an opportunity of displaying a conciliatory attitude toward the spokesman and of making a hostile attack upon Robert while defending the people's demand to be heard. His enmity toward Robert arises from rivalry as to which of them shall eventually inherit Guiskard's crown. Instead of bluntly affronting the people, as Robert has done, Abälard flatters them adroitly in an endeavor to win their favor. He poses as their friend and calls upon them to remain and to present their plea. Robert, who knows thoroughly well what motives actuate Abälard, endeavors to undermine his rival's attempt to ingratiate himself with the multitude. Haughtily he reminds them that he is their ruler's son and calls upon them to state whose word carries greater weight with them, Abälard's or his own. His rival maintains that he, too, is the son of a Norman duke, since his father Otto ruled before Guiskard, who was instituted merely as guardian to reign until Abälard had arrived at his majority. On being called upon by both to decide between them, Armin praises the personal traits of Abälard, who seems to bear resemblance to their admired leader, Guiskard, but concedes the greater authority to Robert as son of their ruler. The people are ready to obey the latter, not because he is Robert but because he is Guiskard's son. Hence they will leave, though Armin expresses the desire to bring them back at an opportune moment. Robert, who has blustered and stormed, now withdraws his former command and weakly agrees to allow them to return on the following day, on that very noon or even within an hour, provided Guiskard, on having dispatched important business, is ready to see them. Thereupon Abälard first taunts Robert for his vacillation and then turns to the throng and announces that Guiskard is ill. When asked in terror by Armin whether it is the pest, Abälard replies evasively in the negative, saying that he scarcely fears it is the pest, although the physician manifests uneasiness and believes it to be so. For this disclosure Robert curses his hostile rival as a traitor; he then enters the tent.

The growing suspicions of the people have been confirmed; now they are seized by a panic. Without Guiskard they count themselves hopelessly lost. Breathlessly they ply Abälard with questions: Is Guiskard really ill with the plague? Is he feeble? Has he a fever? Is he consumed by thirst? To the first question Abälard replies equivocally, saying there can be no certainty as yet, and since death is the only certain index, they may be sure that Guiskard will deny it, deny it even at the point of death. Yet, he adds, the physician, the duchess, the daughter, and the son himself, as the people have seen, do not doubt it. Abälard affirms that all the dread symptoms are present in marked degree, but that in spite of his weakness Guiskard is still gazing longingly at the battlements of the imperial city, that he is still consulting the map in his hand and weighing plans of gigantic conquest. One significant circumstance betokens a change, he adds. Until today Guiskard has steadily refused to negotiate with two Greek princes who had secretly offered to hand over the keys of Constantinople on one condition. (This condition is appended by Kleist in a footnote which explains that the traitors were to admit Guiskard to the city on the promise that Guiskard himself was to wear the crown rather than to give it to his daughter Helena, the exiled Queen of Greece. It had been the duke's intention to have Helena, who had been driven out by Alexius Komnenes, seize the crown in behalf of her children.) Now, in spite of Guiskard's past honorable steadfast refusals, he has today sent forth a messenger agreeing to this stipulation. And so, if nightfall finds him still alive, they may count on his ordering an attack upon the city. Crafty as he is, Abälard has not succeeded in achieving his obvious desire to arouse rebellion against Guiskard's plans for continuing warfare in the face of the menacing pestilence. The danger of losing their chieftain has entirely dispelled thoughts of turning back; their one desire now is that he may order the attack, that they may follow him, and that he may lead them in many a future battle to victory and to death. Hypocritically, Abälard voices the same desire, but launches one more dart at his young rival by adding that Guiskard's empty boot could take the city more readily than could Robert without the aid of his father.

At this moment Robert returns with the announcement that Guiskard has transacted his affairs and will appear at once. Abälard is terrified at this news but tells Armin that only a few moments ago Guiskard was lying in his tent unable to move a finger. By way of further characterization of the duke's strength of will, he adds that Guiskard's spirit triumphs over his body and over destiny. At last the duke, upon whom interest has been focused for nine scenes, is seen coming from his tent; he is full of vigor, deep-chested, broad-shouldered; he is clad in armor and wears a tall plumed helmet. With transports of joy the people hail him. His first words, accompanied by a gesture of authority, are directed to Abälard, whom he commands to maintain silence and to step behind him. The prince, who has sought a place in the multitude, obeys, while Guiskard fixes his gaze upon him and tells him they will subsequently have a word in private. Armin does not present the people's request at once but expresses their happiness at seeing the rumor of his illness dispelled. The duke laughs, refers to the strength of his body and to the clarity of his voice, and asks jestingly whether they can conceive of the idea of dragging his vigorous frame over to the pest-stricken corpses on the field. He adds that they will never bury him in this camp; he will stop in Constantinople and not before. He admits that he has felt a little less vigorous today but claims that this is the effect of his great efforts in behalf of his army. No malady, he asserts, has ever triumphed over his physique; the very pest would fall ill from gnawing at his bones. Armin pleads with Guiskard to desist from further exposure, but the duke's reply contains the implication that he bears a charmed life and that they need entertain no fears for him. He now directs Armin to proceed with the request of his subjects but to be brief because momentous affairs demand his return to the tent. Scarcely has the spokesman begun his recital when Guiskard looks around. The consternation of the duchess and Robert and the surprise of Abälard find expression in broken question and exclamation. Helena has enough presence of mind to draw up a drum; Guiskard sits down, thanks her half audibly, and urges the spokesman, who has stood lost in thought, to continue. After a moment's reflection the latter describes the ravages of the plague in such terrible colors that the duchess is overcome with horror, falls into the arms of her daughter, and has to be led to her tent. Armin's sinister picture is more than she can bear. He portrays the victim of the plague, whose poison-laden bones collapse beneath him, who sinks down again and again, whose mind becomes horribly deranged, who gnashes his teeth at God and man and rages at friend, brother, father, mother, and children. Armin closes with the entreaty that Guiskard lead his subjects out of this vale of anguish back to their own land, flight being the only means of saving the faithful army.

The spokesman's recital is interrupted by the byplay of Guiskard and his family in such a way as to rob it of all tedium; in fact, the description of the pest gains in impressiveness because of the veiled action accompanying it. With rare skill Kleist has lent interest to a speech of some length whose general import was known beforehand. As it is, the spectator's concern is increased by being centered about the condition of Guiskard, whereas the attention of the people is fixed primarily upon the speaker. In this manner the danger of their discovery of the duke's feebleness is somewhat lessened.

From these ten scenes, which comprise the torso, the plot cannot be inferred in its entirety. Yet there can be no doubt that Guiskard has actually been stricken by the plague. If his plans for the conquest of Constantinople are to succeed by an attack on that very day, then his illness must be kept from the people and he must endeavor to dominate all outward signs of illness and weakness. The repeated reference to the pestilence, to Guiskard's symptons, and to the sudden, hideous end of those attainted, points, however, toward his death as the only possible outcome. But his demise will be accompanied by the miscarriage of his stupendous plan of conquest at the very moment when his goal is within reach. The tragic element lies not in mere death but in the duke's heroic and unsuccessful struggle to triumph over the ills of the body long enough to achieve his aim. Everything depends upon his physical strength. For, in spite of the menacing plague, the people have reaffirmed their readiness to follow him to battle, victory, and death. Moreover, Abälard, cowed as he is, can provide no great opposition as long as Guiskard retains his vigor. Consequently the main outlines seem to be established as pointing to the duke's death without the realization of his ambitions. But the complications of the plot and the details of its development remain a matter of surmise. An element of intrigue is disclosed in Guiskard's acceptance of the terms described above, whereby two Greek princes are to betray Constantinople into his hands provided he will seize the Greek crown instead of giving it to his beloved daughter. Rather than see his plans frustrated by an untimely death, he will accede to this condition, which hitherto he has persistently refused to accept. By doing so, he will rob his daughter Helena who, of all his family, is most affectionately devoted to him. Moreover, at the same time, he will be thwarting Abälard's desires of coming to power as her husband. Whether Guiskard would have adhered to this agreement in the event of a victory connived at through the treachery of the Greek princes is in no way foreshadowed in the fragment. It might not have been out of keeping with the crafty, unscrupulous nature of the historical Guiskard to refuse subsequently to abide by the agreement. Another complicating element lies in the rivalry between Robert and Abälard. Yet, whatever might have been the outcome of their hostility, it seems obvious that neither one can be regarded as capable of carrying Guiskard's plans to successful completion in the event of his death. And even if the duke should succeed in dominating his pest-ridden body long enough to take Constantinople, the incapacity of his successors will undo all he has achieved. What the outcome of these implications was to be is problematical, although secondary conflicts linked up with the central theme are definitely foreshadowed. The tragic effect is heightened by the spectacle of a family torn by inward dissension while its head is struggling with death.

Comparisons have frequently been made between *Robert Guiskard* and Sophocles' *Oedipus Rex* with a view to pointing out the influence of the Greek tragedy upon Kleist's fragment. Investigation has disclosed that from June 18 to July 15, 1803, Kleist borrowed a translation of *Oedipus Rex* from the Dresden library.[2] Although this points toward his interest in the Greek tragedy while he was at work on *Robert Guiskard*, the fact remains that outward similarities in plot are at bottom casual enough. Matters of form and style probably interested him far more in his reading at the time than did incidents of plot. In both tragedies the people as a whole are threatened with extermination by a plague, incense is burning on the stage, and people of various ages appear on the scene headed by a spokesman who is to present their plea for alleviation of their distress. Yet the differences between the two are much more significant than are a few superficial similarities. At the very opening of the Greek tragedy the king appears in person before his subjects to ascertain the cause of their torments, but in Kleist's fragment the people are addressed in turn by Helena, Robert, and Abälard before Guiskard, upon whom attention has been centered throughout, finally appears in the tenth scene. By raising doubts as to whether he will come at all and as to whether he can come, Kleist has created suspense. Oedipus is entreated to discover some remedy or other, whereas Guiskard's followers have sent a delegation with a definite petition, to be seconded, if necessary, by the insistent demand that they be led away. The Greek king manifests grave concern for the well-being of his people, but Guiskard is occupied primarily with the success of his plans of conquest. There is far more concrete realism in Kleist's portrayal of the ravages of the pest and more rhetorical emphasis in the picture of the plague as given by the chorus of Sophocles. The latter description is couched in much more general terms and is marked by far greater restraint. In *Robert Guiskard* the plague and its dangers are decidedly more imminent and menacing; Kleist never allows one to lose sight of the horrors of the pestilence, which stalks along in gruesome, fear-inspiring, dread personification, active, all-pervading, and ever attacking new victims. In the tragedy of Sophocles the plague is soon lost sight of, and interest centers more and more upon discovering the meaning of the oracle and the author of the misdeeds in punishment of which the plague has been sent. This endeavor to discover the identity of the impious murderer relegates the pestilence to a position of minor importance, whereas in

Robert Guiskard the threatening danger arouses constant fear and suspense. In Kleist's tragedy the people are vitally concerned in the action; they surge about restlessly and irresistibly, representing power in spite of their fears; they are not an impersonal chorus but human beings endowed with characteristic traits. They appear not only as a mass, but individuals as such stand out, thereby giving the impression of particularization. The sonorous quality of the opening scene spoken by the people in unison, and the different motifs introduced by the subsequent speech of individuals, produce a musical effect of greater variety than does the chorus of Sophocles. Kleist's people voice a concrete demand; in keeping therewith they indulge in no rhetorical reflections or generalizations, nor do they recite formal lyric passages. They are not spectators in an action but are decidedly a part of it; indeed, they never lose sight of the fact that their lives are at stake and are intimately bound up with the development of events. Furthermore, the spirit and mood of *Robert Guiskard* differ altogether from the tragedy of Sophocles. Kleist makes no reference to oracles, gods, and their decrees, or to mysterious powers which must be appeased if a curse is to be removed from the people; no strange personal identity need be revealed and no far-fetched curse or evil deeds require atonement. Since he eliminated such impersonal directing agencies he had to concern himself much more with careful characterization as the mainspring of the action. This is apparent both in the differentiation of individuals in the multitude and in the particularization of the small number of major personages. These are sharply drawn because their character is to have a decisive bearing upon the course of events.

The fundamental difference lies in Kleist's greater emphasis upon concrete realism, upon individuality of characterization, and upon variety. Nevertheless, he made concessions of a formal stylistic nature which he must have felt more and more as so many shackles on his tendency to individualize. He seems very definitely to have striven for greater harmony, for more regularity in rhythm, for continuity and euphony, for uniformity, elevated style, and refined diction. Thus the meter of *Robert Guiskard* is more regular than in any other of his dramas. It varies but little from uniform iambic pentameter; only two lines of irregular length are to be found, both of them having six feet. There are fewer instances of enjambement, the rhythm is smooth, the tempo is less hasty, there is less tendency to break up lines, and there is no tossing back and forth of words for the sake of emphasis as in *Die Familie Schroffenstein*. This restraint is not at all in conformity with Kleist's nature. Such moderation, together with the simplicity of plot and the presentation of a final catastrophe, rather than the progressive detailed portrayal of a richly varied action, marks an approach to ancient classical tragedy. That such concessions, for concessions they clearly are, involved Kleist in difficulty is not surprising. His insistence upon reducing drama, as far as possible, to action causes him to do away with monologue and long epic narrative. But the latter, in particular, he could not easily dispense with in an analytical exposition necessary to an understanding of a final catastrophe. In dealing with an historical or mythological subject, the Greek dramatist could assume that his spectators were familiar with the general facts leading up to the catastrophe. Kleist, however, could assume nothing of the kind in presenting Guiskard as the hero of a tragedy. Nevertheless, he surmounted such obstacles by terse, compact presentation of expository data. As a result, the action develops so speedily that the inevitable catastrophe looms up almost too rapidly. But fundamentally, Kleist's difficulty goes back to his temperament and to his personality. Regularity of a conscious sort, regularity arising out of careful design, is foreign to his nature; hence the unity and reasoned harmony of classicism are scarcely to be expected in his dramas. If, as Wieland implied, *Robert Guiskard* represented an attempt on the part of Kleist to effect a synthesis between what is best in ancient tragedy and in Shakespeare, then Kleist's failure to carry such a project to its conclusion must have resulted in part, at least, from his inability to introduce a sufficient amount of the restraint of Greek tragedy. Moreover, Kleist's genius is much more closely akin to Shakespeare in the tendency toward individualization in character portrayal. His characterization is marked by a wealth of details whose purpose is to motivate action out of character. In the very nature of the case such efforts at psychological motivation cannot be harmonized with a determinism which has its basis in the decrees of gods and in oracular ambiguities. But, beyond the difficulty or impossibility of harmonizing two types of drama rooted in entirely different social conditions, there remains another factor which lies in Kleist's nature.

While at work on *Robert Guiskard*, Kleist had not yet realized that, for the naïve, spontaneous artist, content can scarcely be divorced from form. He subsequently saw that immediacy in the transmission of thoughts is essential and that spontaneity of production is irreconcilable with profound conscious reflection upon formal considerations. For Kleist form and content are inseparable; they constitute a single entity. He was much less interested in formal elements, as such, than in powerful human emotions, in the range of their manifestations, and in the extremes to which they might be pushed. Obviously enough, such surging emotions cannot be constrained by cold, statuesque formalism of diction, style, rhythm, meter, and tempo. Kleist portrayed his own emotions and much of himself in his dramatic personages. Their actions and reactions were his own, or at least such as he was capable of. To subject them to formal considerations was to subject himself to such considerations. The result could be only something un-Kleistian. And, indeed, as far as can be judged from the fragment, *Robert Guiskard* is altogether different from Kleist's other works. Although the tendency to individualization in diction crops out here and there, and although restless, unruly nervousness is incipiently present, one is conscious of a restraint which runs counter to the author's nature and does violence to it.[3] *Robert Guiskard* lies outside of the general line of dramatic development foreshadowed by *Die Familie Schroffenstein*. There is no sudden bursting forth of elemental passion which irresistibly sweeps everything before it; though varied, the dialogue and diction lack the range so characteristic of Kleist; the cadence is too regular and the tempo is too moderate to be in keeping with his tumultuous, passionate, intense nature. *Robert Guiskard* is impressive, magnificent, and grand, but not truly Kleistian. It resembles the powerful surging of a great stream rather than the precipitous dashing of a mountain torrent over irregular, steep cascades. Kleist's failure to complete this fragment can be attributed only to his endeavor to produce something which ran counter to himself. Restraint imposed by conscious formal considerations paralyzed his productivity.

Although in some respects *Robert Guiskard* lies outside of the line of Kleist's development, it nevertheless represents definite progress in other particulars. The motivation is marked by a surer touch, the action is concentrated, and melodramatic effect is absent. Kleist has omitted monologues altogether, has refrained from sententious statements, and has placed the emphasis more and more upon the action as such to the exclusion of everything undramatic. There is development also in the positive conception of life which is reflected here. Man is no longer weak, passive, and baffled but is actively engaged in shaping his own destiny. He struggles heroically with adversity, asserts his will, and achieves great success. With a definite goal in view, he falls only after a gallant, determined, ennobling conflict, which redounds to his greatness. Moreover, the conflict is with natural forces, not with error that arises out of blind and base passions. The pestilence that thwarts the hero is a natural phenomenon and does not represent a fatalistic conception any more than do sunshine, flood, frost, and rain. And Guiskard's final destiny is the outcome of his character quite as much as was his rise to power and eminence. His intrepidity, his resolution, ambition, and firmness of will have brought him into prominence; these very same qualities make it impossible for him to turn his back on a plan to which he has set himself. The fearlessness and devotion with which he cares for his pest-stricken followers expose him to contagion and result in his becoming attainted. This is but another instance in which death halts a human being just as his endeavors are about to be crowned by an impressive, climactic success. To regard this frustration of a gigantic, ambitious plan as the work of a jealous, inexorable fate or as punishment for guilt incurred by double-dealing represents a conception of life, morals, and art that does grave injustice to the author of *Robert Guiskard*.

Allusion has already been made to Kleist's despair at his inability to complete his tragedy satisfactorily. His letters contain a pathetic account of the height of his ambitions and his overwhelming disillusionment at failure to reach the pinnacle of dramatic success at a single bound. On May 20, 1802, he writes from Switzerland to his fiancée, Wilhelmine, that there is one word in the German language which, as a rule, women do not understand, namely ambition. He will return to his fatherland only in the event that he can satisfy certain expectations of other people. If he cannot reappear as an illustrious person, he will never come back. In a letter from Weimar of December 9, 1802, he tells his sister Ulrike that the beginning of his poem arouses the admiration of everyone who hears it. But already he seems to entertain doubts as to his ability to conclude the drama. For he exclaims: "If only I could complete it! Let heaven grant me this one desire; then it may dispose of me at will." The next month he writes to Ulrike that he will shortly have much joyful news to impart, for he is about to realize all human happiness. In a letter of March, 1803, he writes with great satisfaction of the enthusiasm which Wieland manifested on hearing his tragedy. Kleist's sheer joy at the inward emotion of the old poet was such, he says, that he was unable to speak; he fell down at Wieland's feet and showered fervent kisses upon his hands. On July 3, 1803, in a letter to Ulrike, he refers to a certain discovery in the field of art which he hopes will rank him among the immortals. But less than three months later, on October 5, these hopeful utterances are followed by a letter of utter despondency. It is literally true, says he, that he would gladly give a drop of his heart's blood for every letter of an epistle which might begin with the words: "My poem is completed." He has devoted a half thousand successive days and most of their nights to the endeavor of winning another wreath that might be added to the many wreaths of his family; now its sacred patron saint tells him to desist. Deeply moved, she kisses away the perspiration from his brow and consoles him, saying that if every one of her beloved sons did as much, the family name should not lack a place among the stars. He adds that it would be folly for him to expend more effort upon a work which, as he is finally forced to admit, is too difficult for him. In bitter anguish he cries out: "Hell gave me my semi-talents; heaven gives man a full talent or none at all. I cannot tell you how great my grief is. With all my heart I should gladly go whence eternally no man returns." Three weeks later, on October 26, 1803, he again writes to his sister: "What I am about to write, may cost you your life, but I must, I must, I must do it. In Paris I read my drama, as far as it had been completed, rejected it and burned it: and now everything has come to an end. Heaven denied me fame, the greatest of this world's goods; like a stubborn child I cast away all others. I cannot prove myself worthy of your friendship and yet without this friendship I cannot live: I am rushing to my death."

Kleist now resolved to enlist under Napoleon, who was reported to be planning an attack upon England; he rejoiced at the thought of finding death in this hazardous undertaking. But, having proceeded to Boulogne-sur-Mer in search of the French fleet, he was rescued by a friend from the danger of being seized and shot as a spy, was taken to Paris and provided with a pass to Potsdam. On arriving at Mainz, however, Kleist collapsed completely and became critically ill. This illness was one of several which followed upon grave crises in his life; his body gave way under the intensity of the nervous and mental strain to which it was subjected.

Some years later, on December 17, 1807, Kleist wrote to Wieland that the proudest moment of his life was when he declaimed his *Robert Guiskard* for the old poet. Wieland himself wrote a letter on April

10, 1804, to a physician in Mainz named Wedekind, in whose care Kleist had been at the time of his breakdown. This letter deserves to be reproduced in part, at least, because of the light it sheds upon Kleist and upon his work on his tragedy. On coming to Weimar, Kleist had visited Wieland, to whom he seemed mysterious and a good deal of an enigma. Hearing that the young man's quarters were very undesirable, the old poet invited him to come to Ossmanstedt, just outside of Weimar, and live with him. This Kleist did, and became a member of the Wieland household for some nine or ten weeks. Although he seemed to have a filial love and respect for his host, he remained distant and reserved. Among various noticeable peculiarities of his was a strange form of absent-mindedness; in the course of a conversation a single word seemed to suggest a chain of ideas in such vivid fashion that he would become oblivious to everything that was said. He had a most peculiar manner of mumbling to himself at table as if he were all alone or far removed and occupied with some very different matter. He finally confessed to Wieland that at such moments of absent-mindedness he was busy with his drama but that he had in mind so high an ideal that as yet it had been impossible for him to put it in writing. To be sure, he had written down many scenes from time to time, but he had always destroyed them because of his constant dissatisfaction with them. Wieland made every effort to persuade him to develop and complete his drama in accordance with the plan he had outlined; he urged Kleist to submit it for his friendly judgment or at least to complete it so as to be in a position to view it as a whole and to be able to make necessary changes. After many vain requests to be permitted to see but a single scene, Wieland finally succeeded in persuading his guest to recite from memory a few of the most important scenes. The host was astounded, and assured Wedekind that if the spirits of Aeschylus, Sophocles, and Shakespeare combined to create a tragedy, it would be what Kleist's death of Guiskard the Norman was, provided all of it conformed to what Kleist then recited. From that moment Wieland was convinced that the young man was born to fill the great gap in German dramatic literature which, in his opinion, had not yet been closed even by Schiller and Goethe. He used all his persuasive efforts to induce Kleist to complete his drama. The latter had seemed tremendously pleased at the impression his recital produced upon Wieland, and made many promises, but nothing came of them. Afraid of tormenting him, Wieland henceforth referred to the drama as little as possible while Kleist remained his guest. Wieland's praise, however, continued to be a source of comfort and a stimulus to the young, struggling poet, whose dramatic genius was misunderstood and unappreciated.

Robert Guiskard is a tragedy of greater depth than *Die Familie Schroffenstein* partly because of the impressive character of the hero, whom Kleist has most convincingly endowed with true greatness and authority. Moreover, the thwarting of an ambitious plan of conquest and dominion on the very eve of its successful achievement is far more tragic than the fitful calamities befalling rather passive, short-sighted creatures whose passions blind them and lead to error.

While at work on this tragedy, Kleist came under the spell of Guiskard's destiny to such an extent that he himself began to fear that death might overtake him before his stupendous ambition to win undying literary fame at a single bound had been satisfied. Like the capture of Constantinople by the Norman duke, Kleist's burning desire to complete his tragedy was destined to remain unachieved.

CHAPTER FOUR

AMPHITRYON

AFTER the mental and physical collapse which followed his failure to complete *Robert Guiskard*, Kleist was for a time too broken in health and spirit to devote himself to new literary projects. At Königsberg, where he resided from May, 1805, until the end of the following year, Kleist busied himself with French literature and translated into German Lafontaine's fable of the two pigeons and Molière's comedy, *Amphitryon*. Like other sons of aristocratic Prussian families of his time, he had been schooled in French; moreover, he had spent some time in Paris and was well read in the literature of France. Consequently he was well equipped for the task of translation. Having apparently lost confidence in his belief that his was a great genius destined to make a singular contribution in the field of drama, he now devoted himself for a time largely to literary activity of a less original nature. Yet so strong was his individuality that it transformed, to a considerable extent, the works he translated. In both translations Kleist took the liberties which characterize his sovereign use of source materials in general. The two pigeons of Lafontaine became lovers who clearly represent Kleist and Wilhelmine. His former fiancée had meanwhile become the staid wife of an industrious professor of philosophy, who had in time succeeded to Kant's chair at the University of Königsberg. Kleist's version of the fable reflects some of his feelings upon meeting anew the girl whom he had requested in a letter to write to him no more.

Kleist's translation of the French play bears the title *Amphitryon. Ein Lustspiel nach Molière*. In a letter written to the poet Wieland on December 17, 1807, he refers to *Amphitryon* as a recasting of Molière's comedy. Unfortunately his correspondence sheds no light whatsoever on his work or on his intentions as a translator. He writes that his friend, Rühle von Lilienstern, had to sell the manuscript for twenty-four louis-d'or, which in Kleist's opinion was but a third of what it should have brought. Even this meager sum was paid only after long delay by the purchaser, a Dresden publisher named Christoph Arnold. On September 17, 1807, Kleist writes to Ulrike that his translation has been read repeatedly in Dresden social gatherings where it finds favor. He estimates that Arnold's profits, derived from the publication of *Amphitryon*, are six times as high as the price he received for the translating. It is quite possible that this figure is exaggerated by the author who, at the time, was planning to establish a publishing house with the optimistic expectation of realizing large profits from printing his own and other works.

The theme of Molière's comedy was a favorite among the ancients who were fond of regarding their legendary heroes as conceived by gods. According to Greek mythology, Zeus assumed the likeness of Alcmène's husband, Amphitryon, and, appearing to her in this disguise, begot a son, Heracles, during her husband's absence. Molière's comedy is based upon Plautus' *Amphitruo* and bears the influence of Jean de Rotrou's comedy, *Les deux Sosies*, of the year 1636. Molière's *Amphitryon* was first given in January, 1668, with the author playing the rôle of Sosie; shortly afterward it was published with a dedication to Condé. His *Amphitryon* is a light, sportive comedy in which Jupiter seeks amorous adventure much in the manner of a *grand seigneur* of the time of Louis XIV. It is reported that, on reading it for the first time, Voltaire laughed so heartily that he fell back on his chair, turned over backwards, and narrowly escaped serious injury.

Molière's play opens with a prologue in which Mercury bids the night retard her flight so as to prolong the joys of Jupiter who, disguised as Amphitryon, is profiting by the absence of the Theban general and is playing the rôle of an amorous young husband. His predilection for the charms of Alcmène is but a passing one, for Dame Night informs Mercury with a slight disapproving shake of her head that Jupiter is not content with assuming human form to satisfy his desires but that he becomes a bull, a serpent, a swan, or anything else to suit his fickle fancy. To this Mercury retorts:

> Laissons dire tous les censeurs:
> Tels changements ont leurs douceurs,
> Qui passent leur intelligence.
> Ce dieu sait ce qu'il fait aussi bien là qu'ailleurs;
> Et dans les mouvements de leurs tendres ardeurs,
> Les bêtes ne sont pas si bêtes que l'on pense.

These lines serve rather well to characterize the Jupiter of Molière as an Olympian roué who is in the habit of neglecting the heavens for the sake of variety in the gratification of desire. Mercury regards the god's amorous adventures as a welcome relief from imprisonment in grandeur and takes pleasure in the thought that the highest deity has a hundred happy, ingenious ways of gaining acquiescence from even the most haughty daughters of earth. And the ending of the comedy, in which the identity of the celestial pleasure-seeker changes the aspect of things, is foreshadowed by Mercury's words:

> Lorsque dans un haut rang on a l'heur de paraître,
> Tout ce qu'on fait est toujours bel et bon,
> Et suivant ce qu'on peut être
> Les choses changent de nom.

In the play proper, Sosie, Amphitryon's valet, who is endowed with less courage than nimbleness of tongue and wit, is seeking his way home with the aid of a lantern in order to carry a message to Alcmène from her husband. The latter has just defeated the enemy in battle and sends word to his wife of his impending return. Poor Sosie, who is frightened by every sound, first discourses on the hard lot of a valet and then, addressing himself to his lantern, rehearses the message he is to bring to Alcmène. While engaged in his recital, he is amazed at seeing Mercury appear disguised as his double. By dint of many blows, executed with enviable skill and precision, Mercury disabuses Sosie of the notion of being Amphitryon's valet and prevents the interruption of Jupiter and Alcmène by the messenger. Jupiter is now presented in the act of taking leave from Alcmène. He would like the assurance that she has conferred her favors upon him with the spontaneous ardor accorded a lover rather than as the mead due a husband and that he is indebted for the passionate felicity of the night to his own irresistible charming person rather than to his disguise. Such subtleties remain unintelligible to Alcmène, who makes no distinction between husband and lover. Subsequently, comic scenes result from mistaken identity and from Sosie's attempts to explain his adventures with his other "I." On his return, Amphitryon hears with consternation that Alcmène fancies having entertained him the preceding night and that she has showered upon her nocturnal visitor the full extent of her marital favors. Hurt by this affront to the honor of his home, the general leaves to summon his wife's brother, who is to prove an alibi for him. Meanwhile Sosie's wife, Cléanthis, whose carnal appetites are greater than her charms, upbraids her husband violently for his indifference toward her during the past night when Mercury, disguised as Sosie, turned his back upon her. Nothing could have offended her more than such stubborn, disdainful continence. Jupiter subsequently appears to Alcmène in disguise a second time and obtains forgiveness for the doubts voiced by her husband. During this second meeting Mercury, disguised as Sosie, refuses Amphitryon admission to his own palace. When Jupiter emerges, the two Amphitryons are face to face. Enraged, the real Theban general leaves to summon his friends so that his identity may be established. The situation is finally cleared up, and from a cloud the god declares:

> Un partage avec Jupiter
> N'a rien du tout qui déshonore.

He announces that he himself, crowned with immortal glory, was unable to triumph over Alcmène's fidelity and that he received from her only what she believed to be granting her husband. She is to give birth to a son, Hercules, and all the world will envy Amphitryon's lot. Sosie, who has the rare gift of setting forth things as they are, observes dryly that Jupiter knows how to sugar the pill and that it is the part of widsom to pass such affairs over in discreet silence.

The above summary, which is far too cursory to do justice to Molière's play, is necessary to an understanding of Kleist's version. What was there in this comedy that interested the German dramatist primarily, and wherein lies the fundamental difference between the French original and the German adaptation? Kleist was deeply interested in manifestations of emotions and especially in emotions evoked under unusual, trying circumstances. Consequently he was attracted by the sensibilities and reactions of a woman of innate purity like Alcmène who, although incapable of fickleness or of wanton desire, found herself in the incomprehensible situation of outward infidelity committed with the profoundest innocence of heart and intention. With this psychological conflict in mind he portrays her as a somewhat pensive young woman of incomparable charm and sweetness, of touching purity and innocence. All her thoughts and emotions center about her husband; her love for him is such that it excludes all else and that she can imagine the deity himself only in the image of Amphitryon. With such a central figure in mind, Kleist obviously had to devote especial care to her portrayal. Moreover, the deepening of her character necessitated a corresponding change in Amphitryon and in Jupiter as well. Such transformations introduce a serious element which was quite foreign to the comedy of Molière and which places the emphasis much more strongly upon character and less upon outward situation.

As in Molière's play, the entire action takes place in Thebes before the palace of Amphitryon. The personages include Jupiter in the guise of Amphitryon, Mercury in the guise of Sosias, the Theban general Amphitryon, his servant Sosias, Alkmene, Sosias' wife Charis, and several generals. In the original as well as in the translation the scenic background is entirely neutral. In its main outlines the first act does not differ essentially from Molière's comedy.

At the opening of the second act Sosias is giving a report of his experiences, which Amphitryon is totally unable to decipher. Sosias, who cannot comprehend how he was confronted and beaten by his own double, naturally is unable to make his master understand his singular encounter. He narrates that it was impossible for him to enter the palace because his other I blocked his entrance and beat him mercilessly. This devilish I, this I that insists upon being the only I, that I of the palace, the I of the stick, the I that beat me half to death, says he. It is not at all surprising that Amphitryon can make neither head nor tail of this mad gibberish. All that he ascertains is that Alkmene has not been apprised of his coming.

At this juncture the two are spied by Alkmene who is leaving the palace to worship the gods and to pray for their blessing upon her husband. On seeing him, she exclaims in surprise: Back so soon? He, however, reminds her that he has been absent for five full months. But she replies that he can scarcely charge her with giving him a cold greeting, since during the past night with warm bosom she richly accorded him every favor. Furthermore, she reminds him of the words with which he had expressed the boundless measure of his joy; never had Hera rendered Jupiter as happy as she had made him. She concludes that he owes her an explanation because of his sudden unannounced return and because of his denials of his presence with her during the night. As evidence of their meeting she exhibits the diadem of Labdakus which he had taken from the enemy and given to her. But Sosias, who has been commissioned to bear this gift to her with Amphitryon's message, draws the case from his pocket. Strange to say, the seal is undisturbed but the diadem has vanished. The general no longer denies his visit to Alkmene but insists upon hearing all the details, alleging that he has certain reasons for making such a request. But when she narrates what has happened, he cries out in anguish that whoever stole in at dusk in disguise is the greatest of scoundrels. He casts aside all moderation; henceforth—like Rupert Schroffenstein—he will revel in rage and revenge. With torn, bleeding heart Alkmene thereupon declares her intention of leaving him and of freeing him that very day of any bond which unites them.

A comic scene enacted by Sosias and his wife, Charis, now affords relief from the harrowing torment just portrayed. The tender couple is shortly joined by Alkmene, who shows Charis the diadem of Labdakus. Alkmene, who has begun to doubt, has seized the jewel as invaluable evidence of her fidelity; but just as she is about to press it to her lips she discovers the initial J. She insists that she cannot have been mistaken, and that the letter originally was an A. Yet even if she was mistaken in the initial she was not mistaken in the person. For without eyes she could still behold Amphitryon, without ears she could hear him; devoid of all senses, her heart and her innermost feeling would distinguish him from the entire world beyond all possibility of error. She is as certain of not having been mistaken as she is of the purity of her soul. The only difference of which she was aware was that she considered him handsomer than ever before, more like a picture of himself drawn from life by the hand of an artist and brought closer to the divine. She recalls the unspeakable feeling of happiness which came over her on seeing him return as a glorious victor; never had he seemed quite so exalted, and quite as if he had flown down from the stars. But she cannot drive out the recollection of his repeated ambiguous reference to a difference between himself and Amphitryon. She cannot be comforted, she has neither witness nor evidence, for even the jewel bears testimony against her. This use of the initials on the diadem as evidence designed to shake Alkmene's confidence in herself is Kleist's own invention and addition.

Jupiter now returns in the guise of Amphitryon. When appealed to by Alkmene to tell her whether he, her husband, gave her this jewel bearing the initial of another, he endeavors to reassure her by telling her that he himself appeared to her in the night. Yet she senses an evasion in the words that it was her lover, no matter what she may have felt or thought, and that whoever crossed her threshold was received by her as Amphitryon. She cannot live without the conviction that she is innocent in act as well as in thought. Since she cannot bear to remain longer in the home of him whom she has unwittingly wronged, she must leave him. And now Jupiter realizes that his jealous hopes have been deceived, that Alkmene thought of him only as her husband and that he owes nothing to any transcending super-identity which might have differentiated him from the husband. The god was nothing, the husband was all in all to her. When he then tells her that Jupiter himself appeared to her, she deems such words blasphemous or at best a magnanimous attempt to distract her thoughts. Since her soul constantly reverts to the grievous error, he comforts her by saying that only a god could have approached her and that even a god was forced to adopt her husband's features in order to be received by her. He then suggests that Jupiter may have appeared to her to punish her for visualizing the deity in the form of Amphitryon. But she justifies herself by saying she can think of God only by visualizing him and lending him features. Henceforth, says Jupiter, she is to think of God at the altar in the likeness of him who appeared to her that night. More than ever he now realizes that even a god, as such, cannot tempt her to any thought or act of infidelity. Desirous of being loved by the purest of women, he feels repulsed and lonely on a Mount Olympus devoid of love. He tells her of the joys the deity showers down upon mankind and asks, in case she were destined to reward Jupiter for all his bounty to humankind, whether she would requite his generosity with a single smile. With reverent humility she replies that she would not refuse to fulfill a sacred duty if chosen to do so by the decrees of the gods. Let him who created her, rule over her, says she; yet if she had her free choice, she would give reverence to Jupiter and love to Amphitryon. Not yet satisfied, the Olympian insistently pursues his aim. He now asks: If I as God held you in my embrace and Amphitryon should appear, how would your heart declare itself? Under those circumstances, says she, I could but wish that he were God and that you might remain Amphitryon as you are. This reply fills Jupiter himself with an admiration akin to awe. In Alkmene he sees his creation, so sweet and so adorable as to approach the divine conception of human perfection. He declares that everything shall be cleared up and orders Sosias to invite all in the camp to appear as guests at a feast of conciliation.

Strangely enough, Sosias and Charis have been witnesses to this entire scene. Although their presence is entirely out of place, it gives rise to splendid comedy. For the thought now comes to Charis that a god may have appeared to her as well. So she immediately sets about to test Sosias in an effort at determining whether he is a deity or just plain Sosias. Perceiving signs of humility and contrition in her which he had never before noted, her husband manifests an unusually authoritative manner. From this she concludes that he is godlike. And when wrath flames forth from his eyes she is convinced that he is divine and falls at his feet. But Sosias, the realist, whose interests center upon cheese and cabbage, is unequal to playing the exalted rôle of an Olympian deity. One makes a dog of me, says he, and another would see a god in me. I am the old well known ass, Sosias! As soon as Charis hears this admission she is convinced of her husband's identity; her sense of inferiority vanishes into air, and she again is the shrew who tyrannizes her poor ass of a husband. This scene, with its splendid comic effect, is also of Kleist's invention.

The third act opens with a monologue by Amphitryon, who declares his conviction that his wife is as incapable of deception as a turtledove; he could more readily believe in the honesty of knaves who have escaped the hangman's noose than in any malice on her part. The sole conclusion at which he can arrive is that her mind must be deranged; at daybreak he will have to summon his physicians.

Mercury now appears disguised as Sosias. Bored with following Jupiter on his amorous adventure, he decides to have a bit of sport at Amphitryon's expense. Aroused by the commotion outside, Jupiter leaves the palace and confronts his amazed double. The generals behold two Amphitryons and cannot decide which is their leader. Sosias steps to the side of Jupiter and proclaims him the real master. Enraged, Amphitryon draws his sword in order to solve the riddle by a duel. But his generals refuse to permit such conflict, and Jupiter announces his intention of assembling the entire people in order to prove to them who he is. Likewise, Amphitryon is going to summon his friends to support his cause against the impostor.

In the final scene Jupiter enters with Alkmene, Mercury, and the generals. One of the colonels now suggests that Alkmene be called upon to decide which is her husband. She pronounces Jupiter her husband and, in the bitterest terms, denounces Amphitryon as a vile impostor. This denunciation is devoid of restraint; yet its very harshness reveals the depth of her outraged feelings. Surprisingly enough, her words do not wound her husband as might be expected, but serve to assure him all the more of her truthfulness. He swears that he would place more credence in her sincerity than in the oracle or in the voice of thunder. She has convinced him beyond the slightest doubt that she has innocently taken Jupiter for her husband. Alkmene, who requests Jupiter to dismiss her and spare her the further ordeal of confronting a thousand eyes, is detained by him so that she, whom he deems more resplendent than the sun, may celebrate a triumph unparalleled in Thebes. After telling Amphitryon that he is Amphitryon indeed, Jupiter asks Alkmene whether she is of the opinion that her husband appeared to her. She begs him ever to leave her in that belief lest her soul be shrouded in eternal darkness. The god of heaven finally reveals himself, Alkmene swoons, and all prostrate themselves at his feet. At Amphitryon's request Jupiter promises that Alkmene shall bring forth a son, Hercules, whose fame shall eclipse that of all heroes before him. Mercury, in turn, reveals his identity to Sosias and departs after Jupiter. Alkmene's final word is a sigh: Alas! Like other characters of Kleist, she is rendered speechless by the overwhelming stress of events. Her one sigh is a trembling echo of troubled emotions and of a tortured soul. At the same time it denotes relief at seeing her innocence of heart and intent established and at hearing the assurance that things will remain as they were. But it also seems to voice a doubt that they may ever again be as of old.

A general outward similarity between original and translation is apparent. The main incidents of Molière's plot have been preserved; monologues and asides, though not in accord with Kleist's own general preference, are retained and, with the exception of the three principal personages, the characters retain their old identity fairly closely. With ironical humor the name of Cléanthis has been changed to Charis. Certain external changes are in evidence. Kleist eliminated the prologue between Mercury and Dame Night and retained the division into three acts, but he designated certain monologues as independent scenes. This accounts for the third scene of the first act and for the seventh and ninth scenes of the third act. In the main, Kleist's first act adheres to the original, but in the other two acts he institutes rather sweeping changes, eliminating some of Molière's scenes and essentially transforming the character of the last half of the second act and of the two closing scenes of the play.

What is the basis for this transformation? It lies fundamentally in Kleist's conception of the character of Alkmene. Molière's heroine was, after all, a conventional dame of the seventeenth century who observed the proprieties but chanced to receive Jupiter because she was deceived by his disguise. There is no conflict within her soul, since she does not become aware of the fact that she has embraced a god rather than the mortal entitled to share her couch. And with due regard for certain *convenances* Molière has spared her the embarrassment of appearing on the scene after the substitution has become known to others. As a result she does not figure in the third act at all. The conventional though lightly frivolous tone of the French comedy as a whole becomes all the more apparent when compared with John Dryden's play of the same name; this appeared in 1690 and is based upon Plautus and Molière. The rollicking humor of Dryden's *Amphitryon* is broad and coarse; with Anglo-Saxon directness he bluntly revels in licentious crudities and would quite evidently have preferred vulgarisms even if the English tongue had evolved the same clever, insinuating suggestiveness with which the French idiom playfully and elegantly refers to the salacious. Molière was interested primarily in presenting in entertaining, sportive fashion the amours of Jupiter with Alcmène and the resulting discomfiture of Amphitryon until the god should choose to reveal his identity and thereby put an altogether different face on the deception practised. It merely happened to be Alcmène this time rather than the wife of another. Consequently there was but little need of characterizing her whose turn it chanced to be to satisfy the god's desire. His Alcmène is a faithful little wife whose sincerity and absence of frivolity is evidenced by her failure to comprehend Jupiter's subtle distinctions between husband and lover. And, after all, those few traits of her character are necessary to an understanding of Amphitryon's wrath and his wounded feelings at the thought of a breach of fidelity on her part. Yet there is nothing in her nature which would fill Jupiter himself with touching admiration for her and which would serve to convince Molière's Amphitryon of her profound innocence of heart and intent. Doubt as to her own innocence never arises in Molière's Alcmène, whereas, with the merciless insistence so marked in him

Kleist spared his heroine nothing, but placed her in the most trying situation that can be conceived for a woman of her integrity. Her soul is torn by the very thought that unwittingly she may have been guilty of an act of infidelity. Since outward evidence, even in the form of the diadem, points against her, the sole means of bringing conviction to her husband lies in the utter sincerity of her nature. And Kleist stressed her character with just this in view.

Amphitryon, likewise, had to be raised to a higher, more serious level to be in keeping with Alkmene and to be worthy of her regard and affection. Invested as he is with a more sensitive nature, Kleist's Amphitryon suffers keenly, whereas his prototype manifests more of the wrath characteristic of the deceived husband of comedy. The unselfish greatness of Kleist's Amphitryon is in striking contrast with the usurpation of Jupiter, for he declares that if Alkmene recognizes Jupiter as her husband, he is willing to free her from all embarrassment at once by ending his life. Moreover, only a man of great, noble, and forgiving character could have been so profoundly impressed with his wife's innocence at the very moment when from the depth of her outraged sensibilities she denounced him as a shameless impostor.

The deepening of Alkmene's character necessitated a corresponding change in the character of Jupiter as well. In the first act he differs but little from the god of Molière's comedy, although, in keeping with subsequent development, Kleist's Jupiter places a greater emphasis upon the distinction between the joys of this and of other nights. Though a god, he desires assurance that he has aroused in Alkmene the fullest response of passion. He desires to be loved for his own sake; he asks her to promise to remember this night as one apart from all others and not to confound it with those which are to follow. Yet, at bottom, here as in the first act of the French comedy the god produces very much the impression of a happy lover who has been given to fond imaginings while separated from the object of his passionate ardor. In the first act of both plays, Jupiter's questioning seems to be prompted largely by a feeling of masculine *amour-propre;* having received more than ever before, the male desires the happy assurance that he, too, has aroused and given more than ever before or than anyone else has done. It is in the fifth scene of the second act that Kleist introduces the most significant change in the character of Jupiter. This becomes necessary because a frivolous god bent only upon the gratification of desire at the expense of others could not possibly be so moved by Alkmene's touching purity and by her yearning for assurance of her innocence. And although the subsequent spontaneity of Jupiter's admiration perhaps reflects less of the god and more of Kleist's own involuntary enthusiasm as it was evoked by this beautiful creature of his poetic imagination, it nevertheless represents an influence emanating from her which commands profound respect for her character. It is impossible for Jupiter to regard her as a beautiful daughter of earth who will feel flattered by being chosen to dispel the boredom of a god. Such vanity belongs to Charis and not to Alkmene. In the second act Jupiter is portrayed as lonely and as yearning for the love of mankind. But the fact remains that he courts this love in women only and is indifferent to the affection of man. Moreover, in spite of this alleged love for mankind he deals harshly with both Alkmene and Amphitryon; he delays his revelation of himself and thereby prolongs their torture to the utmost. And from a modern viewpoint he has clearly wronged them both by abusing his omnipotence. Thus Kleist's conception

AMPHITRYON 97

of Jupiter, because ennobled, presents contradictory aspects.

The difficulty in presenting the character of Jupiter with consistency arises out of the fact that he combines elements which are irreconcilable to the modern mind. In his origins he is a god of ancient mythology whose anthropomorphism manifests itself in the form of sensual desire. The modern dramatist consequently has to struggle with the ethical aspects of the situation which were of no concern to the ancients. Furthermore, it is a difficult matter for a dramatist of the nineteenth century to lend dignity to a Greek mythological deity without endowing him with attributes suggested by the religions of modernity. Therefore, the moment Kleist set about to deepen the character of a god engaged in amorous pursuit he was beset with complications of a contradictory nature. And yet Jupiter had to be transformed from a celestial wanton in order to harmonize with Kleist's heightened conception of Alkmene. For if the god had appeared merely as a pleasure-seeker, the violation of her peace of mind and innocence would have seemed nothing short of brutal. Hence inconsistencies in portrayal were bound to arise. It has already been pointed out that in the first act Jupiter is very much like the frivolous god of Molière's comedy. Yet the second act contains a pantheistic reference. The difficulty in arriving at a single satisfactory formula covering Kleist's polymorphic deity has perhaps misled critics into giving undue stress to an alleged mystical tendency. The very nature of the relation between the seen and the unseen involves a mysterious element that defies rationalistic analysis, for the human mind cannot comprehend the infinite with which it has been pleased to endow the invisible godhead. Yet despite the much more serious portrayal of Jupiter in the second act and the triumphant authority with which he is invested in the last act, he remains at bottom less a mystically conceived transcendent being than a god of classical mythology having the desires of man. And the longing that draws him down from the loneliness of Mount Olympus is not mystical but remains essentially the desire to gratify human instincts. His *amour-propre* prompts the desire to be loved by the gracious Alkmene for his own sake, and all his arguments, all his varied presentations of himself, all his powers of imagery, of eloquence and persuasion are exerted in the vain hope of wresting from Alkmene the admission that he, a super-lover, has granted her felicity hitherto unexperienced and that her love goes out to him. Kleist's legacy from older sources barred the way to consistent, convincing, serious portrayal of the deity in the given situation. And quite apart from the difficulty inherent in the peculiar situation, it is not surprising that Kleist's presentation of the deity should be lacking in unity. For ever since the collapse of his rationalistic view of the godhead as an abstraction of perfection, absolute truth, and omniscience, he had regarded the spirit underlying the universe as quite unintelligible to man.

Those stressing the mystical element in Jupiter are prone to link it up with Christian views of an immaculate conception. Again, this seems to grow out of the tendency to read religious views and doctrines into an externally analogous situation. The ancients were given to regarding legendary heroes as begotten by gods; as a result of religious teachings, modernity almost unconsciously associates divine origin of man with immaculate conception. That Kleist's friend, Adam Müller, a romanticist converted to Catholicism, asserted that the drama dealt with the immaculate conception of the holy virgin just as much as with the mystery of love as such, is not surprising in view of romanticism's penchant for such religious symbols. Yet there is nothing tangible in Kleist's drama that lends itself to such interpretation. Moreover, there is nothing in Kleist's letters and writings to indicate that he thought of a union of the divine and the human through an immaculate conception.

By transforming the character of Alkmene and of Jupiter, Kleist has made the drama more profound; yet he has done so at the expense of unity, harmony, and consistency. Not only are there irreconcilable traits in Jupiter, but the comic element is not in keeping with the tragic aspect of the scenes in which Alkmene figures. In the case of Amphitryon and Alkmene, mistaken identity causes great anguish and intense suffering, but in the scenes centering about Sosias confusion of personality gives rise to broad comic effects. To be sure, Sosias and Charis thereby furnish comic relief, but the gulf between the two situations created by similar means is too wide. Kleist's drama acquired a dual character which is foreign to Molière's unified comedy.

Kleist broadened the comic element supplied by Mercury, Sosias, and Charis. He did this by making the diction more vigorously concrete, by giving it wider range, and by rendering it somewhat coarser and more popularly realistic. Sosias is invested with the clownish traits of carnival comedy but, at the same time, has some of the clever wit and shrewdness of a court jester. He is not as discursive as his prototype, expatiates less on the hard lot of a servant, and does not discourse on the reasons given by medical authority for continence as cited by Molière's Sosie to Cléanthis. He is less of a *raisonneur* than the valet of the French comedy.

In the main, Kleist's translation, as such, is decidedly felicitous; it is characterized less by literal exactness than by the ability to seize upon the significant and reproduce it in a form that takes cognizance of the difference in spirit of the two languages. A comparison of the original with the translation serves to bring out in bold relief the colorful, picturesque realism of Kleist's diction and his ability to intensify by substituting concrete wealth of incident for generality. He is fond of adding intimate details by way of particularization. Thus Alkmene's narration of the arrival of Jupiter in disguise evokes the background so well suited to an appreciation of her serene nature. She refers to the evening twilight, to the quiet room in which she was spinning, to the sound of the spindle, to her dreams of the field of battle, and to the entrance of Jupiter-Amphitryon who stole in unobserved and woke her from her revery with a kiss.

Kleist's tendency to take liberties with iambic pentameter is again marked. There are lines of one, two, three, four, and six feet. Verse accent and word accent often fail to coincide and rhyme occurs frequently. Irregularities in verse need never occasion surprise in Kleist's dramas, least of all here, since Molière's comedy is written in *vers libres*. Heinrich Füser points out that the translation is well adapted to the content but is inclined to be unmindful of the versification; either Kleist was unconscious of such shortcomings or he was unwilling to give up a good translation for the sake of the integrity of the verse.[1] Due perhaps to the influence of the original, there is less broken dialogue than in *Die Familie Schroffenstein*. Nor is there the same fondness for the repetition and the tossing back and forth of a significant word or phrase.

Amphitryon was published in the spring of 1807 under the direction of Adam Müller while the author was still held by the French as a prisoner of war. The publication was accompanied by a preface from the pen of Müller. Goethe's comments were unfavorable. According to him, Kleist was intent upon confusing Alkmene's inner feelings. In his opinion, ancient and modern tendencies were not harmonized in *Amphitryon* but were placed in opposition to each other. If, by dint of contortion, said he, the opposite ends of a living being are brought together, no new type of organism results; at best, the result is only a strange symbol like that of a serpent biting its tail.

Goethe's first observation is inaccurate. Kleist has indeed portrayed Alkmene as confused and deceived. Yet this is not the end he seeks but is an attendant circumstance. Kleist's characters are frequently perturbed, the clarity of their judgments is troubled by untoward circumstance, and, as a result, the universe and life seem inexplicable; yet he is much more concerned with their striving for clarity and their rising above confusion than in leaving them confounded. The difficult situations in which his characters find themselves, and their efforts at maintaining and regaining equipoise reflect the perplexities of his own life and his endeavor to achieve harmony, calm, and a measure of happiness in an indifferent and even hostile world. Like Kleist, Alkmene has an ardent desire for happiness; she will be content to have suffered the grief Jupiter caused her, if only everything will subsequently remain friendly to her as it was before. But there can be friendly assurance and happiness for her only if her innocence is established. In a sense, Alkmene's inner feeling did not deceive her, for Jupiter is the idealized Amphitryon of her fond imaginings; he is Amphitryon at his best, to whom her affection must of necessity go out even more strongly. All throughout, her thoughts and affections have centered about her husband. In Jupiter, Amphitryon has become the incarnation of his ideal self; he has been transfigured into that more ethereal perfection of which she had dreamed. In thought and intent she has remained faithful to herself and to her ideal of him.

CHAPTER FIVE

DER ZERBROCHENE KRUG

AT KÖNIGSBERG, where Kleist recast Molière's *Amphitryon*, he probably resumed work on *Der zerbrochene Krug*, a play of his own invention which is ranked among the leading German comedies of literary merit. He had begun work on this theme early in the year 1802 while in Switzerland but was interrupted by his feverish interest in the tragedy, *Robert Guiskard*. According to his friend Pfuel, who had one day questioned his ability to write comedy, Kleist dictated the first three scenes in Dresden in 1803 as a convincing refutation of the challenge. Kleist seems to have completed the play in the summer of 1806, for on August 31 of that year he wrote to Rühle von Lilienstern that on the preceding day he had sent his cousin Marie a copy of *Der zerbrochene Krug*.

Kleist's letter to his friend Rühle contains significant observations about himself and his relation to poetic productivity. As long as life lasts, declares he, he is going to write tragedies and comedies. He requests Rühle to state his candid opinion of this comedy and to fear nothing from his vanity as an author, for his opinion of his own ability is but a shadow of what it was in Dresden. The truth is that he finds his conceptions beautiful, rather than their execution. If he were fit for anything else, he would seize upon it with all his heart: he writes for the simple reason that he cannot refrain from doing so. He has given up his career as a government official and is going to live on the income derived from his dramatic works; Rühle's unfavorable judgment of his play would grieve him only because that would augur starvation. He asserts that he can write a play in from three to four months, and, if he obtains forty friedrichs-d'or for it, that will suffice to sustain him. But he realizes that he needs to improve his technique, to get more practice, and to learn to produce better things in shorter time. At the moment he is engaged in writing a tragedy. There is nothing more divine than art, he exclaims with fervor. And nothing easier at the same time; and yet, why is it so difficult? Every first movement, everything involuntary is beautiful, but reflection immediately twists and distorts it. O reason! he exclaims, unfortunate reason! He counsels his friend not to study too much, but to follow his intuitive feeling and to put down at random whatever he deems beautiful. It is like casting a die, says he, but there is no other way.

These remarks are profoundly significant because they disclose a definite change in Kleist's attitude. He had yielded to pressure and accepted office but found it incompatible with his temperament and his interests. Unable to resist the impulse to write, he has now decided to give up an employment which has proved irksome; henceforth he will devote his life to dramatic productivity. At the same time he hopes to live on the proceeds from his writings—a hope which doubtless had encouraged him to throw off the yoke of government service. Strangely enough, not quite five years earlier, he had felt the urge to write but had rebelled at the idea of writing books for money, even though he was then in financial straits and felt assured that he could thereby earn more than he needed. A more significant change, however, lies in his attitude toward art. Failure to complete *Robert Guiskard* evidently led to the conclusion that much speculation and reflection on theory is not only futile but paralyzes spontaneous creation. Henceforth the first creative impulse is to have full sway, and other considerations are to be ignored. This letter was written while Kleist was at work on a new tragedy, *Penthesilea*, which bears the impress of this changed viewpoint. And a certain independence, in form and structure at least, is likewise manifest in the comedy which he has just completed. Like *Penthesilea*, it is divided merely into scenes without further grouping into acts. It represents a distinct departure from traditional practice by its intermingling of exposition and action throughout practically its entire extent. And it is the first broadly realistic German comedy of outstanding merit to be written in iambic pentameter. The extent to which Kleist freely followed his creative impulses in writing *Penthesilea* will be discussed in a later chapter.

The beginnings of *Der zerbrochene Krug* date back to the dramatist's sojourn in Switzerland in the winter of 1802 and to his associations with a group of young men having literary interests and aspirations. This circle included Ludwig Wieland, a son of the Swiss poet Salomon Gessner, and Heinrich Zschokke, a writer of prose narratives. In his autobiography Zschokke narrates what prompted Kleist to write his comedy. In Zschokke's room hung a French copper engraving entitled *La cruche cassée*, whose figures seemed to represent a mournful young pair of lovers, a scolding mother holding a broken pitcher, and a judge with a big nose. Wieland was to use this picture as the theme for a satire, Kleist for a comedy, and he for a narrative. Kleist, says Zschokke, carried off the prize in this competition.

An extant manuscript of *Der zerbrochene Krug* in the Prussian State Library contains a preface, which, however, makes no reference whatsoever to such competition. The preface reads as follows:

This comedy is probably based on an historical incident about which I have, however, been unable to obtain exact information. I was prompted to write by a copper engraving which I saw several years ago in Switzerland. On it could be seen, first of all, a judge gravely seated upon his bench; in front of him stood an old woman with a broken pitcher in her hand, seeming to point out the damage that had been done to it. The judge was berating the accused, a young peasant lad, as guilty, and, although the latter was still defending himself, his defense was growing weak; a girl, who had apparently given testimony in the affair (for who knows under what circumstances the delictum had been committed), was standing between her mother and her fiancé, playing with her apron. No one who had borne false witness could have stood there more crushed than she. The clerk (he had probably just been looking at the girl) was looking at the judge suspiciously from the side, as Kreon on a similar occasion looked at Oedipus when the question arose as to who had slain Laius. Underneath the picture stood the words: The broken pitcher. If I am not mistaken, the original was by a Dutch master.

Kleist's memory probably played him a trick, for the picture in question seems to have been French rather than Dutch. On April 25, 1811, he wrote to Friedrich de la Motte Fouqué that his comedy was written in the manner of Teniers; he may have erred in associating the Dutch local color of his play with a Dutch painting rather than with a French engraving. In any case, Zschokke, the owner, may well be regarded as a better authority on the subject. Investigations of Karl Siegen[1] and Theophil Zolling[2] point with a fair degree of conclusiveness to an engraving by

Jean Jacques le Veau as the picture in question. This engraving was made from a painting of Philibert Debucourt which was exhibited in the Paris Salon of 1782; the painting is entitled *Le Juge ou la cruche cassée* and reproduces the girl of Greuze's famous picture, *La cruche cassée*, against another background.[3]

To Kleist's vivid imagination this engraving suggested a highly realistic comedy in which the judge, whom he mentioned first in his description of the picture, plays the principal rôle. The scene of the action is a Dutch village near Utrecht; the setting is a court room. The characters are:

Walter, Counsellor of Justice.
Adam, a village judge.
Licht, a clerk.
Frau Marthe Rull.
Eve, her daughter.
Veit Tümpel, a peasant.
Ruprecht, his son.
Frau Brigitte.
A servant, bailiffs, maids, etc.

An understanding of the synopsis of the play will perhaps be facilitated by a brief preliminary summary of the events which precede the beginning of the action. These events are revealed by degrees throughout practically the entire comedy. Adam, the judge, is an old bachelor with a bald head and a clubfoot. Nature did not endow him with handsomeness, and made matters a bit worse by implanting strong amorous surgings within him which, owing to his uninviting exterior, women are not inclined to satisfy. He happens to covet the favors of a charming village maiden named Eve. Since she is not at all inclined to grant his desires, he resorts to a ruse. He tells her that her lover, Ruprecht, who is about to be conscripted for military service, is not going to serve his time at home but is to be the victim of an underhand scheme and sent to East India, in whose murderous climate most conscripts perish. Adam offers to secure a medical statement setting forth that Ruprecht is physically incapacitated for soldiering. Late one evening he comes to her with this declaration and gains admission to her room. There he bolts the door, loosens his vest, places his wig over a pitcher on the mantel, and endeavors to secure contentment of his insistent, feverish promptings. But Eve, who is a virtuous young lass, proves obdurate, refuses, and defends herself by scratching his face. Ruprecht, her lover, who has come to chat by her window, hears a man's voice within, dashes into the house, breaks open the door, and hurtles into the room just as Adam seizes his wig, jumps out of the window, and makes his escape. The young swain succeeds in rapping his rival smartly on the head twice with the doorlatch, which has yielded to his fury and remains in his hand. But in frantically snatching at his wig, Adam had overturned the pitcher which crashed to the floor unbeknown to him as he plunged out into the night. Awakened by the din, Eve's mother rushes in, sees her precious pitcher in pieces, and accuses Ruprecht of having broken it. She threatens to take him into court on the following day and secure damages. These are the events which precede the opening of the play.

The entire comedy is enacted in a court room, a sanctuary which Adam uses indiscriminately for any and all purposes. As the curtain rises, Adam is bandaging his leg, which was injured in his nocturnal escapade. He explains to his skeptical clerk, Licht, that, while singing his morning hymn of praise and rising from his bed, he stumbled and suffered a sprain. He accounts for his scratched face and his bruised eye by telling Licht that, while grappling with a damned he-goat near the stove, he lost his balance, clutched about in the air wildly like a drowning man, caught hold of his trousers which were hanging there, tore them down, and crashed over headlong on the corner of the stove. To his discomfiture, Adam learns that Walter is arriving unexpectedly to inspect the local court, and that in a neighboring village both judge and clerk have just been suspended because of irregularities. Adam maintains that he is innocent of financial irregularities and claims that his one act that shuns the inquisitive light was only a nocturnal prank. This single case of levity he excuses on the ground that there is no reason why a judge should be as grave as a polar bear when off the bench.

As Adam and Licht are about to establish a bit of order in the office of records, where the disorder of documents resembles the tower of Babel, the imminent arrival of inspector Walter is announced. The judge would prefer to plead illness; fear has actually laid such hold on him as to have almost the effect of a violent purge. He commands his maid to search for his wig, but she reminds him that he had come home late at night without it and that she had had to wash the blood from his bald head. This he denies, and since his other wig is being repaired, he sends the maid to borrow one from the sexton; she is to tell him that their pig of a cat used her master's wig as a lair for her young. The filthy thing is lying under his bed, says he. And in order to make his story more convincing, he invents details. There are five young kittens, he adds; one is white and the rest are yellow and black. He is going to drown the black ones in the river; what else can he do? He even offers one to his suspicious clerk, Licht.

Walter now arrives and declares in somewhat reassuring words that he has come on a tour of inspection to see what the practice is in the rural courts rather than to punish irregularities; he scarcely expects to find everything as it should be, but will be content to find things tolerable. Since people are already assembling for the session of the court, he will attend the hearing and investigate records and funds later on.

While Adam withdraws to make his preparations for appearance in court, Frau Marthe, her daughter Eve, Veit, and his son Ruprecht arrive. The judge returns, clad in his robes of office, but without a wig, since the maid has been unable to borrow one. Taking cognizance of the situation in an aside, he exclaims: Surely, they are not going to accuse me before myself. But this turns out to be the case. His presentiments of evil are being realized promptly enough. In vain he tries to speak privately to Eve, who refuses to listen to him. He next requests Licht to hear the case under the pretext that his illness compels him to go to bed. But Licht, who, true to his name, has seen the light, counsels him to stay unless Walter excuses him. Now Adam turns to Eve once more in an effort at persuading her to maintain a silence which will neither embarrass nor compromise him. Again without success, for Walter directs him to proceed without previously consulting the parties in private. When asked by Walter why he is so distracted, he replies that a pet chicken of his has the pip and that he was merely asking Eve how to nurse the little patient. Finally, he can procrastinate no longer and is forced to conduct the trial. The wily old rascal experiences a sense of relief when Marthe denounces Ruprecht as the culprit. Without ceremony he orders the clerk to note down Ruprecht as the offender. But Walter remonstrates against such gross violation of court procedure, and will not allow Ruprecht to be declared guilty without a fair trial. He insists that if

Adam does not know how to conduct the case, Licht is to have an opportunity of demonstrating what he can do. Adam now directs Frau Marthe Rull to prefer her charges. But before lodging her complaint she insists upon describing the pitcher in detail in order to make clear why she attaches such great value to it. After a verbose yet colorful description of the pitcher and its history she accuses Ruprecht of having broken it. When Adam again tells Licht to write down Ruprecht as guilty, Walter objects, saying that Adam could not be less intent upon brand ng the young man as guilty if he himself were the offender and desirous of diverting suspicion from himself. Ruprecht now narrates his side of the story. On the preceding evening he had gone to Eve's house to chat with her under her window. But on approaching, he heard her talking in the garden with a man. Though unable to recognize him, he assumes it was Lebrecht, the cobbler. Hiding behind a bush, he heard their joking and carrying on, and finally saw them glide into the house. In a fit of rage he rushed in, found the door bolted, and kicked it open. But just as the door yielded with a crash, the pitcher fell from the mantle, and a man jumped through the window. He rushed to the window, found the fellow caught in the trellis, and, with the door latch, dealt him a savage blow on the head just as he fell to the ground. When he started to climb after his rival to prevent his escape, he was stopped by a handful of gravel which struck him full in the face and blinded him. Then Frau Marthe came, and all the neighbors, dogs, and cats came. And when amid the hullabaloo Frau Marthe asked who had broken the pitcher, Eve replied that it was Ruprecht.

Before Eve is heard, Adam makes a further futile attempt at postponing unpleasant disclosures by inviting Walter to drink wine with him, but the latter declines. He then suggests to his superior that the quarrel might be arbitrated without further questioning, but Walter orders him to continue the case and to hear Eve's testimony. The judge counsels her to tell the truth, that is, to name either Ruprecht or Lebrecht as the offender and not to incriminate anyone else. When Eve admits that Ruprecht did not break the pitcher, Adam endeavors to inculpate Lebrecht by suggesting that he must have committed the offense. But with indignation Eve demands how he dares to incriminate Lebrecht who, as he well knows, had to present himself for conscription and whom Adam himself had sent to Utrecht only the day before for that very purpose. The judge is now forced to take another tack, and recommends to Walter that, in view of the friendship between himself and Eve's deceased father, they allow her to go without pushing the hearing any farther. But Walter is curious to get at the bottom of the matter and urges her to declare frankly who the miscreant is. The girl, however, begs to be relieved from making further disclosures although she declares her willingness to swear on the altar that Ruprecht is not the culprit; moreover, she promises to tell her mother everything in due time though her lips must remain sealed for the present. While Frau Brigitte, a new witness, is being called, Adam tells Walter he would prefer to continue the case on the following day. But the inspector insists that it be heard now.

In the interim Adam orders the maids to bring wine and a luncheon. At the same time, he is on the alert to find an opportunity of speaking to Eve in private. His desire of adjourning the hearing and his strange uneasiness have made Walter more and more suspicious. He asks Adam what caused the wound on his head. The judge repeats that he fell out of bed and struck his head on the stove. And when asked how he received the wound on the back of his head, he says he struck his forehead on the stove and then fell over backwards, striking his head on the floor. Not yet satisfied, Walter asks how his face was scratched so terribly. The judge explains that he had hung up some brush in the corner by the stove in order to dry it for his silkworms and, in falling on it, had scratched his face. When asked how he lost his wig, Adam replies that he was reading a document the night before; having mislaid his spectacles, he bent so low over the candle that his wig caught fire. During this entire scene Adam's courage has risen; he exults whenever the situation seems less dangerous. Confident that Eve will not betray him, he jests both openly and in asides, enjoys his wine, and is greatly amused by his own facile lies and inventions.

But Frau Brigitte, the star witness who has been summoned to present a new angle in the testimony, now arrives, wig in hand. While the maids are clearing the table, Adam enjoins Eve in ambiguous terms to be cautious. It develops that Brigitte has found the wig under Eve's window, impaled on a stalk of the grapevine. Confident at last of being on the right scent and desirous of protecting the dignity of the court of justice, Walter asks Adam in a whisper whether he has no private confession to make to him. But Adam assures him on his honor that he has not. Frau Brigitte claims to have seen a bald man with a hoof like a horse rushing from Marthe's garden about midnight, leaving in his wake foul odors of steam and pitch and sulphur. On hearing what had happened during the night, she had gone back to investigate. In the snow near the vine she had found the imprints of a club foot and of a normal foot, leading from the window and through the garden. Welcoming an opportunity of saddling the devil with guilt, Adam avers that although many have denied the existence of God, no atheist has, to his knowledge, ever been able to demonstrate that there is no devil. He recommends that they address the synod at The Hague to ascertain whether the court is empowered to assume that Beelzebub broke the jug. When the judge is directed by Walter to proceed, Brigitte declares that the footprints led directly to Adam's house. To safeguard appearances Walter directs Adam in private to adjourn court. But Frau Brigitte forestalls such a solution by producing the wig. Becoming more and more aggressive, now that he knows Walter is certain of the judge's guilt, Licht places the wig on Adam's head, pronounces it a marvellous fit and thereby directs the attention of everyone to the real offender. Ruprecht now threatens Adam, saying he will not succeed in throwing sand in his eyes this time. Pressed by Walter to conclude, Adam declares Ruprecht guilty and imposes a jail sentence for contempt of court. When Eve sees her lover in danger, she casts all caution to the winds and declares that Adam is guilty of having broken the pitcher. Enraged, she urges Ruprecht to throw the judge down from his bench, but he manages to seize only Adam's mantle as the latter makes his escape.

In the following scene, the twelfth, Walter has restored order. After Ruprecht has begged Eve's forgiveness, she throws herself at Walter's feet in great distress, begging him to help them. At last the reason for her silence is disclosed as she produces a falsified letter from Adam which states that Ruprecht is to be conscripted for military service in East India. The entire situation is cleared up, and the duplicity of Adam is established. In order to prevent greater public scandal, Walter sends out Licht to bring back the judge who can be seen from the window running madly up hill and down as if pursued by wheel and gallows. The judge is to be suspended from office and is to be replaced temporarily by his ambitious clerk. Magnanimously enough, Walter expresses the hope that the accounts are correct so that Adam may not be forced to flee into exile.

In the only complete edition of *Der zerbrochene Krug* printed during his lifetime Kleist published two versions of the twelfth scene. The one included in the comedy proper contains but 58 lines whereas the one appended as a variant has 475. On the stage, the shorter version is obviously preferable, but even so the one-act comedy totals 1 974 lines, a larger number than Kleist's five-act drama, *Prinz Friedrich von Homburg*. Apparently the variant was originally conceived as the twelfth scene but was subsequently shortened as a concession to the exigencies of the theater. Internal evidence seems to indicate that the variant was written earlier, at a time when Kleist was somewhat more under Schiller's influence in matters of style and diction. Eve's much more detailed explanation becomes rather stilted and declamatory, and her account of the hostility between Spain and the Netherlands smacks somewhat of Schiller's rhetorical recitals. The patriotic tinge of her long narrative is reminiscent of Schiller's *Jungfrau von Orleans;* it is out of keeping with her character and with the spirit of the comedy as a whole. Eve's appeal to Walter in the longer version at times approaches the pathos of Schiller. Kleist, who in the main was unconcerned with the ethical aspects of the situations presented in this comedy, went to some length in the variant in justifying Eve's willingness to resort to subterfuge to secure Ruprecht's exemption from military duty in the murderous climate of East India. Since the government was guilty of misrepresentation and trickery, she was compelled to agree to deception for the purpose of protecting her lover's life and health. On the stage one can well spare the added expositional items of the variant in view of the gain resulting from greater brevity and from heightened unity of style, diction, and spirit. Once Adam, about whom the comedy centers, has been unmasked and has fled, the play is bound to gain by a more rapid termination. The comic effect can no longer be heightened by minute, eleventh-hour disclosure of the exact events preceding the action. Although the shorter version makes for slight inconsistency, Kleist did well to curtail the scene for the theater.

The structure of the comedy is deserving of consideration. As has already been pointed out, the play consists of thirteen scenes without grouping into acts. As it happens, the development of the action is such that these scenes cannot well be divided into three acts of anything like equal length. For the action does not progress in a steady line, nor by a series of accelerating leaps and bounds which, by leading to spectacular climaxes, might make for sharp divisions. Its course is an irregular, jagged one. Whenever any disclosure is made that bids fair to jeopardize Adam's position, he diverts the discussion into another channel or endeavors to silence the witness by threats or outbursts of disapproval. On the other hand, as soon as he seems momentarily out of danger, he takes pleasure in retarding developments by facetious remarks. Again, he slows up the action by throwing the pursuit off the right scent, by guiding it into bypaths and blind alleys. In short, he is ever ready to elaborate those suggestions which may ward off discovery. In the very nature of the case an action of this type does not progress rapidly. Although ultimate discovery seems inevitable, it must be delayed, or there will be no drama. It is the very delay, as it is manipulated by Adam, that makes the play. Postponement of the discovery is due largely to the character of Adam and at the same time serves to set forth his character. The presentation of expository details likewise follows an irregular course. In fact, the final items of the exposition are given practically at the close of the comedy, for in the twelfth scene the information that has been revealed piece-meal here and there is ultimately joined together. Nevertheless, for the spectator, Adam's guilt is fairly well established during the course of the first three scenes. From then on the interest centers largely on whether Adam will be unmasked and how. Consequently it is less a matter of past events than of what is to happen and of the manner in which things are to happen. With great dexterity Kleist has, throughout the play, interwoven his exposition of the past with the development of the action itself.

What gives rise to comic effect in *Der zerbrochene Krug?* Its source is twofold: situation and character. The situation, a capital invention of Kleist, is grotesque enough in that judge and culprit are one and the same person. It is singular, indeed, to find plaintiff, defendant, and witnesses appealing to the guilty offender himself for justice. At the same time, the strangeness of the situation is heightened by the fact that two people, Adam and Eve, know who the miscreant is; yet both, though for very different reasons, wish to keep the matter a secret. The case is in reality tried by three persons rather than one, for Adam, Walter, and Licht all take a hand at conducting the hearing. Another amusing feature is contributed by Frau Marthe, who is much more concerned about her pitcher and with seeing the guilty punished than with the safeguarding of her daughter's reputation. It never occurs to her that it might be the part of wisdom to sacrifice the pitcher rather than to have Eve's virtue challenged in public.

Given this situation, Adam's character becomes the mainspring of comic effect. Though a judge, he has no conception whatsoever of truthfulness; much less has he any regard for truth or for the sanctity of a court of justice. His capacity for lying and misrepresenting is astounding and unique. And yet it does not give the impression of baseness or of malicious perfidy; his mendacity seems rather to proceed from an inexhaustibly fertile imagination. It is the very inventiveness of his genius which is striking and amusing. He is never at a loss to discover a new subterfuge which shall take him out of hot water. He constantly proffers a new invention instead of exhausting the possibilities of an old one by dint of undue elaboration or repetition. Naturally enough, these numerous, fanciful, clever explanations fail to agree, yet the presentation gains in picturesque variety whatever it lacks in consistency. Adam so exults in his ability to deceive and in giving free rein to his imaginative genius that he repeatedly throws all caution to the wind; he lies even when it is quite unnecessary. At the same time, there is enough of an admixture of truth in the details he supplies to be disconcerting to Walter even when the latter has become skeptical. Adam has all the earmarks of a sly old fox who can be caught only by being smoked out of his hole. He represents an old rogue rather than a reprehensible villain; he is endowed with a splendid sense of humor, which does not altogether forsake him even when he is in jeopardy. He praises, coaxes, jests, threatens, blusters, and browbeats in most versatile fashion as the situation seems to demand. And he is ever ready to dwell on anything that seems to free him from suspicion, and to distort or pass over that which may serve to incriminate him. His very success in postponing discovery and in thumbing his nose at everyone finally makes him unmindful of danger; he would prefer to continue dodging, squirming, twisting, and evading rather than to make a private confession to Walter. Only Licht, whose insight into Adam's character is based upon closer association and has been sharpened by his ambition to replace the judge, sees clearly through his falsehoods. The comic effect is increased by Adam's grotesque exterior; his ugliness is heightened by his scratched face, a bruised skull, a bald pate, and a clubfoot. He is a splendidly conceived, original figure of comedy.

Ruprecht and Marthe add to the enjoyment by quarreling and scolding in noisy, realistic fashion; they delight in hurling gross epithets right and left. A further comic element grows out of the loud loquaciousness of Frau Marthe and Frau Brigitte; they revel in the opportunity of testifying in court; they dilate on every detail, giving as much stress to the inconsequential as to the significant. The popular realism of their narration and diction is but an expression of their sturdy, rude, vigorous being. Marthe's description of the pitcher is a masterpiece. The historic figures fairly seem to step forth from their background, endowed with life and colorful individuality. Frau Brigitte's testimony about the devil represents a laughable yet convincing blending of peasant shrewdness and superstition. And, ironically enough, Adam has to content himself with being mistaken for Beelzebub in order to ward off suspicion. Eve makes no contribution to the comic element but undergoes an experience which is not devoid of tragic possibilities in her life. She is a naïve, loyal, country girl of charm, sweetness, sincerity, and devotion. From her fiancé she desires that absolute trust and confidence which Kleist had demanded of Wilhelmine. And she is worthy of it and capable of rewarding it by every sacrifice. To have her virtue rudely questioned even by her lover and to refuse steadfastly to clear herself, in order to shield him, is indeed a severe test of love.

In *Amphitryon* and particularly in *Der zerbrochene Krug* Kleist clearly demonstrated his ability as a writer of comedy. Definite progress is discernible in the latter. In part this may be due to the greater freedom with which he was able to develop a comedy of his own invention. At the same time, he achieves broadly realistic comic effects without resorting to such elementary, facile devices as deluges of blows and confusion of identity. Situation, character, and appropriate diction of wide range are here blended into a unified comedy of colorful, realistic originality. Because of his fondness for dialectic and cross-questioning, Kleist was peculiarly suited to do full justice to the possibilities inherent in the situation provided by a court trial. He successfully avoided everything that might jeopardize the unalloyed enjoyment of comic situation and character; he included nothing that might give rise to the duality of impression so marked in his adaptation of *Amphitryon* in which the tragic element that frequently skirts good comedy is too prominent. Kleist does not dwell on the ethical aspects of the situation, indulges in no pathos, remains free from sentimentality, and refrains from all tendency to satirize Adam's open disregard for justice. The spectator soon becomes aware of the judge's guilt and realizes that he is rather sure of being found out, for, due to Walter's presence, he cannot extricate himself from his difficulty with his customary bluff, rough-shod manner of administering justice. At the same time, the spectator knows that no one is going to be dealt with harshly, for Walter has given assurance at the very outset that he expects to proceed with leniency and moderation. Consequently the theater-goer can settle back in ease and enjoy the clever game of hide and seek, knowing full well that the aim of this comedy is amusement and amusement only.

It is a tribute to Kleist's genius that he was able to write so vigorously realistic a comedy as *Der zerbrochene Krug* in verse without loss of picturesque, popular concreteness. This success is due, in part, to the liberties which he took with iambic pentameter. Justly enough, he refused to sacrifice individuality to metrical uniformity. There are lines of four, six, seven, and one of eight feet. Anapests are numerous, and word accent and verse accent often fail to coincide. Kleist's sentence structure in this comedy is likewise characterized by great freedom. Periods, on the whole, are short, and verses are frequently divided among several speakers. One verse, line 1900, is shared by five persons. Constant interruptions, questioning, and repetition of word or phrase not only lend life to the dialogue but, together with loud, violent exclamation, aid in confusing characters rather than in clarifying matters.

Kleist eliminated monologues in *Der zerbrochene Krug* but employed asides very effectively. Adam's running fire of asides is highly entertaining and amusing to the initiated spectator, especially when, with irrepressible glee, the sly judge comments on his own ruses and subterfuges. At such times he has the air of a playful goblin who revels in the mischief and confusion he has wrought.

The diction is popular, concrete, vigorous, and intensely realistic; apart from certain passages in the variant, it is thoroughly in keeping with the characters. Rude vulgarisms are frequent; like the numerous spicy plays on words, they add to the broad humor of certain situations. Proverbial statements and picturesque metaphors abound.

Der zerbrochene Krug is one of the two plays of Kleist which were staged during his lifetime. Plans for an amateur performance in Dresden at the home of the Austrian ambassador did not materialize. But Goethe, who as director of the Weimar Court Theater was searching for suitable comedies, decided to produce the play. On August 28, 1807, he wrote to Kleist's friend, Adam Müller, from whom he had received the manuscript, that the comedy had extraordinary merits and that the whole portrayal was insistently realistic; he regretted, however, that this play, too, belonged to the invisible theater. In spite of the admitted vividness of portrayal, he was of the opinion that the talent of the author inclined more to dialectic, as the stationary court procedure strikingly manifested. Goethe asserted that if Kleist could solve a genuinely dramatic problem and unfold an action before the eyes and ears of the spectator with the same naturalness with which he here unfolded a past action, the result would be a great gift to the German stage. With Müller's permission Goethe agreed to take the manuscript to Weimar to determine whether a performance might prove feasible. He claimed to have an actor perfectly suited to the rôle of Adam, which he regarded as the essential one. The others, he thought, would be easier to fill. The Weimar performance was given on the second of March, 1808, and resulted in a dismal failure. Fortunately, Kleist had abandoned his plan of attending this production. There were various reasons for the fiasco. First of all, the patience of the spectators was overtaxed by a lengthy program, for the comedy was preceded by an opera of one act by Della Maria, entitled *Der Gefangene*. Evidently the long version of scene twelve was enacted, thereby making a total of almost 2,300 lines to fill out an evening after the performance of the opera. To make matters worse, the comedy, which is conceived as a one-act play, was arbitrarily cut into three acts, none of which could possibly have represented an articulate, well-rounded unit approaching a third of the whole. It is easy enough to imagine the impatience of the audience when the curtain rose after each intermission and the action seemed to resume without any marked progress. And worst of all, the actor Becker, who played the part of Adam, was totally unsuited to this important rôle. At the rehearsals, Geothe had found it quite impossible to accelerate the tempo of his slow, tedious, laborious acting. Indeed, he was so wearisome in the leading rôle that his fellow-actors were overcome with boredom. Obviously, Becker's acting alone would have undermined any chances for a successful presentation, for the rôle of Adam must be played with celerity and sparkling vividness. Weimar theater-goers, accustomed as they were to sentimentalism in comedy, might very well have been incapable of appreciating Kleist's comedy even if it had been well staged in lively, realistic fashion. Under the circumstances, the disapproval of the audience is not surprising. When a spectator manifested his impatience by loud whistling, Duke Karl August commanded his hussars to arrest the impudent fellow who dared whistle in the presence of the duchess. The offender, an official, was seized just as he was about to escape through the door and was placed under arrest for three days.[4] Goethe subsequently stated that the failure of this presentation was due solely to the fact that the theme, which in itself was clever and humorous enough, was not embodied in a rapidly developed action.

In the March number of his journal, *Phöbus,* Kleist in 1808 published excerpts from his comedy with the following comment: "In accordance with the original plans for our journal we had intended to insert here the fragment of a larger work (Robert Guiskard, Duke of the Normans, a tragedy by the author of Penthesilea); but since this little comedy, put together several years ago, has just proved unsuccessful on the Weimar stage, it may be interesting to our readers to determine the reason thereof for themselves. And so, may it find a place here as a novelty of the day." The journal contains the beginnings of scene one and of scene six and approximately the first half of scene seven. In 1811, the entire comedy, with the long version of scene twelve appended as a variant, was published in Berlin. The excerpts appearing in the *Phöbus* had been carefully revised, but the entire comedy as published in 1811 seems to have been based more casually on one of the copies in circulation in 1806. Goethe had had a copy of the manuscript as had also Marie von Kleist; it is possible that still another existed for the proposed amateur performance in Dresden. An incomplete manuscript in Kleist's own writing is in the Prussian State Library at Berlin; unfortunately parts of the eleventh and twelfth scenes are missing. The *Phöbus* version coincides with that of this manuscript, which represents a revision and an improvement over the copy subsequently used as a basis for the publication of 1811. Professor Heinrich Meyer-Benfey assumes with reason that Kleist did not have the revised version at hand when hurriedly preparing the copy for the printer.[5]

One of the best criticisms of *Der zerbrochene Krug* written by a contemporary of the author is that by Ludwig Tieck in his foreword to the publication of Kleist's posthumous works. Tieck praises the masterful skill with which the dramatist has spun a network out of a trifle, a network which now becomes more and more and more complicated and now seems quickly to disentangle. It is vivid, writes Tieck, and ever new; all the personages are convincing, and everything arouses the greatest interest, so that the unimportance of the object is lost sight of, and it appears just as significant to us as to the quarreling parties. The conception of a judge as the delinquent who is embroiled by his attempts to clear himself is just as felicitous as it is novel. In Tieck's opinion, diction and iambs are used to better advantage in this genuinely Dutch painting than ever before in the German language.[6]

In 1850, Friedrich Hebbel, a great German dramatist who manifested considerable interest in Kleist, wrote after a presentation of the comedy at the Court Theater of Vienna that *Der zerbrochene Krug* is one of those works in the face of which the public alone can prove a failure. According to Hebbel, the most pleasing invention and the most colorful painting of manners here rise to the heights of genius and are blended like root and fruit; since Falstaff, no figure of comedy has been created worthy to unloose the shoe's latchet of Judge Adam.[7]

Kleist's comedy has had a varied career on the stage. It has already been stated that Goethe did violence to it by a division into three acts for the presentation in Weimar. Incidentally, the programs for this performance did not even mention the author's name. The text has repeatedly been mutilated by those who realized the necessity of producing it as a one-act comedy but who felt the need of reducing its length by more or less arbitrary pruning. Friedrich Ludwig Schmidt, director of the Hamburg Municipal Theater, produced it effectively in 1820 but did violence to it by abbreviations, changes, and additions of various kinds. Other adaptations for the stage have been made by Siegen, Wittmann, Kilian, and Zeiss; more recently, the tendency has been to manifest more regard for the integrity of the author's work.[8]

Theodor Döring, an eminent German comedian, and Adolf Menzel, an artist, contributed much to the interest in Kleist's comedy. The former scored great success in popularizing the rôle of Adam, and the latter drew thirty splendid illustrations which are masterfully conceived in the spirit of the play. These illustrations appeared in a handsome edition of *Der zerbrochene Krug* in 1877, the hundredth anniversary of Kleist's birth, and were reproduced in a French translation of the comedy by Alfred de Lostalot which was published in Paris in 1884.

In *Der zerbrochene Krug* Kleist clearly demonstrated his ability to write comedy of acknowledged originality, to create characters endowed with individuality, and to invent a unique situation. Had he been spared an untimely end and had conditions of life become more endurable, he might have aided signally in establishing a comedy of literary merit on the German stage.

CHAPTER SIX

PENTHESILEA

THE FIRST reference in Kleist's correspondence to a new tragedy entitled *Penthesilea* is in a letter of August 31, 1806, written from Königsberg to Rühle von Lilienstern, whom he tells that he is writing a tragedy. How long he had already been at work on it is unknown. He evidently refers to *Penthesilea* and *Der zerbrochene Krug* when he writes to Ulrike from Châlons-sur-Marne on June 8, 1807, that he has two completed manuscripts. Yet a letter written in the fall of 1807 seems to indicate that this last statement was sanguinely inexact and that he resumed work on *Penthesilea* in Dresden. This letter, presumably addressed to Henriette Hendel-Schütz, a well known actress, gives evidence of the intimate relation between Kleist's experiences and the content of this tragedy. He tells her that into it he put his inmost being, the whole grief and, at the same time, the splendor of his soul. He is curious as to what she will say about Käthchen von Heilbronn, who represents the reverse of Penthesilea, her other pole, a being who is just as mighty in her absolute devotion as Penthesilea is through action. He adds that the heroine actually devoured Achilles out of sheer love. The tragedy, he continues, has already been read twice in Dresden social gatherings and evoked tears in spite of the unavoidable feeling of horror it aroused. On the whole, he considers it better suited to men than women and realizes that not even all men can take pleasure in it. It had been calculated entirely for the warlike temper of his friend Pfuel. Kleist relates further that when he stepped into Pfuel's room and told him that Penthesilea was dead, two big tears came into his friend's eyes. Whether, in view of the demands of the public, the tragedy could be staged, was a question which, in Kleist's opinion, time would have to decide. He did not believe so, nor did he desire it as long as actors were trained only in imitating Kotzebue and Iffland. To Christoph M. Wieland Kleist wrote on December 17, 1808, that he should like to declaim *Penthesilea* for him as he had recited *Robert Guiskard*. He declares that, having coughed this tragedy from his chest, he again feels perfectly at liberty. When both of these tragedies appear, Wieland may tell him which of the two is the better, for he himself, so he asserts, does not know.

Into none of his dramas did Kleist put quite so much of his anguished soul as into *Penthesilea*. That he identified himself in spirit with the heroine is obvious from the close correspondence between her violently passionate outbursts and passages from his letters that are written as with his heart's blood. Her tragic struggle for Achilles is reminiscent of his unsuccessful effort to overcome the obstacles standing in the way of the completion of *Robert Guiskard*. It is as if his own experiences were finding a profound echo and as if he had poured his own unrequited longings, his high ambitious hopes, their sad frustration, and his poignant grief into the very heart of the Amazon queen. The dynamic intensity of his nature, the feverish ardor with which he pursued a goal on which he had staked everything, his oblivion to all else, and the destructiveness of his bitter disappointment are reflected in her.

PENTHESILEA

Although the dramatist created the character of Penthesilea out of his own vivid imagination, her background and outward relationships were derived from Greek mythology. According to ancient legend, female warriors known as Amazons lived on the banks of the river Thermodon. They were independent politically, were ruled by their own queen, and had their capital at Themiscyra. In order that they might draw the bow with greater freedom and vigor, they either cut off or burned off the right breast. To perpetuate their tribe, they had passing relations at intervals with men of neighboring tribes who were subsequently dismissed and to whom the male children were sent. Among the most famous Amazons was Penthesilea, the daughter of Ares and Otrera, who went to the aid of the Trojans and was killed in battle by Achilles. On appropriating her weapons and armor, her victor is said to have been struck by her beauty, to have wept at her death, and to have slain Thersites, who had insulted her dead body. Kleist also made use of a later legend according to which Achilles was slain by Penthesilea. These meager external details about the Amazon state and the conflict between Penthesilea and Achilles were a mere skeleton which Kleist invested with colorful life, throbbing passion, and a dramatic fiction of his own invention. He was much more interested in the conflict waged in the breast of Penthesilea than in exact mythological data, archaeological accuracy, and the avoiding of anachronisms. Kleist did not approach Greek antiquity in the spirit of Winckelmann and Goethe, who regarded noble simplicity and quiet grandeur as fundamental characteristics of its art. Harmony, moderation, restraint, repose, and poise are foreign to *Penthesilea*. True to his nature, Kleist here presented the most extreme violence of passion and outraged feeling of which he deemed the human heart capable.

The main outlines of the plot of *Penthesilea* can be sketched briefly. The action takes place on a battlefield at Troy. In obedience to the command of Mars, the Amazons have gone forth to wage war upon the Greeks encamped about Troy. Tradition has decreed that the female warrior tribe is to be perpetuated by the temporary union of the Amazon with the vanquished hero she chances to capture in battle. But Penthesilea, the Amazon queen, disregards the command that she take whomsoever the fortunes of war cast her way, and attempts to capture Achilles, the most glorious of heroes. On being defeated and captured by him, she is overwhelmed by grief and disgrace, and falls into a deep swoon. When she regains consciousness, she is deceived by Achilles who pretends to have been worsted in combat by her before she swooned away. After she has declared her boundless love to him, she learns that she did not overcome him and that in reality she is his captive. In order to grant her the triumph of having defeated him and in order that he may subsequently be hers at the hymeneal feast of roses, Achilles challenges Penthesilea to a duel in which he will feign defeat. But she cannot believe that Achilles, who knows she is too feeble to vie with him, can be challenging her to combat. Has she thrown away her feeling of unbounded love upon one unworthy of her? Flushed with indignation, she accepts the challenge. Calling down the vengeance of the furies upon him, she calls for her dogs and elephants, for her hooked chariots and mounted troops, for every terrible instrument of warfare that can be used in a battle of annihilation. Foaming at the lips, Penthesilea madly sets her dogs upon the unsuspecting Achilles, pierces his throat

PENTHESILEA

with an arrow, tears his armor, and buries her teeth in his noble body. When she recovers from her madness and hears that she herself slew her lover and tore his body limb from limb, she declares herself free from the laws of the Amazons, calls upon her heart to send forth a powerful, destructive emotion, and dies.

In this tragedy certain characteristic tendencies of Kleist stand out more sharply than in any other of his dramas. It embodies so much of the dynamic intensity of his own nature that it has rightly been pronounced the most Kleistian of his works. With utter disregard for the conventional refinements of art he portrays elemental emotions which know no restraints, and passions that are aroused to fever heat. He is not interested in the psychological analysis of passions but rather in their violence and in their fierce destructiveness. The only regard Kleist manifests for restraint born of esthetic considerations lies in the fact that the most savage eruptions of Penthesilea's madness are not presented on the stage itself but are recounted by eye-witnesses. Yet even these narratives are couched in diction that reproduces every horror as graphically and unsparingly as possible. Neither Penthesilea nor Achilles wages a conflict between the dictates of reason and the white heat of desire. They are devoid of rational faculties, incapable of deliberation, reflection, or even of choice. Impetuously and blindly they follow their instinctive bent. Reason is invoked only by their friends, who vainly endeavor to turn them from their disastrous course; they themselves are deaf to all argument and to every appeal. Blind to the logical exigencies of the situation, oblivious to all responsibility toward others, and forgetful of all other considerations, they respond solely to impulse. Both are so deaf to reason that attempts are made to curb them by force. In the case of Penthesilea all these eruptive, cataclysmic outbursts are more extreme. She is buffeted back and forth from one tempestuous emotion to another, is constantly keyed up to higher pitch and knows no moderation whatsoever. Her whole being centers feverishly about the achievement of a single desire. Her emotions change as this desire approaches fulfillment or seems to be denied her. And since she is without a stabilizing force, one emotion fairly chases another. Her feelings are characterized by enthusiasm, feverish expectation, hope, despair, tenderness, bitterness, rage, hatred, love, anguish, triumphant joy, exultation, momentary resignation, grief, dejection, defiance, ecstatic longing, hysteria, and insane cruelty. Penthesilea's emotions are charged with dynamite; they are volcanic in their wild explosiveness. She is as one possessed when obstacles are thrown across her path. And yet these impetuous outbursts are not the convulsive reactions of jangling, over-wrought nerves but arise out of a superabundance of vitality. In *Die Familie Schroffenstein* the tension induced by suspicion, hatred, and desire for vengeance seem to unnerve the characters, but in *Penthesilea* there is a fullness of youthful, unspent nervous energy which is as irresistible as a hurricane. Much has been written about the pathological aspects of this orgy of passion. The pathological element in the heroine lies in excess; it arises out of a responsiveness to emotion alone and out of the absence of any restraining influence.

Kleist's *Penthesilea* is more than a profound echo of past ambition, disappointment, and suffering. It is possible that, like Goethe's *Werther*, this tragedy meant taking cognizance of tendencies which, if unrestrained, would lead to certain destruction. Werther, too, is pathological in his lack of balance and restraint. He abandons himself to his feelings to the extent that they finally paralyze all initiative and all action. His range of interests becomes more and more restricted; he is driven in more and more upon himself. His attitude is contemplative and lyrical in its morbid subjectivity. On the other hand, Penthesilea's emotions are volcanic in intensity; they give rise to savage outbursts rather than to tears and complaints, and find an outlet in deeds of madness. The one represents a passive yielding to overpowering emotion, the other is spurred on to dynamic, cataclysmic activity by unbridled passion. Too weak and too sensitive to revolt, Werther endures, suffers, and ends his life; impelled by the fullness of her vigor, by the strength of her instincts, and by fierce, uncontrollable rage, Penthesilea is driven to an act of eruptive violence. In both instances, without some stabilizing force, uncurbed emotions run riot and precipitate disaster. *Werther* and *Penthesilea* both represent an act of liberation from dangerous tendencies on the part of their respective authors. Goethe moved toward harmony born of self-imposed restraint, and Kleist ultimately sought a stabilizing force in the service of an ideal outside of himself. Henceforth he turned from tragedy to dramas of a more conciliatory, optimistic type.

The tragedy *Penthesilea* centers entirely about the Amazon queen, her character and the conflict which arises out of the contradictions between her nature and the unnatural laws of her state. Consequently Kleist has portrayed her with great care. Though less concerned with her exterior than with psychological motivation, he nevertheless supplied a variety of descriptive details. Despite her vigor and tenacity, Penthesilea is by no means a giantess in stature, but is portrayed as young, girlish, and endowed with truly feminine grace and charm. In fact, a certain daintiness, slenderness of form, smallness of hands and feet are common to her and to the Amazon warriors in general. They are chosen to go forth into battle with men because of their beauty and vigor, for their state is intent upon developing a finer, handsomer physique by mating the most virile captives with those Amazons who are in the highest bloom of youth. Penthesilea herself has the girlishness of a maiden of sixteen, has a flood of curly, silken locks, cheeks like rose-blossoms, and a small, dainty head. "Young" and "youthful" are the adjectives which are repeatedly employed to describe her. Her body, says Prothoe, is young and adorned with charms. The highpriestess says she was charming when she danced and sang, full of dignity and grace. Even in battle she wears jewels, just as a certain coquettish, seductive charm is common to all the female warriors, who carry tiny mirrors as part of their equipment for conquest. But when aroused, this dainty, girlish queen is half Fury and half Grace; she has the wild *emportement* of a blindly raging tigress. Yet she has a maiden modesty blended with savage pride, and blushes deeply when she first sees Achilles.

Penthesilea is individualized less through external characterization than by her emotional intensity and its manifestations. Like Kleist, she is given to extremes, and knows moments of highest exultation as well as of deepest despair. Stubbornly tenacious, she flies into a rage before any opposition to the pursuit of her goal. When thwarted, she is like an ill-tempered child; misfortune makes her violent and unjust, though no one can be gentler than she when in a happy mood. Her cruel slaying of Achilles and her unkindness to Prothoe call to mind Kleist's exclamation in a letter of May 21, 1801: "Why, like Tancred, am I condemned to offend by every act that which I love?" Adequate motivation of Penthesilea's irrational conduct occasioned great difficulty. To attribute her slaying of Achilles to a momentary fit of insanity was insufficient; the causes of her outraged feeling had to be presented. Kleist linked them up with the conflict waged within her and with her own nature. This conflict between natural womanly instincts and the artificial laws of the Amazon state is precipitated by her meeting Achilles. Had this war been waged with some other tribe, her affections might not have been engaged, and her part in the conquest might have been like that of other Amazons, largely an impersonal incident in the perpetuation of the state. Like others, she might merely have experienced temporary grief at parting from her captive after the festival of motherhood. But a series of circumstances combined to make her part in this expedition a distinctive one. For the first time in her life she had received Mars' summons to join in warfare. Great, general rejoicing greeted the announcement that this combat was to be with the glorious heroes of Greece whose exploits had been sung throughout the Amazon realm. Penthesilea's mother, the dying queen, sent her on her way bidding her capture Achilles contrary to Amazon law which forbade the seeking out of a particular opponent. Henceforth the young girl's thoughts and dreams were of him. And when she first beheld him on the field of battle she felt as if Mars himself had descended from Olympus. She was as if blinded by an apparition of dazzling splendor. In love at first sight, she decided to win him or die. But before long, she lamented her lot which compelled her to woo him on the field of battle when her one desire was to draw him down to her breast. And yet she would have cursed herself if she had ever received a man whom she had not conquered with her sword.

When Achilles, who realizes that he can possess her only by becoming her captive, challenges her to combat, her feelings are cruelly outraged. Her rage and hatred arise out of her feeling that in thought, desire, and avowal she has surrendered herself to one unworthy of such surrender. She, who would rather be dust than unable to charm Achilles, believes herself derided by him after her avowal of love, after having confessed to him with infinite tenderness that the very feelings of her breast are like hands which caress him. His challenge issued to her, a frail maiden, to vie with the great conqueror, is derisive mockery. He is scorning her love; her emotions have betrayed her into a declaration of affection which is being spurned. Now nothing is more sacred to Kleist's characters than their inmost feeling. And so, scorned and outraged in the very depths of her being, Penthesilea is seized by a fury which knows no bounds.

But this motivation of savage revenge evidently did not satisfy the dramatist, who was conscious of the fact that powerful emotions defy rationalistic analysis. For he has Prothoe say of Penthesilea that it is impossible to comprehend her soul; its reactions cannot be predicted or calculated. Again, Prothoe tells the highpriestess that the queen alone knows what is going on within her and that every feeling breast is a mystery. Penthesilea is easily offended, says Prothoe, who fears that in her state of mind the queen may become insane. And again Prothoe points to the extremes of the queen's volatile temperament, saying that joy and grief alike are destructive to her and that both immediately plunge her into madness. By their very intensity they cloud reason and make for temporary aberration. Thus there is something incommensurable in her nature which grows out of the tremendous violence of passions whose reactions are unpredictable. In part, then, Kleist motivated Penthesilea's extreme conduct by logical explanation and characterization. Beyond that, he indicated that certain acts are unreasoned, irrational, and hence unpredictable.

By some, Penthesilea has been pronounced sadistic because of her slaying of Achilles and because of her savage rending of his body. A reply to such unfounded allegations lies in a reference to the beautiful scene between Penthesilea and Achilles in which they declare their love. The poetry and rare charm of this scene and the naturalness of the affection the lovers voice for each other suffice to dispel any such notions as the basis for the queen's subsequent act of madness. It is of interest to note that Lessing endowed the spurned Countess Orsina in the tragedy *Emilia Galotti* with a thirst for revenge which in imagination and desire manifests itself much as Penthesilea's rage actually does when the Amazon believes herself spurned by her lover. Similarly, in the fourth act of Goethe's drama, *Clavigo*, Beaumarchais burns with the desire to wreak vengeance upon the faithless lover of his sister in much the same manner as does Penthesilea. Like a hound he would follow the trail of Clavigo, sink his teeth into Clavigo's flesh, and drink his blood. He has become a raving beast whose every nerve trembles with the desire to annihilate. It should be noted that Goethe conceived the unfulfilled vengeance of Beaumarchais upon one of his own sex exactly as Penthesilea actually wrought vengeance upon Achilles.

Apart from Penthesilea, only Achilles is drawn with any effort at individualization. He is resplendent in his youthful vigor, manly beauty, and fearlessness; he is magnificent in his heedless defiance of all who attempt to turn him from his mad course. In lesser degree Achilles shares some of the queen's traits. His desire is no less strong than hers; like her he is deaf to all reason and to all entreaty. Singleness of desire and purpose characterizes both. He cares no more for the outcome of the expedition against Troy than she ultimately does for the success of the expedition without him as a captive. Achilles' preoccupation with thoughts of Penthesilea is like her own aberration; like somnambulists they are present in body alone and entirely oblivious to their surroundings. Yet for Achilles there is no internal conflict.[1] He feels entirely free to follow his desire to win and possess Penthesilea. She, however, is violating the laws of her state which she, as a sovereign, should safeguard. He yields spontaneously to his impulses, whereas she is divided between her duties as Amazon queen and the natural demands of love and womanhood. Both Achilles and Penthesilea gain much through indirect characterization, through the enthusiastic admiration which their youthful vigor, their striking beauty, and their feats of valor arouse in others. Kleist made Penthesilea a more complicated individual by putting so much of himself into her being; Achilles does not reflect Kleistian complexity of character but is naïvely natural.

Kleist made no effort to individualize other characters of the tragedy; the Greek kings, Antilochus, Diomedes, and Odysseus are types. Among the Amazons the highpriestess stands out as the uncompromising, devoted guardian of the sanctity of Amazon law and tradition. Meroe is colorless, and Asteria merely embodies the warlike spirit of her tribe. Prothoe, the unselfish, devoted, forgiving friend of the queen, shares some of the traits of the confidante and sheds light on the imponderables of Penthesilea's character and temperament. This she does in part by words of direct characterization and in part through the contrast between herself and the queen. Two distinct phases of Amazon life are set forth, its warlike aspects and the sensuous delights of the festival of roses. The preparations for the latter, as directed by the priestess, and Penthesilea's description of its insinuating charm emphasize the feminine qualities of the Amazons. These contradictory traits of Amazon character have not been convincingly harmonized in the tragedy. The political independence of the artificial state is achieved at a high price, namely through the violation of the personal rights of womanhood.

Reference has already been made to the kinship between Kleist's nature and that of Penthesilea. In spirit the dramatist identified himself with his heroine to such an extent that she occasionally seems to echo his own emotions rather than those which grow directly out of the situations in which she is presented. Yet an occasional tendency on her part to overstep the bounds of her rôle is offset by the sincerity of conviction it carries. If Kleist had not injected so much of himself into her seething emotions, their portrayal might well have given the impression of rhetorical bombast. As it is, his own heart's blood courses within her and throbs through her feelings, thoughts, desires, and acts. She is the embodiment of his single-hearted, all-devouring ambition to wrest the laurel wreath from the brow of Goethe, of his high hopes for success, of his despair at failure, and of the madness which drove him to burn his tragedy *Robert Guiskard* after a passionate but vain struggle to reach the pinnacle of fame at a single bound.

There are numerous passages in *Penthesilea* which sound like poetic transcriptions from Kleist's letters. Other lines reproduce the poignant grief attendant upon unsuccessful effort and the renewed struggle for literary fame. One need merely cite a few excerpts from Kleist's correspondence during and after his feverish work on *Robert Guiskard* to become aware of resemblances.[2] Thus he writes that it is unpardonable to awaken ambition in us, for with it we become a prey to fury.[3] Penthesilea's singleness of desire, which prompts her to win Achilles or perish in the attempt, is like the abandon with which the dramatist envisaged his goal. Referring to his unfinished tragedy, he exclaimed: "O Jesus! If only I could complete it! Let heaven fulfill this one wish and then it may dispose of me at will."[4] The queen's wild frenzy seems to be foreshadowed in Kleist's remark that the effect of unsatisfied ambition upon a sensitive nature is incalculable.[5] Her harshness toward Prothoe is like Kleist's when his lack of success fills him with a certain unjust bitterness toward men.[6] Penthesilea and Kleist manifest the same scornful indifference to life and all it holds when their one great desire is frustrated. Having burned his tragedy, he writes: Heaven denied me fame, the greatest good on earth; like a stubborn child I cast away all others.[7] When the Amazon queen's hopes seem impossible of fulfillment, she becomes embittered by her misfortune and revolts against gods and men in incomprehensible rage. Similarly, Kleist writes that unhappiness makes him violent, raging, and unjust, yet no one is more gentle and amiable than he when he is happy and contented.[8] Such passages, bearing greater or less resemblance, might easily be multiplied.[9] Suffice it to add one quotation from *Penthesilea* which seems much more closely applicable to Kleist's vain struggle than to the Amazon's efforts to capture Achilles. To Prothoe she exclaims: "I have done all that human strength is capable of—I have attempted the impossible—I have staked everything on one effort; the die is cast, there it lies, and I must realize that I have lost."

Other incidents in the tragedy reproduce occurrences from Kleist's life. Penthesilea's swooning away and the subsequent recovery of equilibrium after a paroxysm of emotion have suggested the calm awakening of Goethe's Orest or of his Faust. But they undoubtedly had their source in certain experiences of Kleist, who, after periods of tremendous mental and nervous strain, fell into a state of complete exhaustion and collapse from which he arose with renewed vigor. Such was the case just after his attempt to join the Napoleonic expedition at Boulogne-sur-Mer; on recovering from his coma and illness he, like Penthesilea, had difficulty in recalling past events. Penthesilea's mode of death very probably reflects a desire on the part of Kleist who repeatedly wished to die but shrank from the idea of self-annihilation even when life seemed unbearable.[10] How he must have desired to be able to end his life as she did by summoning an emotion powerful enough to extinguish it!

Kleist's tragedy is highly unified in action, since he limited himself to the internal conflict waged in the soul of the heroine. There are no digressions, no episodes, and no secondary action to detract from the central interest. Strictly speaking, there is but one interlude, namely, the sixth scene, in which the highpriestess directs preparations for the festival of roses. Although it seems surprising and inconsistent that such preparations are under way on the battlefield, far away from Themiscyra where hymeneal rites are practised, the scene serves the purpose of setting forth the girlish, feminine side of Amazon nature, which is violated by the unnatural decrees of the state. Although unity of time in itself is an unimportant consideration, Kleist has observed it by portraying events which can well be regarded as occurring in a single day. The artificial unity of place is indicative of the author's lack of interest in the scenic background. He is concerned with inner conflicts and with emotions at the white heat of passion, not with such externalities as local color, decoration, properties, and scenic effects. The scene of the action is designated as the battlefield at Troy. With great indifference to consistency in details, Kleist allows the Greeks to leave the stage at the close of the fourth scene in order to pursue the Amazons, who immediately enter to take the place of their pursuers. The battlefield is to be regarded as extensive, with certain scenes taking place at different localities. Paul Lindau, who has published a stage adaptation of *Penthesilea*, points out that Kleist himself wisely anticipated the danger of monotony which might result from staging the entire tragedy without change of background. By variation in light effects—such as are produced by golden sunlight, threatening thunderstorm and flashes of lightning—by illumination which changes from early dawn to sunset, the action can be presented in a variety of moods and effects which give somewhat the effect of actual change of scene.[11]

Kleist's dramatic technique in *Penthesilea* presents a curious admixture of indifference and of singularly effective devices. In spite of his careful attention to unity of action and of interest, Kleist was unmindful of consistency in details, even of motivation. Fascinated by the overwhelming primitive savagery of outraged sensibilities, he manifested no concern for the practical demands of the stage nor for accuracy in minor matters. Hence there is little virtue in exploiting incidental contradictions, anachronisms and slight inconsistencies which the ordinary meticulous technician can rectify but which do not detract from the poetic power, from the wild horror, and from the impressiveness of the tragedy as a whole. Kleist, who so skillfully interwove exposition and action in *Der zerbrochene Krug*, here presents exposition in obvious fashion by long narrative interrupted only

PENTHESILEA

here and there by question or by stilted exclamation. Although events preceding the beginning of the action are rehearsed largely in the first two scenes, the history of the Amazon state and the purpose of Amazon warfare as recounted by Penthesilea in the fifteenth scene constitute additional expository material. Though these recitals contain speeches of varied length, Kleist makes no particular effort to avoid long, uninterrupted discourse. Since most of the outward action, namely such deeds as the pursuit of Achilles by Penthesilea, the battle between Greeks and Amazons, the combat between the queen and Achilles, and the horrible death and mutilation of the hero's body, occur off stage, all such events must be recited by eye-witnesses who have been immediately present or who, stationed on the stage at some point of vantage, describe them while they occur. This facile device is used extensively but does not succeed in covering up the paucity of action on the stage itself. Uninterrupted speeches of some twenty and thirty lines are frequent; Meroe's account of Achilles' death contains a single unbroken discourse of seventy lines. Other speeches numbering over forty and fifty lines occur. In spite of a certain monotony which these recitals produce, they are frequently of vivid, dramatic intensity. Moreover, occasional impressive pauses made by the speakers, the silent gestures of listeners, as well as interruptions by exclamations and questions, add variety and heighten the effect. Breathless excitement on the part of the narrator is reflected in violent outbursts, in halting, irregular sentence structure, in broken lines, in choppy meter, and in the tendency to doubt the incredible impressions conveyed by the senses.

Kleist makes use of a skillful device to facilitate the communication of images from scenes which the hearer does not have before his eyes. Just as in *Der zerbrochene Krug* Adam adds details based on fact in order to make his misrepresentations seem more plausible, so here the narrator supplies occasional concrete data which are easily visualized by the listener. They afford relief to the imagination and add vivid lifelikeness to the picture portrayed by serving as tangible points of support. In the third scene a good example of such introduction of concrete detail occurs in the account of Achilles' successful escape from Penthesilea: Covered with dust he leaps from his seat! He hands over the reins! He turns! He takes off his helmet which weighs down his head! And all the kings surround him! Moreover, Kleist takes pains to render descriptions more vivid by linking them up with and translating them into action.

A further technical device employed with admirable skill for the purpose of heightening the dramatic intensity of a tragedy replete with recital is the use of silent gesture. The tragic effect of the final scene is due in large measure to the pantomime of Penthesilea; this silent acting on her part becomes all the more impressive because of its visible effect upon the Amazons. With great care Kleist supplied detail after detail of such pantomime in the stage directions. This is all the more surprising because he did not write *Penthesilea* with an eye to its production on the stage of the time. Silence, accompanied or unaccompanied by gesture, is to be found in others of his dramas. When subjected to tremendous emotional stress, when overcome by an all-powerful feeling, Kleist's characters frequently swoon or are reduced to silence. Instead of baring their inmost soul in long monologue they become mute; their tragic suffering is heightened by their inability to communicate it by words. Stricken dumb as they are, they seem all the more lonely in a world which fails to understand them and which is incomprehensible to them.

Although the tragedy numbers over three thousand lines, its twenty-four scenes are presented in a single act. Like *Der zerbrochene Krug* it does not lend itself to partition into groups of scenes representing units of anything like equal length. Two scenes, the sixth and the fifteenth, are somewhat in the nature of interludes because of their quiet peacefulness and because the action itself is not advanced in them. The sixth marks the preparations for the festival of roses and the fifteenth presents the meeting of Penthesilea and Achilles with their avowal of love. These somewhat idyllic scenes afford relief from the hectic storminess of over-wrought passion but do not dispel the growing feeling that a tragic outcome is imminent. Parallels between Achilles and Penthesilea, both of whom are actuated by ardent desire, who revolt against all restraint, refuse to listen to reason, and rush headlong into conflict, produce an effect of structural symmetry akin to division. In spite of its length, the tragedy was written in one act partly because of the author's temporary indifference to the demands of the theater but more particularly because its precipitately violent tempo made it unsuited to division into acts.

Although comparatively little outward action is presented on the stage, the tragedy is not lacking in the vividness that can be gained by diction, meter, verse, and rhythm suited to reflect breathless, halting, surging, throbbing emotion. In general, Kleist's use of these aids is masterly; yet he sometimes employs them to the extent of making of them an obvious, hackneyed device. This is true of his recourse to expletives in an attempt to enliven long narrative and to break it by exclamations of utter amazement, dismay, and disapproval on the part of listeners. The tragedy is replete with expletives; scores of them are uttered by Greeks and Amazons alike. Kleist introduced a certain variety by addressing appeals to different gods, by employing various adjectives before the same name, and by combining two or more in a single invocation. Even a partial enumeration constitutes a formidable mythological array; such as, by Jupiter, by our God, by Hades, by the Styx, by all the great gods who protect us, by Zeus, by the Erinnes, by the eternal gods, by the god of thunder, ye Olympians, by the gods of Olympus, ye gods, ye gods of Olympus, ye eternal gods of heaven, Aphrodite, Diana, Artemis, by the terrible powers of Olympus, and by the locks of Zeus, the thunderer. Varied as these exclamations are, they become a fatiguing, obvious artifice, especially when heard on the stage. Referring as they do to Greek mythology, they sound particularly artificial in a modern tongue. And their very variety makes a studied impression.

In general, however, Kleist's diction in *Penthesilea* is marked by dynamic power and an astounding ability to find words capable of denoting a wide range of the most intense emotions. He indulges his fondness for hyperbole, invents unusual compound words, employs occasional realistic vulgarisms, places adjectives after the nouns they modify, uses bold imagery and gains emphasis through repetition of word or phrase. The highest pathos is achieved neither by rhetorical device nor by sentimental appeal calculated to stimulate the lachrymal glands, but by portraying emotions so overwhelming that they rob the tragic heroine of speech. Gestures become far more eloquent than words. The musical effect of Kleist's diction in this tragedy is particularly marked. It has none of the sonorous euphony so noticeable in *Robert Guiskard*. There are shrill, discordant notes born of violent, screaming passions, of flaming hate, and wild savagery. And there are tones of rare sweetness, of melting tenderness, of love and devotion. The wide gamut of emotions has been reproduced not only in striking diction but with acute sensitiveness to sound as well.

Strangely enough, the verse of *Penthesilea* is less irregular than might be expected in a tragedy of such surcharged emotions. Füser has counted forty-four lines of six feet, many of which could very easily have been reduced to pentameter. He lists a total of but fifty-eight lines of irregular length, a smaller proportion than in any of Kleist's dramas with the sole exception of *Robert Guiskard*.[12] The iambic pentameter is irregular; anapests and trochees are frequent. The dialogue is decidedly broken, with many lines divided between two and three persons. But the fierce savagery, the eruptive vehemence of delirious passion, is manifest less in irregularity of verse and meter than in the jerky, chopped rhythm and the throbbing, uneven, racing tempo. This tempo is induced to a considerable extent by irregular sentence structure, by short, hacked units, pauses, parenthetical phrases, expletives, exclamations, and questions. At times the effect is almost comparable to that of sharp, staccato-like, frequently and briefly interrupted machine-gun fire. One can scarcely become more strikingly aware of this restless rhythm and tempo than by reading aloud a few broken, irregular lines from *Penthesilea* and the opening scene of Goethe's *Iphigenie auf Tauris* with its harmonious, smooth cadence. Each of these dramas has a tempo and rhythm admirably suited to the spirit in which it is conceived. And, singularly enough, both deal with Greek antiquity.

Penthesilea has a number of rather distinct points of contact with Kleist's first tragedy. The wild, unreasoning rage of Rupert Schroffenstein is a forerunner of blind, irrational violence on the part of the Amazon queen. In both tragedies the voice of reason is unheeded, and emotions are lashed into a fury of frenzied destructiveness. In both, tender love and furious hatred present a striking contrast. Hacked and choppy lines, broken dialogue, surging, furious tempo, irregular meter, throbbing cadence and jerky rhythm are common to these two tragedies and reproduce violent passions at fever heat. On recovering consciousness, both Sylvester and Penthesilea experience a feeling of peacefulness and relief, as if they had been transported to another world. But, in spite of such outward resemblances in the treatment of tempestuous feeling and primitive instincts, *Penthesilea* represents marked development and greater maturity. Kleist's command of language has become such as to do ample justice to a wider range of emotions; his motivation is more convincing, because it leaves less to chance and is less inclined to melodramatic effect. With its heightened tragic intensity *Penthesilea* rings truer; this tragedy is not made, but is of the very life and blood of its author.

On January 24, 1808, Kleist sent Goethe a copy of the first number of his journal, *Phöbus*, which contained an "organic fragment" from the tragedy, *Penthesilea*. It was accompanied by a letter in which Kleist humbly wrote that he was making this presentation on the "knees of his heart." He added that he had been diffident about placing the tragedy before the public in its entirety. *Penthesilea*, he remarked, was written just as little for the stage as his earlier drama *Der zerbrochene Krug*. The other German theaters, he continued, were not equipped to produce it, and much as he would like to belong to the present, he was obliged in this case to look to the future, for otherwise the prospects would be altogether too discouraging.

Goethe's reply, dated February 1, 1808, was outspoken in its disapproval. After stating that he could not as yet get on friendly terms with Penthesilea, he proceeded as follows:

> She is of so strange a race and moves in such unaccustomed regions that I require time to adjust myself to both. Moreover, you will allow me to say (for if one were not to be sincere, it would be better to be silent) that I am always saddened and grieved on seeing young men of intellect and talent who are waiting for a theater that is to come. A Jew who is waiting for the Messiah, a Christian awaiting the new Jerusalem, or a Portuguese waiting for Don Sebastian do not cause me greater displeasure. Before every boardstaging I should like to say to the genuine theatrical genius: *hic Rhodus, hic salta*! At every annual fair, with planks laid across barrels, I should undertake *mutatis mutandis* to give the educated and the uneducated mass the greatest pleasure with Calderon's plays. Pardon my abruptness: it is indicative of my sincere good will. Such things can of course be said in kindlier fashion and more agreeably. But I am satisfied nowadays if I can get something off my heart. More, shortly.

This blunt commentary contains no attempt at evaluation or appreciation of the tragedy from a literary or artistic viewpoint, but concerns itself merely with Kleist's statement that he scarcely considered the drama such as to meet with success on the contemporary stage. It may be that Goethe's reply does constitute something of an evasion and is less frank than it purports to be. For his judgment of *Penthesilea* from an esthetic viewpoint would undoubtedly have read even more unfavorably. By its boundless vehemence, its unhesitating portrayal of maddened, outraged feelings and of savage cruelty, by its disregard for all harmony, restraint, and moderation, and by the violence it did to his refined sensibilities it must have reminded Goethe strongly and unpleasantly of his own youthful, titanic, insurrectionary attitude. No doubt his chastened sense of beauty was rudely offended by the monstrous excesses to which unbridled passion was irresistibly swept in Kleist's tragedy. From his point of view such extremes seemed to transgress the boundaries of art and lead to riot and chaos. Kleist, who had approached Goethe with veneration and humility, was angered by Goethe's reply and directed bitter epigrams at him in the *Phöbus*. Thus a permanent breach arose between the two men. When one recalls what Wieland's commendation and good will meant to Kleist, it is quite apparent that Goethe's kindly interest and encouragement might have had a highly salutary, stabilizing effect upon Kleist in his subsequent struggles.

The appearance of excerpts from *Penthesilea* in the *Phöbus* was followed by the publication of the entire tragedy. Karl Gärtner, a Dresden publisher, began the printing at the author's own expense, but financial difficulties compelled Kleist to make arrangements with the house of Cotta for its completion. It is reported that Cotta did not interest himself in the advertising and sale of the tragedy, and that even after eighty years copies of the first edition could still be bought directly from the publisher.[13] A manuscript of *Penthesilea*, not in the author's handwriting, but bearing numerous corrections made by Kleist himself, is in the Prussian State Library at Berlin. This is an older version than that of the *Phöbus*.

Penthesilea has not met with popular success on the stage. It was first presented in May, 1876, in Berlin where an arbitrary adaptation of the tragedy, with a division into three acts by S. H. Rosenthal, proved an utter failure.[14] For a time Kleist critics were divided as to the feasibility of staging *Penthesilea*. Thus a

French biographer of Kleist stated in 1894 that the representation would offer some difficulty, for the chariots and elephants in the twentieth scene would require a vast space, these enormous quadrupeds would cost considerable money, and the training of the howling dogs would demand much patience.[15] Elsewhere he asserted positively that the tragedy cannot be presented.[16] In answer to such objections Professor Meyer-Benfey suggested with reason that verses 2421-2426, with their reference to these formidable properties, be omitted[17]—an easy solution of the difficulty. Although successful performances of the tragedy have been given, nevertheless, even under the most favorable conditions, the dearth of outward action and the numerous, lengthly recitals make for a certain monotony. *Penthesilea* must still be regarded as a better book-drama than stage-drama.

CHAPTER SEVEN

DAS KÄTHCHEN VON HEILBRONN

DAS KÄTHCHEN VON HEILBRONN, the most optimistic of Kleist's dramas, is at the same time farthest removed from the realities of life. It is of a popular nature, varied and spectacular, and, according to its author, is more on the order of the romantic play. It is written with little of the restraint imposed by careful dramatic technique and logical motivation. Instead, Kleist gave his imagination free rein and drew lavishly on the supernatural, the fairy realm, folk-lore, popular beliefs, miracles, dreams, somnambulism, and the occult, mysterious attraction between individuals that defies rationalistic explanation.

The first reference to this drama in Kleist's correspondence is in a letter written presumably to Henriette Hendel-Schütz in the late fall of the year 1807. On June 7 of the following year, the author offered it to Johann Friedrich Cotta for publication. One may assume, therefore, that it was written early during his sojourn in Dresden.

It will be recalled that, in his letter to Henriette Hendel-Schütz, Kleist had referred to Käthchen as Penthesilea's other pole. Similarly, he wrote on December 8, 1808, that Käthchen and Penthesilea belong together like the plus and minus of algebra; they are one and the same being merely conceived

DAS KÄTHCHEN VON HEILBRONN 153

under opposite conditions.[1] Penthesilea throbs with dynamic activity, with the desire to conquer and win; defiantly she hurls herself at every obstacle that stands between her and her goal. Käthchen, too, is characterized by absolute abandon, but hers is passive, unreflective, and virtually unconscious. Having no goal in mind, she need formulate no plans for its achievement; she undergoes no inner struggle, but is undivided, her one desire being to remain in the presence of the man to whom she is irresistibly drawn. Her blind, unswerving devotion is as signal and impressive as the violent, vigorous, aggressive, combative nature of the Amazon queen. One may truly say of Käthchen that she lives, moves, and has her being in the man she loves. It is not at all surprising that Kleist created this character, for she is endowed with many of those qualities which he admired in women; hers are the traits which he emphasized in his correspondence with his fiancée, Wilhelmine, and with his sister, Ulrike. His ideal woman was one who, without question or hesitancy, would sacrifice herself utterly for those she loved. He believed that in woman at her best the finer qualities such as devotion, spontaneity, unselfishness, loyalty, unwavering affection, kindness, gentleness, and generosity were more highly developed than in man. A cold, calculating woman intent upon her own advantage and pleasure was loathsome to him; nothing seemed to him more hateful, unnatural, and catlike in a woman than selfishness.

More than any of Kleist's characters, Käthchen is the embodiment of his human ideal of childlike simplicity, spontaneity, naturalness, and youthful, unconscious charm and grace. She reflects the conclusion that the wisdom of the world lies in becoming as a child. Kleist was profoundly impressed by the conflict between reason and emotion, between thought and action; he was keenly aware of the inhibition of action by reflection. How to restore original immediacy of reaction and spontaneous yielding to first unerring impulse was a question which kept recurring to him. Having become conscious of himself, could man regain the primitive naïveté in which he was never at variance with himself, in which he unhesitatingly obeyed instincts, and in which desire was consequently promptly translated into action? Desirable as this was, it seemed to have become impossible, once man had eaten of the tree of knowledge. At the age of twenty-four, Kleist, who had become interested in Rousseau, wrote: "Many centuries had to elapse before enough knowledge could be gained to lead man to the realization that he ought to have no knowledge. Now then, one should have to forget all knowledge in order to repair the damage, and thus the misery would begin anew. For man has an indisputable need of enlightening himself. Without enlightenment he is not much more than an animal."[2] In his essay, *Über das Marionettentheater*, Kleist deals at some length with this problem.[3] Having eaten of the tree of knowledge, man has lost his naïve innocence, has become conscious of his acts, and is given to reflection about them and about himself. His movements have lost their primitive naturalness and grace because he is no longer a creature that blindly obeys instinctive desire. The marionette has an advantage over man, for it has no choice of movement, and responds promptly and infallibly to impulsion. It is incapable of affectation, hesitancy, or false movement because its soul is at its center of gravity, from which alone its movements are governed. Since the manipulator has control only of the center of gravity, all other members of the marionette's body are merely

DAS KÄTHCHEN VON HEILBRONN 155

dead pendulums and follow the law of gravity only. Consequently, a marionette could never be as lacking in grace as a human dancer, whose soul is in his elbow as he stands between the three goddesses in the rôle of Paris and presents the apple to Venus. Such distortion is the inevitable result of conscious effort. And since the garden of paradise is locked and a cherub bars its entrance, it becomes necessary to journey around the world to see whether it may possibly be open somewhere on the other side. Only a god can vie with marionettes in that natural gracefulness which is independent of matter. Since the force which raises them into the air is greater than that which draws them to the ground, they merely touch the earth as do the elves in order to animate their members anew by momentary pausation and not for the purpose of resting upon it from the exertion of the dance. In the organic world, writes Kleist, grace becomes more resplendent and dominant in proportion as reflection becomes dimmer and feebler. But just as after passing through infinity, the image in a concave mirror suddenly stands close before us again, so also does grace reappear when knowledge has, so to speak, passed through infinity. And thus it appears purest in that human body which has either no consciousness or an infinite consciousness; that is to say, in the marionette or in God. The final chapter in the history of the world will be written when man again eats of the tree of knowledge in order to revert to the state of original innocence.

This whole essay reads like an elaboration of a passage in a letter to Rühle von Lilienstern of August 31, 1806, to which reference has already been made. In it Kleist encouraged his friend to let himself be guided solely by his feeling for the beautiful in translating Racine, and asserted that every first movement, everything involuntary, is beautiful; everything is crooked and distorted as soon as it becomes conscious of itself. Kleist took delight in portraying Käthchen as the embodiment of that spontaneity, charm, naturalness, and grace which humanity has lost and strives in vain to regain. Significantly enough, this unity and harmony, of which Käthchen herself is unconscious, does not exist in the world of everyday reality, but is linked up with the fairy realm of dreams, visions, and miracles. And thus, underlying this happy state of unconscious bliss and natural innocence, there is Kleist's tragic recognition that such perfect accord and harmony are not of this world. Käthchen represents a compensatory rather than an expressive ideal.

The full title of Kleist's drama is *Das Käthchen von Heilbronn oder die Feuerprobe. Ein grosses historisches Ritterschauspiel*. The double title with its reference to a test by fire was evidently intended to serve as a drawing card for the public, for the dramatist wrote this play with an eye to its presentation on the stage. Moreover, the subtitle, a great historical spectacle of knighthood, was likewise designed to arouse interest by falling in with the popular predilection for such picturesque scenes of medieval life. As a matter of fact, there is nothing historical about the incidents portrayed in the drama; yet the colorful background of medieval knighthood, the Vehmic Court, the imperial city of Worms, and the gorgeous pomp of royal procession are reminiscent of the spectacular grandeur of past history. The personages are not historical but are of the author's own invention; even the emperor is designated merely by title rather than by name. The cast of characters includes numerous people of varied rank and station, of whom the more important are Count Friedrich Wetter, Kunigunde von Thur-

DAS KÄTHCHEN VON HEILBRONN

neck, Theobald Friedeborn and his alleged daughter, Käthchen. The scene of the action is in Swabia, which had come to be regarded as the land of romantic adventure. Käthchen, who has been reared by the armorer Theobald Friedeborn, sees her future husband in a dream. Subsequently she recognizes Count Wetter vom Strahl, who comes to Theobald's smithy, as the knight who has thus appeared to her. Count Strahl has likewise seen his future wife in a dream, but he does not recognize her as Käthchen, the humble daughter of an armorer, for she has been proclaimed to him as an emperor's daughter. Irresistibly impelled, Käthchen now follows him wherever he goes, although he attempts to rid himself of her both by kind words and by cruel harshness. But she will not be repulsed, and Strahl is forced to defend himself before the Vehmic Court against charges of abduction by sorcery, as preferred by Theobald. Blinded by considerations of rank and station, and ensnared by seductive wiles, Strahl becomes engaged to an ugly adventuress, Kunigunde von Thurneck. By discovering an attempt upon their lives, Käthchen succeeds in saving Kunigunde and Strahl. As the castle of Kunigunde is fired during the attack, Käthchen unselfishly risks her life to save important papers for Kunigunde. In doing so, she is protected by an angel whom she has seen in her dream. In time, Strahl is apprised of the sordid, selfish ambitions of Kunigunde, and discovers that it was Käthchen who had appeared to him in a dream as his future wife and as the emperor's daughter. Inquiries reveal that she is the natural daughter of the emperor and that Friedeborn is merely her foster-father. Kunigunde is unmasked and disgraced, whereas Käthchen wins Strahl's hand and the greatest happiness.

What was Kleist's source for this complicated, varied action, and what impelled him to write in so fanciful a vein? His writings give no information whatever as to the sources upon which he may have drawn. Because of certain outward similarities in detail, various critics have assumed that the theme was suggested by Bürger's version of Percy's ballad, *Child Waters*. As usual, however, Kleist drew upon his own fecund imagination to portray incident, character, background, and atmosphere to suit his own ends, thereby utterly transforming any source materials he may have used. Again, there are tendencies in the drama which led to the assertion that Kleist was more or less strongly influenced by lectures given in Dresden by Gotthilf Heinrich von Schubert entitled *Ansichten von der Nachtseite der Naturwissenschaften*. In these lectures Schubert dealt with occult, mysterious phenomena such as dreams, somnambulism, forecasting the future, states of ecstasy, and hypnotic states. Doubtless Kleist was greatly interested in Schubert's discussions of such subjects. In *Das Käthchen von Heilbronn* the dramatist, however, is not greatly concerned with such pseudo-scientific presentations. Here he takes pleasure in ignoring the logic of a rational universe and in drawing freely upon the fanciful, the miraculous, and the phantastic. Various resemblances to Goethe's *Götz von Berlichingen*, to Schiller's *Jungfrau von Orleans*, to the double dream in Wieland's *Oberon*, to other writings of Wieland,[4] to Stilling's novel, *Theobald oder die Schwärmer*,[5] and to the fairy tale[6] have been cited and substantiated in such a manner as to carry conviction. Yet the fact remains that Kleist's individuality transcends any such materials that he may have consciously or unconsciously adopted from others.

Kleist's evident original intention was to portray a character so utterly under the domination of irresistible love that everything but her affection would be excluded from her consciousness. Having lost confidence in reason, he had turned to feeling and intuitive judgment as a guide. Hence he was interested in presenting Käthchen as following her intuitions unwaveringly; untroubled by reflection, sense impression, and external influences, she was to trust to her feeling, obey her first impulse, and achieve happiness. This idea seems to have prompted him as he began work on the drama. But not being as single-minded as his little heroine, he allowed other considerations to detract from this central conception of characterization. He appears to have become thoroughly imbued with the desire of writing a drama that would be successful on the stage. It may be that Goethe's adverse criticism of *Penthesilea* and the failure of *Der zerbrochene Krug* stimulated an ambition to demonstrate that he could achieve popular success. With an eye to such success on the Vienna stage, Kleist may have combined the presentation of his ideal of feminine devotion with an amount of romantic fustian and chivalric hurly-burly which he subsequently regretted as detracting from the portrayal of character that had originally been uppermost in his mind. How eager he was to have *Das Käthchen von Heilbronn* produced is evidenced by his letter of December 8, 1808, to Heinrich Joseph von Collin, through whose efforts he hoped for a presentation of the drama in Vienna. He writes, in part: "*Käthchen von Heilbronn* which, as I myself realize, must necessarily be shortened, could fall into no hands to which I should rather entrust the undertaking than yours. Proceed with it just as the needs of your stage demand. The Berlin theater, which is producing it, is shortening it, and I may do the same thing myself for other theaters." Imbued as he now was with the desire of having his drama played, Kleist did not approach his theme with the same freedom that had characterized his work on earlier plays. Several years later, in a letter presumably written in August, 1811, Kleist referred to influences that marred his plans for this drama as originally conceived. He declared his intention of once more taking up something decidedly fantastical, now that he felt a renewal of energy stirring within him. In doing so, he would follow his heart wherever it might lead and be mindful only of his own inward satisfaction. He admitted that the opinions of various people had dominated him too much in the past, *Käthchen von Heilbronn*, in particular, bearing numerous marks of such influences. Henceforth, he added, he was going to allow himself to be entirely permeated by the thought that if a work proceeds quite freely from the inmost recesses of the human spirit, it must of necessity belong to all mankind.

There have been different conjectures as to the meaning of this statement. Some have inferred that Kleist was referring to a change in his portrayal of Kunigunde who, they maintained, was first conceived as a supernatural, witchlike creature of extreme hideousness of character and person rather than as an ugly, scheming mortal who owed her seductive charm to artifice. Again it has been assumed that Kleist had in mind the ultimate repetition of expository reference to the Count's vision. For, as first published in the *Phöbus*, the second act lacked Brigitte's narration of Strahl's dream. The final version, printed in 1810, contains not merely Brigitte's long account in the ninth scene of the second act but also Strahl's own recounting of the incident to Käthchen in the second scene of act four. It is quite possible, however, that such conclusions as the above do not go far enough, and that Kleist's regrets were based less on the presentation of Kunigunde or of individual scenes

DAS KÄTHCHEN VON HEILBRONN 161

than upon deviations in the general treatment of the theme he had had in mind. Kleist did, in fact, make regrettable concessions to popular taste. Careful motivation through character is replaced to a considerable extent by a wealth of outward action, spectacular effects, a predilection for the *coup de théâtre*, sharp, overdrawn contrast, outward pomp and display, frequent disjointed change of scene, rhetorical bombast, exaggerated pathos, hackneyed stage tricks, and obvious device. This drama might have rendered good service to a French romantic writer of melodrama like the elder Dumas. It is such excesses which Kleist may very well have had in mind when referring to the lamentable distortion of his original excellent conception. Moreover, they strike deeper than do the details commonly cited as the basis for his statement of profound regret.

With the exception of Käthchen, Strahl, and Kunigunde, the characters are rather shadowy types lacking in particularization. The emperor appears somewhat in the rôle of one who has played a trick on himself and has been found out. Theobald is touching in his loyal affection for Käthchen, in his devotion to her well-being, and in his stubborn, doughty defiance of Strahl. In his unselfish, charitable, forgiving disposition, Gottfried Friedeborn, Käthchen's fiancé, calls to mind Johanna's lover, Raimond, in Schiller's *Die Jungfrau von Orleans*. The galaxy of knights is devoid of individualization. Kunigunde is conceived largely as the antithesis of Käthchen. She has charms, a certain majestic beauty, an impressive presence, and a tall, slender figure; like Käthchen, she is attractive to men. Yet she owes such outward attractiveness entirely to artifice, to seductive wiles, deception, dissembling, and shrewd, hypocritical ingratiation. She is an ambitious, vain, selfish, acquisitive, scheming, cruel, frigid being, devoid of any spontaneous, generous impulses. Her whole nature is one of cold, hard calculation; her one aim is to exploit others in order to further her desire for power and self-aggrandizement.

Kleist makes effective use of contrast in portraying Käthchen and Kunigunde. He characterizes the heroine, in large part, through her impression upon others as narrated by Theobald and as seen by her growing ascendency over Strahl's affections. Just as Frau Marthe Rull gives a detailed description of her beautiful pitcher in order to impress the court with the enormity of the offense of breaking it, so Theobald gives a preliminary detailed characterization of the charm and beauty of his daughter in order to make the crime of abducting her seem all the more appalling. The heroine is a mere slip of a girl, less than sixteen years of age, sweet, tender, lovable, pure, natural, modest, of ineffable grace, and charmingly naïve in her girlish simplicity. She is as healthy, sane, and sound in body and soul as the first human beings, declares Theobald emphatically. She is thoroughly Kleistian in her feminine devotion, in living in a world which centers about the man she loves, and in caring for nothing but to be near him. This desire to be with him is not of her own choosing but is involuntary, as if imposed from without. She follows Strahl unquestioningly wherever he goes and is ready to render him any service even though he may know nothing of it. Käthchen does nothing for the purpose of ingratiating herself, is forgetful of self, has no aggressive scheme or plan, and in her waking moments seems entirely unconscious of any thought of marrying Strahl. She is not given to reflection, but, being a creature of instinct, she follows her intuitions unhesitatingly. During her waking moments Käthchen is unconsciously under the spell of her vision.

DAS KÄTHCHEN VON HEILBRONN 163

In the literature of romanticism love at first sight is frequently taken for granted as requiring no explanation. Of this, Schiller's Johanna is a typical example. But Kleist motivates the heroine's affection, which outwardly seems love at first sight, by basing it on her vision of Strahl. The attraction which the Count has for her by virtue of this dream is like an irresistible, magic power. It is mysterious and, after all, about as inexplicable as romantic love at first sight. But for Käthchen, the dream is born of heaven and carries divine assurance, for with childlike faith she believes that in answer to her prayer God has allowed her future husband to appear to her in a dream. Hers is a profound faith in the ultimate goodness of things. Like the lilies of the field, she neither toils nor takes thought of the morrow. In her unselfish devotion she calls to mind the attitude of Natalie, in *Prinz Friedrich von Homburg*, who implores the prince-elector to spare the prince's life, not that he may be hers, but merely that he may be near by, independent, and free like a flower that gives pleasure. There is no erotic desire in Käthchen; her virgin modesty and childlike innocence are nowhere more manifest than when Strahl finally voices his powerful, passionate desire for her. Even in her waking hours she retains some of the characteristics of the somnambulist, for she is unmindful of the cold, harsh, disillusioning realities of the everyday, waking world. She is torn by no conflict, has but one desire and trusts in its fulfillment. For her, grief lies merely in separation from the man to whom she is irresistibly drawn. There is no discordant element in her nature; she is never at variance with herself because of the sureness of instinct which impels her. Herein she represents an ideal which Kleist never achieved. He was frequently a prey to conflicting desires because reason and emotion seemed to be in eternal conflict. Life at times seemed to him like a lottery bag full of blanks; harmony, unity, and peace appeared humanly unattainable. In the world of harsh reality, reason had proved incapable of triumphing over the vicissitudes of life; it could not afford a basis for that constancy and calm for which Kleist had striven. Hence in a fanciful world of poetic fiction he endowed his heroine with that absolute reliance upon feeling, instinct, and intuition, and the resulting unity which the world of reality had denied him. Reason and reflection, plans, cares, and ambitions here give way to the spontaneous, trusting, naïve, unhesitating following of natural impulse.

Standing between Käthchen, the embodiment of naturalness, and Kunigunde, a caricature of hateful artificiality, is Count vom Strahl. He is a straightforward, manly, valorous knight, whose chivalrous attitude is clearly manifested by his rescue of Kunigunde from her captors and by his subsequent generosity toward her. Rich, powerful, courageous, and handsome, he has much that might make for contentment. Nevertheless, he was once seized by a strange melancholy whose cause no one could fathom. What had hitherto remained his own secret was subsequently revealed in the delirium of fever when the inhibitions of consciousness were removed. Unfulfilled desire and unrequited affection were at the bottom of his melancholy. Lying there unconscious, he declared he was content to die; no maiden lived who might be capable of loving him, and life without love would be death. The insistence of his desire was evidenced by the threefold recurrence of his dream with the assurance that on Saint Sylvester's Eve he should see the girl who loved him. Yet after his recovery nothing came of the dream. Engaged in the activity of knight errantry and warfare, he doubtless gave less and less thought and credence to this vision; all the more so because the possibility of his marrying an emperor's daughter probably seemed a remote one.

But Käthchen gains the ascendency over his affections. At their first meeting he looks at her contemplatively, kisses her on the forehead and invokes heaven's blessing upon her, quite as any proud knight might on seeing a beautiful, charming daughter of the people. Yet her utter devotion to him as she follows him from place to place, the feeling of his power over her as it becomes clearly manifest in the trial, and her beauty of body and soul at length produce their effect upon him. Nevertheless, though he is attracted to her, the thought of marrying beneath his rank presents an insurmountable barrier which he recognizes unquestioningly. He does not think in terms of espousing her but rather of finding a wife of his station who equals her charm. His outward harshness and cruel threats are defense-mechanisms, unconsciously prompted by the fear that he may be coming under the spell of her affection and beauty. How he is torn by an inner struggle is graphically portrayed in the sixth scene of act three. When Käthchen seeks him at Castle Thurneck he seizes his whip and savagely threatens her. But on learning that she has come to notify him of the attack on the castle he is all the more deeply moved by her affection. Obeying an impulse, he removes his scarf with the intention of lending it to Käthchen, who is overheated from the exertion of her errand. But after an instant's reflection, he tosses it on the table and tells her to use her apron. Then he sees the whip with which he has threatened her. In wild rage he hurls it through the window-pane. He finally caresses her cheeks, weeps at his harshness, and hands her his scarf. His conduct is marked by similar instability at the thought of the risk Käthchen incurs by proposing to seek the picture for Kunigunde. He endeavors to detain her by words, blocks her path, offers Kunigunde ten other pictures, and finally allows the girl to go, saying that it serves the fool right—what business has she here anyhow? Yet she has scarcely gone when he is terrified at the thought of the danger to her life. He calls for a ladder, tosses away his sword, and is about to climb the ladder when the castle crashes into ruins. Thereafter he no longer struggles to shut out thoughts of her. But blinded by conventional decree, which prevents him from yielding to impulse, he decides to marry Kunigunde who, he has been told, is the daughter of an emperor. Although Käthchen has won his affections and Kunigunde has been unmasked, his scruples against a mésalliance have not been overcome. It is only when she is found to be the emperor's daughter that he decides on the course toward which instinctive desire has long vainly urged him. In contrast with Käthchen, Strahl is at variance with himself; conventions have robbed him of the naïve spontaneity which determines her conduct.

The question has been raised repeatedly why the effect of the double dream is so much more powerful in the case of Käthchen even though the visions are practically identical. Röbbeling has pointed out that, after all, Strahl considered his vision but a fleeting dream and attached little significance to it. Moreover, Käthchen had seen the form and face of the knight, which were impressed on her memory. The count, however, had had no distinct view of her features because the vision vanished just as, trembling with infinite rapture, he placed his hand upon her chin to raise her face and gaze upon it. Since he was absorbed by the duties of his knightly calling, the tender emotional side of his nature, which had so suddenly become manifest, no longer had an oppor-

DAS KÄTHCHEN VON HEILBRONN 167

tunity to assert itself.[7] It must be emphasized as well that even if Strahl had continued to attach significance to his vision, the only remaining index was bound to lead him astray, for he could not have thought of Theobald's daughter as an imperial princess. He was just as determined that his wife should be of noble birth as Penthesilea was to give herself only to a hero whom she had conquered with her sword. Such views of rank and station were accepted as absolute and binding by him as well as by the many knights who wept because Käthchen was not of noble birth. There has been a tendency to criticize the final solution as based upon the discovery that Käthchen was the daughter of the emperor. Yet in view of a certain undeniable kinship between this fanciful drama and the fairy tale in which such strange, unexpected discoveries frequently effect a dénouement, this objection need not be taken too seriously. In fact, the drama as a whole is of the type which is to be enjoyed by suspending one's logical, critical faculties while one spends a holiday in the land of romance.

In *Das Käthchen von Heilbronn* Kleist manifests a marked indifference to unity, to careful motivation, and to the refinements of dramatic technique. The wealth of concrete, descriptive stage directions is indicative of a desire to produce a colorful effect by dint of the pomp and splendor of the background. The somewhat disjointed wealth of outward action and the attendant frequent changes of scene are a concession to the fondness for the spectacular on the part of the wider theater-going public. Moreover, the rôles of Kunigunde and Käthchen jeopardize the fundamental unity of action. The motivation is frequently casual and amateurish in its obviousness; vraisemblance is sacrificed for picturesque violence of effect. Strahl's revenge upon Kunigunde at the end of the drama is a glaring example of sensationally theatrical mannerisms. The delayed announcement to Käthchen by Strahl that she is to be his wife is of a piece with Kleist's tendency to keep from the interested characters information of which they should long have been aware and which has long since become obvious to the spectator. Examples thereof are the hide-and-seek game of identity between Ottokar and Agnes Schroffenstein, between Jupiter and Alkmene, and the delayed discovery of Judge Adam as the offender. Kleist even deigns to use the timeworn device of an interchange of letters as an aid in motivation. Details of exposition are recited to the audience across the footlights with little effort to conceal them as obvious rehearsals of facts. Three long informative monologues and one brief monologue occur. Such weaknesses have been condoned and explained away on the ground that this is essentially a fairy drama in which careful, natural, convincing motivation and technique are not to be expected. Unfortunately, however, it is not a pure fairy drama but, like the character of Kunigunde, a combination of diverse elements which have not been blended into harmony. Interchange of letters can scarcely be termed a fairy device, neither is the rationalization of Kunigunde's horrible ugliness to be regarded as such. There is not enough of the fairy element in the play to make it good fairy drama.

Das Käthchen von Heilbronn is written in prose and verse with no discernible basis for the change from one to the other. Kleist imposed no restraint upon himself in this particular, and evidently yielded entirely to the preference of the moment. As usual, the iambic pentameter is decidedly irregular; anapests and trochees are numerous, and lines of two, three, four, six, and seven feet occur. Enjambement is

DAS KÄTHCHEN VON HEILBRONN 169

frequent and many lines are divided among several speakers. Broken dialogue is enlivened by exclamations, questions, commands, and repetitions. Kleist's predilection for penetrating, inquisitorial cross-questioning is evident in Strahl's cross-fire of interrogations hurled at Käthchen. The harrowing effect of such passages is in sharp contrast with the warm sensuousness of desire and passion presented in other scenes. Kleist indulged his fondness for antithesis, rhetoric, extravagance in diction, and hyperbole to the full, without overmuch regard for its appropriateness. The rhetorical tirades and swollen bombast of Theobald in the opening scene are entirely out of keeping with his station. And Strahl's extravagant monologue at the beginning of the second act savors of strained eloquence and pompous artifice. Style and diction are frequently marked by violence, extremes, and mannerisms. The diction is decidedly varied; it is, in turn, vigorously realistic and poetic, concrete and fanciful, moderate and exaggerated, simple and rhetorical, popular and archaic. In none of his other dramas does Kleist give quite so much the impression of consciously striving to be effective in diction and imagery as in parts of this uneven play. A quotation from Count vom Strahl's long opening monologue in Act II presents a striking example of rhetorical prose diction:

Count vom Strahl.—
Verily! I will delve in the lexicon of my mother-tongue, and ransack the whole rich column under the caption Emotion,—so plunder it that no rhymester ever after shall be able to find a new way of saying, I am sad. I will put under conscription every jot of pity that sorrow bears; blithe joy and death-harboring grief shall alternate, and shall guide my voice, like a graceful dancer, through all the intricate movements

that enchant the soul. And if the trees are not moved by this, and do not drip down the gentle dew like rain from heaven, then they are mere wood, and all that the poets tell us of them is relegated to the realm of lovely fable. Ah you—how shall I call you? Kaethchen! why can I not call you mine? Kaethchen! my Kaethchen, why cannot I call you mine? Why can I not lift you in my arms and bear you off to the canopied bed that my mother has made ready in the state-chamber at home? Kaethchen, Kaethchen, Kaethchen! you whose young soul, as today it stood divested before me, seemed all adrip with sensuous beauty, like the anointed bride of the Persian king, when dropping fragrance at every step, she is led to his bridal chamber. Kaethchen, my Kaethchen! What keeps me from doing the like? Oh beauty, more charming than I can sing, I will invent some special art and weep it. I will open all the phials of feeling, of this world and the next, and compound such a mixture of tears, an effusion so particular, at once so holy and yet so sensuous, that everyone on whose neck I weep for her shall instantly say: These tears flow for Kaethchen of Heilbronn.

Das Käthchen von Heilbronn, one of the two dramas of Kleist to be staged during his lifetime, was first presented in Vienna on March 17, 18, and 19 of the year 1810. It was likewise produced at Graz and Bamberg before the author's death.[8] Efforts to effect presentations in Dresden and Berlin miscarried. In August, 1808, Kleist wrote to his sister Ulrike saying that he did not expect to have the drama staged in Berlin where nothing but French playlets were being given in translation; in Cassel the German theater had been supplanted by a French one. August Wilhelm Iffland, director of the Berlin National Theater, to whom Kleist sent the drama, was unfavorably disposed because of Adam Müller's attacks upon him in the *Phöbus*. After waiting for some time for a reply from Iffland, Kleist demanded the return of his manuscript and was told that the play could meet the demands of the stage only if completely revised. Thoroughly provoked, Kleist wrote Iffland a letter on August 12, 1810, calculated to give the greatest personal affront by its allusion to the director's perversion.

Kleist had requested the dramatist, Heinrich Joseph von Collin, to use his influence in securing a performance in Vienna. He received 300 gulden for the play, which, however, was produced in modified form in the Theater an der Wien only after a long delay. Opinions in Vienna as to the merits of the play were divided although the performance as such was praised. Two of three journals referred to the play as disjointed, and a third reviewer remarked that although a distressingly faithful imitation of Schiller's *Jungfrau von Orleans*, it nevertheless stood out above the ordinary spectacles of knighthood and occupied the first rank among the new productions of the year.[9]

In Bamberg the drama was first given on September 1, 1811, under the direction of Franz Holbein. Ernst Theodor Amadeus Hoffmann, at that time musical director of the theater, planned and carried out the decorations for the performance. Holbein's first adaptation of the play was less arbitrary than a later one made at Karlsruhe, which did shameful violence to the drama. Because of the condensation and simplification which facilitated its production, this version was unfortunately played widely for decades. Moreover, it set a bad precedent for numerous other adaptations. In 1876 the company of actors directed by the Duke of Meiningen began a series of successful presentations based on the original which was merely somewhat shortened and very slightly changed.[10] In various adaptations the drama maintains its place in the repertoire of the German theater and demonstrates that the success of a play on the stage is not at all determined by the approbation of learned and pseudo-learned critics.

On January 12, 1810, after considerable delay, Kleist fulfilled his agreement to send the manuscript to Cotta for publication. At the same time he requested the publisher to send him any sum of money in return, although Cotta had stipulated that he wished to decide only after a year what amount he was to pay. When Cotta subsequently declared that it was impossible to print the book during the course of the year, Kleist requested that his manuscript be returned. He then offered it to Georg Andreas Reimer of Berlin in a letter of August 10, 1810, in which he stated that the drama had first been produced in Vienna on the seventeenth, eighteenth, and nineteenth of March and, as friends advised him, had been frequently repeated since that time. He added that the *Moniteur* and several other newspapers had commented on it. Obviously enough, his reference to the Paris journal was intended to impress Reimer favorably. As a matter of fact, the allusion to Kleist's drama in the *Moniteur* was anything but flattering. The journal for May 2, 1810, merely reprinted a news item from another Paris daily paper, the *Courrier de l'Europe* of April 30. A Vienna correspondent reported that for two months local theaters had been presenting many new plays, some of which, however, such as *Catherine de Heilbronn* by Kleist, *Rochus Pombernickel, la Famille Pumbernickel*, etc., were beneath all criticism although they attracted an immense number of spectators each time. Kleist subsequently stated his willingness to accept eighty or even sixty thaler if only Reimer would print the drama by Michaelmas. A day later he wrote again saying: "The times are bad, I know you cannot give much; give what you wish, I am satisfied with anything, only give it at once." He finally received seventy-five reichsthaler.

Meanwhile Kleist had published parts of his drama in the *Phöbus*. The first act, together with the opening scene of the second, appeared in the April—May number for 1808; the remainder of the second act was printed in the September—October issue. These parts, as published in the *Phöbus*, differ considerably from the final form as printed in 1810. The latter is more condensed and its diction is more moderate. Moreover, in the later version the ninth scene and most of the tenth scene of the second act as published in the *Phöbus* have been omitted.[11] On the other hand, in the later version, the ninth scene of the second act contains Brigitte's account of Strahl's vision—a rather lengthy addition involving repetition.

By and large, *Das Käthchen von Heilbronn* is Kleist's most uneven drama. It was not written at fever heat; it is not one of those works which he was irresistibly impelled to write. And yet, despite its obvious defects and weaknesses, it contains scenes of great poetic beauty and charm. Above all, Kleist endowed the heroine with traits of rare sweetness which are as haunting as the fanciful dream-world of which she forms a part. In the more subtle, illusive touches, suggestive of the realm of fairy myth, of child-like wonder, unquestioning optimism, and happy faith in the ultimate goodness of this world, lies much of the insinuating charm of this drama. Kleist's theme might have lent itself better to treatment as a pure fairy play than as a hybrid including the shopworn figures of medieval knighthood that had stalked the German stage ever since the advent of Goethe's *Götz von Berlichingen*. Nevertheless, *Das Käthchen von Heilbronn* has proved to be the most popular of Kleist's dramas and will doubtless continue so. It makes its fresh, youthful appeal to the theater-goer who can leave behind his critical mask, become as a child, and enter naïvely into the world of the fanciful.

CHAPTER EIGHT

DIE HERMANNSSCHLACHT

FROM the fanciful dream world of *Das Käthchen von Heilbronn*, with its picturesque background of medieval knighthood, Kleist turned to the harsh political reality of the day in writing his next drama, *Die Hermannsschlacht*. This drama is born of the author's ardent patriotism and of his violent hatred of Napoleon as invader, usurper, and oppressor. Conceived in the fever heat of passion, it was rapidly written, most of the work on it being done during the second half of the year 1808. The transition from the world of visions, miracles, and romance to that of contemporary politics and wars of aggression was somewhat more abrupt but scarcely more striking than the change which Kleist himself had undergone. From a pronounced individualist, whose ideal was that of culture and self-development, he had developed into an ardent patriot imbued with the desire to aid his country in her struggle for liberty from tyrannical oppression. Of this profound change Kleist's correspondence gives a faithful and graphic record.

At the age of twenty-one, Kleist wrote a lengthy epistle to his former teacher, Christian Ernst Martini, setting forth his reasons for leaving the Prussian army and abandoning the military career which had become traditional in his family. The life of a soldier, for which he had never had any fondness, ran contrary to his whole being and, in time, had grown odious to him. He had come to the point of viewing the greatest achievements of military discipline with scornful disdain; he regarded the officers as so many drill-masters, the soldiers as slaves, and the skillful manoeuvres of the regiment as a living monument to tyranny. As time went on, the young lieutenant of the Prussian guards began to feel more and more keenly the evil effect which this anomalous situation was having upon his character. He was often compelled to punish when he would have been glad to pardon, and forced to pardon when he should have punished; in both situations he felt culpable. At such moments the desire naturally arose in him to abandon a career in which he was constantly tortured by principles at variance with one another; he was ever in doubt whether to act as a human being or as an officer, for in view of conditions obtaining in armies he deemed it impossible to reconcile the two. And since he considered his moral and cultural development a most sacred duty upon which his happiness was to be founded, he saw himself obliged to resign his commission and devote himself to the pursuit of knowledge and the search for truth. In April, 1799, Kleist, as already stated, received his discharge from military service. He profoundly regretted the seven years spent in the army as so much time irretrievably lost. Army life had been sorely trying and irritating to one of his intelligence, independence, refinement, and sensitive temperament. It had meant galling servitude rather than any ideal of service to his country.

For some years after his discharge Kleist was under constant pressure on the part of his family to accept a civil appointment. To them it was unthinkable that a scion of the nobility should refuse to serve king and country either as a soldier or in government office.

The young man's courageous desire for independence was sorely tried, and all the more so because, poor as he was, he repeatedly needed help from the family purse which at times was but grudgingly opened to so useless a citizen. In his desire for freedom he regarded government office in much the same light as the enslavement of military life. On November 13, 1800, he wrote to his fiancée that he would not accept a civil appointment, for he could not be a mere tool in the service of unknown ends which his reason was forbidden to scrutinize. He could not lend himself to doing what the state required without determining whether what was demanded of him was good or bad. He would be sure to take pride in asserting his own judgment and reason against his superiors. Interested only in his cultural development he would steal time from his work to devote to his ideal of happiness. A few days later he wrote to his sister Ulrike in a similar vein, asserting that he was too unskilled to seek and fill an office and that in the end he would scorn the beggarly happiness to which it might lead. With an air of mystery he informed her that he had much on his heart that he had to keep from everyone, but which he would like to impart to her, who would probably not misunderstand him altogether. He implied that a nobler fire was burning within him and that this made him unsuited to civil service. Haughtily he referred to the king's recent ungracious attitude toward him, saying if the king did not need him, he needed the king even less, for it might be less difficult for him to find another sovereign than for the ruler to find other subjects. At court, he continued, people are classified as metals formerly were by the chemist—namely, into those that can be stretched and expanded, and those that cannot be. Then the pliable ones are beaten with the hammer of arbitrariness, but the others are rejected. For even the best kings may like to develop the slumbering genius, but they constantly suppress the developed genius; they are like the lightning which enkindles inflammable bodies but puts out the flame. Moreover, said he, the Prussian commercial system, with which he would have dealings if he accepted an office offered him in the bureau of finance, is very military, and he doubted that such a system would find an eager supporter in him.

For some time Kleist was too deeply absorbed in the broad, humanitarian, cultural ideals of the enlightenment and its individualistic assertion of self to be able to conceive of the state as deserving of service and sacrifice. For him, service to the state meant loss of independence and entailed intellectual and moral enslavement. During a period of years he was concerned first with his own development in the pursuit of knowledge and the search for ultimate truth; subsequently he was absorbed by his ambitions for success as a dramatist.

The Napoleonic menace to Prussia brought about a striking change. Kleist, who in 1803 had wanted to enlist under Napoleon in order to find death in an expedition against England, later became an ardent champion of his country's rights against the invader. In December, 1805, he asks Rühle von Lilienstern in a letter why no one shoots a bullet through the head of this evil spirit of the world. He suggests that the king might have obtained the enthusiastic support of his people against Napoleon by an appeal to their national spirit. That would have been an opportune time to explain that this was not an ordinary war but a matter of existence or non-existence. Supposing, says he, that the king had had all his gold and silver services melted up, and had gone without chamberlains and horses, that his entire family had followed his example, and that he had then asked what the nation was willing to do. What effect would such an example have produced upon the people? In this letter the thought of individual sacrifice for the common cause is already clearly manifest. Kleist's letter to Ulrike of October 24, 1806, reflects the general misery and depression caused by the war. He exclaims that it would be terrible if the tyrant founded his empire. Only few people, says he, realize how ruinous it is to come under such domination. The parallel between the present situation and that at the time of Arminius is already suggested by his statement that the Germans are the peoples subjugated by the Romans. The intention, he remarks, is to plunder Europe in order to enrich France. Another letter to Ulrike of December sixth of the same year indicates clearly the warm interest which the nation's plight has aroused in Kleist. He writes that he does not know whether his physical condition is improving or whether the consciousness of his illness is merely being dimmed by the terrible phenomenon of the moment. It seems to him that the general misfortune is educating human beings; he finds them wiser and less cold, and their view of the world more generous. He is unable to think of the queen without being deeply moved. Her character is being developed in a manner truly worthy of a queen, for she, who but recently had been interested in mere trifles, has now grasped the seriousness of the situation and gathers about her all the great men whom the king neglects and from whom alone deliverance may be expected; indeed, it is the queen who is keeping things intact. On June 8, 1807, while held at Châlons-sur-Marne as a French prisoner of war, Kleist writes to Ulrike that it is repulsive to speak of one's own need under existing conditions.

His natural aversion to the French is heightened by the treatment they accord him during his imprisonment. Kleist's profound interest in the affairs of his country is revealed in a further letter from Châlons-sur-Marne to Marie von Kleist to whom he writes:

> In view of the seclusion of my mode of living you have always considered me as isolated from the world, and yet probably no one is more intimately linked up with it than I. . . . How disconsolate is the vista that opens before us. . . . Can one even presume to be happy when everything is in misery? As you may imagine, I am working, but without pleasure and love for what I am doing. When I have read the papers and again take up my pen, then with a heart full of grief I ask myself as Hamlet did the actor: what is Hecuba to me?

In view of the apathy induced by the hesitation and dilatoriness of the Prussian king, Kleist subsequently desired to publish a patriotic weekly journal entitled *Germania;* this, as has been stated, was to aid in arousing the country to the necessity of throwing off the tyrannical yoke of Napoleon. To Ulrike he wrote on July 17, 1809, that he had never before been quite so shaken. He had left Dresden with the intention of casting himself directly or indirectly into the tide of events but was most strangely blocked at every step he took. In Prague, however, whither circumstances had driven him against his wish, friends who had heard him read some of his articles welcomed his plan of establishing a patriotic journal and undertook to find a publisher for him. But just as the venture seemed assured, the defeat of Wagram and its aftermath crushed this undertaking and destroyed his whole activity.

In September and October, 1811, Kleist writes that he has applied to the king for a commission in the army; he hopes to become an adjutant to the king or to be placed in command of a company. This represents an entire reversal of his former attitude. Now that his country is in need, he is willing to serve it by re-entering the army from which he had once resigned on the ground that a military career hampered him in the free development of his personality and enslaved him body and soul. Kleist, the former individualist, has meanwhile become an ardent patriot burning with the desire to plunge into the events of the day with the full weight of his influence and to contribute in every possible way to the liberation of his fatherland. But since the vacillating king declared no war of independence Kleist's hatred of the enemy was compelled to vent itself in patriotic writings, in poems, journalistic articles and in drama.

Of Kleist's patriotic lyrics the most intense is the poem *Germania an ihre Kinder*.[1] As the mother of many German people, Germania calls upon her children to rush to arms, to leave huts, homes, and every pursuit and to surge over the foe like a boundless sea. They are to avenge the countless wounds dealt by the haughty, scornful enemy, to whiten the land with their bones, to dam the Rhine with their corpses and to rid the country of them. It is to be a savage carnage, a wild chase of wolves. Slay the enemy! is to be the slogan. Throw off the yoke of servitude which the son of hell has laid upon them; reign free on German soil or die in defense of liberty! Posterity, sitting in judgment, will demand no reason and no accounting for such an act of deliverance. In these patriotic lyrics Napoleon is branded as the spirit of murder against whom every weapon is to be used. In a poem to Archduke Charles of Austria Kleist urges war: Helplessly standing on the edge of the abyss, the German does not demand victory but merely a struggle, which, flaring up like a torch, may make him worthy of his grave.[2] The tragic inability of Kleist and other patriots to stir their lethargic rulers to action and to unite all Germans in a war of liberation is voiced in *Das letzte Lied*.[3] Here the minstrel, who has vainly sung of the joy of fighting for one's fatherland, is overcome with sadness as his song dies away unheard and unheeded; he ends his chant, desires to die with the ebbing notes, and, with tears in his eyes, lays down his lyre. With the exception of the ode to Friedrich Wilhelm III, these patriotic lyrics were not published until after Kleist's death.[4]

Although Kleist's proposed patriotic journal, *Germania*, never saw the light of day, a number of articles and a prefatory statement intended for it have been preserved. The latter states that the journal is to be the first breath of freedom. It is to voice everything, all the cares, hopes, and misery of brave Germans which have remained unexpressed during the three years sighed away under French oppression. The journal is to thunder forth a battle hymn, to sing of the fatherland, of its sacredness and grandeur and of the wave of destruction surging over it. It is to descend into the fury of battle, to animate the courage of the warriors and to pour fearlessness, endurance and contempt for death into their hearts.[5] The fiercest denunciation of the enemy is to be found in the *Katechismus der Deutschen*[6] written for the *Germania*. In the grilling, insistent fashion for which Kleist had a strong predilection, a father catechizes his son on Germany, on love of country, on the destruction of the fatherland, the arch-enemy, the restoration of Germany, the war against France, the admiration for Napoleon, the education of the Germans, voluntary contributions to the cause of freedom, etc. The parent wishes to drive home the thought that a Saxon is not merely a Saxon but a German as well—an idea that recurs in *Die Hermannsschlacht*, in which all the different tribes need to be impressed with the thought that they belong to a larger Germanic unit. It is one's duty, says the father, to love one's country not because it is blessed with riches and beautiful works of art, not because it has been glorified by heroes, statesmen, and others, but simply because it is one's fatherland. The enemies of the country are Napoleon, and the French as well, so long as he is their emperor. The sole cause which has any rightful claim to the undivided attention and efforts of the Germans is the restoration of the empire; it is the duty of their children to pray for the success of this undertaking. Let internal disputes be forgotten and forgiven until the empire has been restored! Napoleon, who has enslaved the country, is an object of loathing, the beginning of all evil and the end of all good; human language does not suffice to accuse him of all his wickedness; he is like the spirit of parricide risen from hell, stealing about in the temple of nature. Another favorite idea of Kleist, who has long since come to the conclusion that spontaneous acts are better than knowledge, is echoed here. The Germans, the son tells his father, are to be censured for their tendency to reflect when they should act; the enlightenment has robbed them of the old mysterious power of the human heart to feel and to react with spontaneity. Their idols are money and this world's goods. They are interested more in calm, comfortable, carefree living than in the highest ideals such as God, fatherland, freedom, love, fidelity, beauty, science, and art. The indifference of the times is scored in the dictum that he who loves shall go to heaven, he who hates shall descend to hell, but he who neither loves nor hates shall be consigned to the seventh, deepest, lowest hell. Emphasis is placed upon the duty of everyone to take arms at the emperor's command and to emulate the brave Tyrolese in slaying the French wherever they are to be found. Moreover, it is the duty of everyone blessed by God with this world's goods to give everything he can spare for the carrying on of the war. What is dispensable? All but bread, water, and raiment, for money and property are nothing as compared with freedom. If they are not staked in a war for liberation they will only be confiscated by the enemy after all. Everything is to be risked in a war for freedom; let everything perish, including men, women, and children, for it is pleasing to God to see men die for their liberty, but it is an abomination in his sight to have slaves live. Much of this catechism reads like a prose dialogue version of the theme of *Die Hermannsschlacht*.

An article bearing the title *Was gilt es in diesem Kriege?* sets forth the aims of the war which is to be unleashed. Its purpose is to awaken the national pride of the Germans in their past, in their virtues, in their great men, artists, scientists, poets, and religious reformers. The war is not one for fame, conquest, petty, political considerations, or sordid ambitions but is destined to save a nation from annihilation. Moreover, this nation, whose existence is at stake, belongs to all humanity.[7] In all these articles Kleist is aiming to drive home his burning conviction that a war against Napoleonic domination is a war for God, liberty, law, and morality. These are goods of inestimable value and must be defended at any cost against every enemy.[8] But like *Die Hermannsschlacht* these minor patriotic writings remained unpublished until after Kleist's death; they were written for a time which was not ripe for them, and when they did see the light of day the war of liberation had already been fought and won. They are a monument to Kleist's intense patriotism and to his burning desire for freedom; at the same time they bear witness to a fateful destiny which thwarted his efforts to be of service to his country. But even if published, it is not likely that his patriotic writings other than *Die Hermannsschlacht* would have appealed to the popular imagination and elicited a response at all in keeping with the intensity of spirit that prompted them. In mournful recognition of his failure to achieve the desired aim Kleist wrote a dedicatory distich on the first page of his manuscript of *Die Hermannsschlacht*. This dedication voices his sadness and regret at not being permitted to sing of the fame of his country.

Die Hermannsschlacht owes its title to Hermann or Arminius, prince of the Cherusci, who in the year 9 A.D. led the Germanic tribes in their successful uprising against the Roman invaders under Quintilius Varus. As conqueror of the Roman legions and as liberator of his people from foreign aggression, Hermann came to be regarded as a German national hero. Before Kleist, Johann Elias Schlegel, Möser, von Ayrenhoff, and Klopstock had celebrated him in drama.

Of the numerous personages designated in the list of characters the more important are the following:
    Hermann, Prince of the Cherusci.
    Thusnelda, his wife.
    Marbod, Prince of the Suevi, ally of Hermann.
    Wolf, Prince of the Chatti.
    Thuiskomar, Prince of the Sicambri.
    Dagobert, Prince of the Marsi.
    Selgar, Prince of the Bructeri.
    Quintilius Varus, Roman general.
    Ventidius, Legate from Rome.

The drama opens with a scene which graphically portrays the dissension, jealousy, and greed of various Germanic princes who ally themselves with the invader against their own peoples. This scene bears out Kleist's assertion that France was pursuing the old policy of Rome by taking advantage of internal dissension, dividing a nation, and dominating it. As the princes Thuiskomar, Dagobert, and Selgar quarrel among themselves, Wolf sadly exclaims that a beast of prey is attacking the country and its herds, while the shepherds squabble over a mere handful of wool. Hermann declines to ally himself with these petty, selfish chieftains merely for the protection of property. He demands that they sell and pawn their holdings, destroy their fields, slay their herds, and burn their huts, that they sacrifice everything for the sacred cause of liberty. Hermann would rather lose his life in murderous carnage and die an heroic death in the shadow of an oak of Wodan than to lose his freedom and be compelled to serve the enemy.

Hermann endeavors to unite the Germanic chieftains in warfare against the common foe, in order to annihilate the Roman invaders. To win the support of Marbod, the most powerful of the Germanic princes, he promises to render homage to Marbod on bended knee as soon as they meet over Varus' dead body; he would rather become the vassal of a German prince than the ally of Rome. To arouse and quicken the hatred of the invader, Hermann spreads exaggerated rumors of atrocities committed by the Roman legions and sends out men disguised as Romans who are to follow behind Varus, pillaging, burning, and destroying. He resorts to any and every ruse to accomplish his end, and even encourages his wife's flirtation with Ventidius, the Roman legate, in order that the latter may be lulled into a false sense of security. At Hermann's command the body of Hally, a girl defamed by Romans, is cut into fifteen pieces, and one is sent to each Germanic tribe so that all may be incited to revolt against the common enemy. An episode indicative of the wild fury of revenge kindled by Hermann is the vengeance of Thusnelda upon Ventidius, who has trifled with her affections. Outraged by his duplicity, she entices him to an enclosed garden where he is killed by a bear. The Germanic tribes which have been allied with Varus desert him, the Roman legions are annihilated in battle, and the way is paved for the reconstruction of a united realm.

In writing *Die Hermannsschlacht* Kleist was by no means concerned with glorifying the hoary past of his country or with erecting another literary monument to the memory of a hero already widely celebrated in German literature. This drama is born of Kleist's desire to arouse his fatherland to action and to unite all German peoples in a war for liberty. It is a drama prompted by love for his country and by hatred for Napoleon, its oppressor. Much of his wrath was due to his antipathy toward the French; primarily, however, the fanatical violence of his hatred arose out of seeing himself condemned to the very inactivity at which he scoffs in his portrayal of the petty princes who make a great ado but accomplish nothing. It is possible, too, that his intense feeling was in part a savage reaction from his own former indifference to the state and from his concern with nothing but personal ambitions. To substitute action for contemplation and reflection was the goal to which his patriotism impelled him. The immediate success of a revolt against tyranny seemed a matter of much less moment than bringing about the revolt itself. War, struggle, and deeds, even if leading to defeat, Kleist regarded as preferable to the hesitation, lethargy, and indifference of the times.

In writing *Die Hermannsschlacht* Kleist was in the vanguard of those ardent patriots who wrote with the intention of inciting their countrymen to a war against

Napoleon. Poetry, which had long remained aloof from political realities, was but beginning to include them in its domain. In a letter of March 12, 1806, to Friedrich Baron de la Motte Fouqué, August Wilhelm Schlegel had scored the laxity, indecision, and indifference of the times, the dissipation of energy in petty diversions, and the incapacity for great, resolute participation in movements for the common good. He stressed the need of a literature which should be wide-awake, energetic and, above all, patriotic rather than dreamy and idly fanciful. Schlegel inclined to the opinion that it might be well for poetry to be supplanted by eloquence so long as German national independence was so severely threatened. He asked: Who will give us plays like the historic dramas of Shakespeare which will deal with epochs in German history in which similar dangers threatened us, dangers which were overcome by probity and heroic courage? While other poets were still seeking refuge from the unpleasant facts of existence by living in a world of the fanciful and the ideal, Kleist found some compensation in envisaging a world of activity. Denied an opportunity to serve in a war of liberation, he vented his violent hatred and his need for action in a patriotic drama of intensity and sincerity. His aim was to effect a union between Austria and dismembered Prussia in which all German states would unselfishly join for the purpose of ending the galling Napoleonic domination.

Die Hermannsschlacht was written with intense enthusiasm to serve an immediate purpose. Obviously, therefore, Kleist, who was not at all inclined to make careful historical and documentary studies, was particularly unmindful of exactness in details. Writing under the pressure of his enthusiasm and at high speed, he was interested largely in the general similarity between temporary conditions and the repulsion of the Roman invader by Arminius. Consequently there are numerous glaring anachronisms and inaccuracies which have been welcome targets for detractors and pedantic critics. There is no great virtue in pointing out that in the year nine, of the Christian Era, Arminius' wife did not ring for her ladies in waiting and that her warrior husband was not in the habit of citing Cicero or comparing himself with the Shah of Persia. Nor does one require much knowledge of the civilization of the times to conclude that traveling salesmen and letters written in cipher were unfamiliar objects to the ruler of the Cherusci. Kleist concerned himself here neither with the faithful reproduction of historical facts and relationships nor with presenting the past with an eye to accurate local color. As a matter of fact, he was quite indifferent to the matter of decoration, properties, and stage setting in this drama. In contrast with *Das Käthchen von Heilbronn* its background is decidedly neutral; externalities are subordinated to the ideal of liberty.

Whether Kleist used the *Germania* of Tacitus or some compendium as a basis for his historical references is a matter of argument, although the latter conjecture seems to be advanced with greater reason. Striking and significant parallels in general situation between the drama and the first book of Samuel have recently been set forth.[9] Both Hermann and David of old are filled with zeal from above to rid their land of enemies. In pursuance of this inspired goal they feel entitled to avail themselves of any means, any cunning and deception that may be necessary. Called by Wodan and Jehovah respectively, they are to fulfill a higher mission for which they are endowed with steadfastness, courage, and a religious fatalism which ignores ordinary caution. Both are unsparing in the treatment of the enemy; the bard and the prophet alike demand that the foe be dealt with harshly and that personal feeling be suppressed. Kleist had the same consciousness of belonging to a people with a high destiny as did the Jewish prophet. There is further similarity between the fate of Hally and an incident in the Book of Judges XIX, 26-30. Although Kleist borrowed certain outward details from Klopstock's *Hermanns Schlacht* there is no kinship in spirit and execution between the two.[10] As usual, Klopstock's characters are shadowy phantoms while Kleist's leading personages are endowed with life, vigor, and individuality. Shakespearean influence is manifest in the frequent changes of scene, in the large number of characters, in the freedom with which the action is developed, in the mysterious, ominous words of the alruna and their effect upon Varus, in mass scenes, in the elemental, instinctive reactions of personages, in the range of passions, and in the vigor of expression. Nevertheless, Kleist's originality transcends all such influences and materials, and gives its own individual, particularizing impress to character and incident. Above all, he is more intense, extreme, and heedless of esthetic considerations than Shakespeare.

In this drama character portrayal is of greater significance than dramatic plot. The principal personages about whom the interest centers are Hermann, Thusnelda, Ventidius, and Varus. Like the elector in *Prinz Friedrich von Homburg* Hermann represents an ideal of unwavering stability, firmness of purpose, and inner harmony for which Kleist struggled in vain. Another of Kleist's characters, Käthchen, never was at variance with herself and was subject to no inner conflicts, but she differed from Hermann in blindly and unconsciously following her intuitive feeling. He, however, is not a creature of instinct but is given to reflection as well. Fortunately for him reason and emotion are intent upon the same end. Moreover, the power of his ideal is such as to transcend all else and to eliminate internal struggle. Yet as a truly Kleistian hero, he fears a clash between reason and emotion or between contradictory impulses, and consequently endeavors to eliminate every discordant possibility. The good Romans, he tells Thusnelda, are the worst; he curses every noble deed of the enemy because it affects his emotions, thereby momentarily making him a traitor to Germany's great cause. He declares he will not love this scornful progeny of hell. As long as the defiant foe is present, hatred becomes a duty and vengeance a virtue. Moreover, the chorus of bards urges him, who is so mild by nature, to yield to no gentler impulse, for that would be treason. Hermann is an idealist who is violently scornful of those who place property and petty ambitions above the sacred cause of liberty. He is ready to make any sacrifice for freedom. If necessary, he will devastate his own lands, raze every hut, destroy herds, and convert everything into a desert waste as he defends his territories inch by inch. To win support in crushing the Romans, he unselfishly offers to do homage to Marbod, who is but his peer. He runs the risk of losing his wife's affections in the deception of Ventidius and jeopardizes the life of his sons as he sends them to Marbod as hostages. His idealism endows him with a religious confidence in the gods which is nothing short of fatalistic. Convinced of the sacredness of the cause of freedom, he is confident of the aid of the gods. Why send three messengers to Marbod when Wodan can destroy three as readily as one? Why await an affirmative reply from Marbod when such delay will mean loss of opportunity to annihilate the enemy? Why leave forces behind to guard his territory from other enemies when the foreign invader is to be crushed in the wilds of the forest? Such passages reflect the thought expressed in Kleist's *Katechismus der Deutschen,* in which he exhorts his countrymen to let everything perish, including men, women, and children; for it is pleasing to God to see men die for their liberty, but an abomination in his sight to have slaves live.

But Hermann is not only an idealist; he is a practical realist as well, who never loses sight of concrete means of achieving his goal. A superior judge of human nature, he succeeds in winning the support of others for his cause. Moreover, he exploits every weakness of his enemies. In the service of a sacred cause and in a war with a ruthless foe, he uses any and every means of attaining the desired end. Hermann fights fire with fire and becomes altogether unscrupulous in resorting to dissimulation, ruse, misrepresentation, and falsehood. In such particulars the drama calls to mind Baron vom Stein's recommendation of October 12, 1808, that the king of Prussia employ cunning against the infamy and violence of the enemy. In support of this recommendation, Stein, the king's minister, asked whether Napoleon alone was to be permitted to substitute arbitrariness for justice and falsehood for truth. And Hermann, whose one desire is for liberty, maintains that in a struggle for freedom every strategy of war, every ruse and deception are permissible. His hatred sharpens all his faculties in the exploitation of every weakness on the part of the foe. He flatters Ventidius, the Roman legate, who is at Teutoburg in the capacity of a spying observer. By this flattery, by feigned indifference to the fate of his country, and by appearing to be stupidly blind to Ventidius' flirtation with Thusnelda, he disarms the Roman's suspicions. The legate becomes so thoroughly convinced of Hermann's artlessness and sincerity that he assures Varus the prince of the Cherusci can be trusted implicitly. As a result, the general leaves his legions exposed to attack from the rear by Hermann's forces. In the presence of Ventidius, Hermann simulates a certain hesitancy about admitting the enemy's forces into his territory although he is desirous of luring them into the bogs of his forests. Wishing to impress Varus as peaceable and cordial, he excuses himself for not having advanced to meet him. With a display of cushions and tiger skins he feigns to be fond of luxury and ease rather than of warfare. Deeds of violence committed by Roman soldiers are magnified at Hermann's command, as exemplified in the cruel dismembering of Hally's body described above. He not only rejoices at every Roman atrocity that can be exploited, but sends out his own soldiers disguised as foes to pillage, burn, and destroy. Nevertheless, Hermann, who has become an obsessed fanatic in the service of his ideal, is at heart reverent, sensitive, and profoundly susceptible to finer impulses. The song of the bards moves him so deeply that, in true Kleistian fashion, he becomes speechless with emotion. Although essentially a man of action who puts aside everything that may hinder him in the accomplishment of deeds, he has the farsighted vision of the statesman. Everything is to be avoided which may jeopardize the permanent amity and union of the Germanic tribes; the present emergency does not blind him to the demands of the future. His patriotism sees beyond a war of liberation and envisages an empire in which all these peoples are to be united in harmony.

Hermann's attitude toward Thusnelda is somewhat humorously playful and indulgent. Kleist has endowed him with such evident superiority, even among men, that beside him she becomes dwarfed, and for a time seems little more than a naïve child. In keeping with Hermann's firmness of purpose, his determination, and unswerving devotion, he undergoes no change. His wife, however, experiences a significant psychological development. Although convinced of her fidelity and devotion, Hermann does not take her into his full confidence with regard to his plans. He is fond of her, but treats her somewhat as a being of the second order. Without admitting her to any place of influence in his projects, he uses her as a pawn in the game by encouraging her in her flirtation with Ventidius, who is to be thrown off his guard. With his superior refinement, flattery, and gallantry this superficial Roman impresses Thusnelda, who has hitherto known only the ruder, vigorous men of her own people. Her vanity takes delight in his descriptions of Rome's feminine arts of costuming and hairdressing. Although she entreats Hermann to relieve her of the necessity of playing a rôle with Ventidius, she almost unconsciously plays it well as the result of being naïvely caught in the game of her husband's choosing. While her fidelity to Hermann remains unassailed, her affections do become engaged. On learning of the perfidy and mockery of the legate, her feelings are cruelly outraged. It is more than wounded vanity; her sensibilities have been toyed with by a man devoid of respect for her individuality. The man whose life she desired to save has proved unworthy of her childlike sincerity and fondness. Had she merely played a game with him, she could not have taken offense at his trifling with her. Thusnelda's interest in Ventidius has become pronounced; her genuine concern for him is betrayed by her hesitancy to ask Hermann at once and outright to spare his life. The violence of her revenge presupposes deeply offended feelings with which is mingled a sense of treason to the cause of her people.

Like Penthesilea, Thusnelda stops short of nothing in her frenzied madness. And when she has been avenged she, too, is overcome by the cruel deed and the emotional upheaval which precipitated it. The horror of her revenge is frequently criticized on esthetic grounds. But Kleist cared little for esthetic considerations in his presentation of the lengths to which outraged sensibilities might carry. Cold, statuesque beauty and repose held but little interest for him as compared with savage, unreasoned, eruptive outbursts of primitive violence.

Ventidius is vain, dissimulating, pleasure-loving, and desirous of tricking and possessing Thusnelda. A superficial fop, he is unworthy of serious affection and of the mission entrusted to him by Augustus. Sent to observe the situation, he falls an easy victim to the wiles of Hermann. His incapacity and lack of judgment are responsible in considerable measure for the defeat of Varus, whose suspicions he allayed. On the other hand, Varus is an impressive character who calls to mind the sombre, fatalistic gloom of Schiller's Wallenstein and the superstition of Macbeth. He is a brave soldier, unafraid of death and ready to sell his life dear without complaint. He obeys his emperor without inquiring into the political motives and ethics of an empire which waxes fat by taking advantage of the dissensions, greed, and pettiness of the German princes. Wounded and defeated, he regards Rome's arrogant ambition of world dominion as a mad caprice; dashed as it is by savage wits, it is but a reflection of the vanity of things. Kleist's portrayal of the enemy is, on the whole, marked by considerable restraint. Although the Roman soldiers commit occasional acts of violence, Hermann himself rages because these are too few in number to excite violent hatred of the invader.

The attitude of the German princes, whom Rome plays off against each other by exploiting their jealousies and sordid greed, is well characterized. Here again there is individualization and differentiation. Although remarkably high-minded and magnanimous in his final reactions toward Hermann, Marbod, like the other personages of the drama, is overshadowed by the personality of the central hero. An understanding of the allusions to specific rulers of German states and to contemporary incidents is not necessary to an appreciation of the drama as such. The question of the final leadership among the German states is left unsettled. For the moment the important thing is to dispose of the enemy; after that, the matter may be decided by a vote of the council.

The drama is lacking in a carefully developed central conflict with suspense, turning points, climax, and reversals of fortune. The fundamental theme is the endeavor of a prince to arouse his subjects and neighboring peoples to a war of liberation and the successful carrying out of such plans. Although he encounters some opposition, nothing hinders the fortunate, smooth achievement of this project; there are neither unforeseen obstructions nor retardations. On the whole, the central theme, as such, is epic rather than dramatic. But Kleist introduced a secondary action centering about Thusnelda and Ventidius with a dramatic conflict of considerable intensity. Thusnelda, rather than Hermann, experiences an inward struggle. Kleist neither staged the battle with Varus' legions nor did he attempt to describe its progress through eyewitnesses as he had done in *Penthesilea*. There are, however, colorful scenes of great vividness, such as those centering about Hally who, after having been dishonored by the Romans, is killed by her own father. This interruption of the stillness of the night, the flickering torchlight, the influx of masses of people, their growing horror at the revelation of what has happened, the arrival of the father, his slaying of Hally, and the resultant rage of the people form a scene of powerful climax. The action as a whole proceeds rapidly, without check or prospect of failure. The last two acts, with their changes of scene and of central personage, are more disjointed and consequently somewhat lacking in unity of interest. Thusnelda's song and the chorus of bards represent exceptions on the part of Kleist, who ordinarily avoids lyric interludes as undramatic. Nevertheless, the song of the bards is decidedly impressive through its effect upon Hermann and its revelation of a gentler, more sensitive side of his nature.

Individual speeches and the reports of messengers are much briefer than in *Penthesilea*, although only a limited amount of outward action is staged in both dramas. Kleist employed four monologues, varying in length from four to eighteen lines; with the exception of the longer one by Varus, these could have been eliminated without loss. Ventidius' monologue (V, 17), as he comes to his rendezvous with Thusnelda, reveals a sensuous passion which hitherto has not been disclosed as part of his nature; his words contain much the same imagery as that employed by Count vom Strahl in his declaration of the depth of his erotic desires (V, 12). The only significant monologue is spoken by Varus after he has been wounded and defeated (V, 21); its reference to the vanity of power and earthly ambition seems to have been inspired by Schiller's Talbot, who discourses somewhat similarly on being routed by Joan of Arc. The stage directions are intended almost altogether as guides to the actor; Kleist made no attempt whatsoever to introduce local color and to provide picturesqueness of background and decoration. In discussing the diction and meter of *Die Hermannsschlacht*, Ludwig Tieck wrote that they were characterized by greater freedom than any other drama of the author, and that at times Kleist was altogether unconcerned with the regular length of lines. To Tieck this irregularity seemed productive at times of an heroic, hymn-like rhythm, although some of the deviations appeared to result from the haste with which the drama was written.[11] Kleist, who never allowed metrical uniformity to stand in the way of freedom of expression and particularized effect, was particularly hostile to such restraining regularity in this drama. Although the meter is predominatingly iambic, lines vary in length to such an extent that the designation iambic pentameter would be incorrect. It has been computed that approximately nine hundred, or one-third of the verses, are of irregular length; Füser has counted 283 lines of six feet, 603 of four, and a few lines of two and three feet.[12] Word accent and verse accent frequently fail to coincide, especially in the case of proper names. From the standpoint of metrics *Die Hermansschlacht* is the most irregular of Kleist's dramas. Obviously enough, such lack of uniformity arises from design and indifference, and not from inability to conform to a rigid scheme. The diction is devoid of the oratorical flourish, rhetorical flights, and flamboyant bombast found at times in *Das Käthchen von Heilbronn*. Such artifices would have been out of keeping with the sincerity and seriousness of purpose which prompted the writing of the drama. Although similes, metaphors, and imagery are more restrained than one might expect in view of Kleist's common use of hyperbole, the language is decidedly vigorous. In fact, here restraint makes for sincerity. The man of action rather than the rhetorician in Kleist is in evidence.

More than any of Kleist's other dramas, *Penthesilea* and *Die Hermannsschlacht* were written with the very heart's blood of the author. He scarcely expected that the former would prove successful on the contemporary stage, but the latter was written for the theater with the intention of producing an immediate, stirring, patriotic effect. Like so many of Kleist's eager desires, this one of effectively serving the great cause of his day likewise remained unfulfilled. Scarcely had the drama been completed when on January 1, 1809, he sent it to Collin with the request that his friend use his influence in securing its production in Vienna. Kleist did not consider it better than *Das Käthchen von Heilbronn*, whose presentation Collin was sponsoring, but regarded it as more certain of success, and was anxious to have it staged first if possible.

On April 20, 1809, he writes to his friend a third time about *Die Hermannsschlacht*, telling him of his profound desire to have this drama, which was written solely for the moment, produced at once. He begs Collin to notify him soon that it is to be given, adding that he is indifferent to financial considerations; he will give it to the Germans if only it is staged. In a despondent letter of July 7, 1809, Kleist writes to Ulrike of his unsuccessful efforts to sell the manuscripts of *Das Käthchen von Heilbronn* and *Die Hermannsschlacht*. The latter, says he, will hardly find a publisher because of its relation to the times, and the former will be of little interest because it lacks such connection. Almost thirteen months after mailing *Die Hermannsschlacht* to Collin, Kleist again writes to him asking whether in view of changed conditions there is any possibility of its production. If not, he desires to have the manuscript returned. Although the drama was circulated among the author's friends, it was neither produced nor published until years after his death. In the year 1821 it was published posthumously with others of Kleist's works by Ludwig Tieck. All manuscripts of it have been lost.

In the form of an adaptation by Feodor Wehl the drama was first produced in Breslau in 1860. Another version by Rudolf Genée was first presented in Munich on January 6, 1871. Other adaptations have been played from time to time. Although as a patriotic drama with a thesis *Die Hermannsschlacht* has unusual artistic and esthetic merits, it is not surprising that interest in its production depends largely upon political conditions in Germany. In 1914, eleven performances were given in Germany before the war; from then on until the end of that year forty more are recorded. During the following year there were thirty-five, whereas it was staged but three times in 1916 and 1917.[13] Although widely read in the schools of Germany, *Die Hermannsschlacht* can be expected to come into its own on the stage only in times of national crisis.

CHAPTER NINE

PRINZ FRIEDRICH VON HOMBURG

KLEIST'S last drama, *Prinz Friedrich von Homburg*, is his masterpiece and one of the outstanding dramas of German literature. In the limited compass of less than nineteen hundred lines the author has succeeded in portraying an intense dramatic conflict, the clash of opposed conceptions of life, marked evolution of character, significantly individualized personages, subtle psychological motivation, fanciful somnambulistic vision, pronounced realism, colorful scenes of court and military circles, and a wealth of concrete detail. Like *Die Hermannsschlacht*, *Prinz Friedrich von Homburg* is rooted in German soil; both dramas grow out of patriotic devotion to state and country. The former deals with the liberation of a people from foreign oppression under the self-sacrificing idealism of a great leader; the latter presents an ideal of steadfast devotion and enlightened service through which alone the state can be maintained. The one bears the marks of being hastily written in the fever heat of passion with the intention of aiding in arousing an immediate uprising; the other is a maturer work with a high degree of artistic perfection. The tendency to extremes has been considerably tempered and, as a result, *Prinz Friedrich von Homburg* attains a far greater harmony than do other dramas of Kleist. While much of the author's own development is reflected, the conflict, as such, is portrayed with surprising objectivity.

The drama was probably written during the winter of 1809-10, a period of Kleist's life about which relatively little is known. The first reference to it in his correspondence is to be found in a letter to Ulrike of March 19, 1810, in which he tells her that a play of his, taken from the history of Brandenburg, is to be given at the private theater of Prince Radziwil. Whether this performance actually took place has never been established.

The theme of the drama may have been suggested to Kleist by a copper engraving of the year 1790 by Chodowiecki or by a painting of Kretschmar which was displayed and awarded a prize at the Berlin exhibition of 1800. Both present Friedrich Wilhelm, known as the Great Elector of Brandenburg, and one of his officers, Prinz Friedrich von Homburg. Kretschmar's picture, which was discovered in 1908 in the palace of the crown prince in Berlin, has no great merit or originality. It reproduces legend rather than historical fact, legend presented as history by Frederick the Great in his *Mémoires pour servir à l' histoire de la maison de Brandebourg*, which appeared in 1751. According to this account, at the battle against the Swedish allies of the French at Fehrbellin in 1675, Homburg, who had orders not to attack, impetuously led a charge which might have ended disastrously if the elector had not come to his aid. The sovereign pardoned the prince for having exposed his whole state to such danger, saying: "If I were to judge you according to the rigor of military laws, you would merit death; but may I not displease God on so happy a day by shedding the blood of a prince who has been one of the principal agents in my victory." Kleist departed from historical fact even further than had the author of the memoires, for he presented Homburg not merely as having attacked contrary to command but as actually having been sentenced to death for this alleged disobedience. Fiction and legend once more proved to be more poetic than the facts of history. Moreover, Kleist rejuvenated Homburg, who was over forty years of age at the time of the battle of Fehrbellin and who, because of an amputation, was known as the landgrave with the silver leg. For his purposes, the dramatist needed a young officer, a mere youth, rather than a middle-aged married man with a large family. With a poetic end in view Kleist, as usual, was indifferent to actual occurrence.

The more important personages of the drama are as follows:
Friedrich Wilhelm, Elector of Brandenburg.
The Electress.
Princess Natalie of Orange, his niece, chief of a regiment of dragoons.
Fieldmarshal Dörfling.
Prince Friedrich Arthur of Homburg, general of cavalry.
Colonel Kottwitz of the regiment of the Princess of Orange.
Hennings, Count Truchss, } Colonels of Infantry.
Count Hohenzollern of the elector's suite.

The first act opens at night in a formal French park at Fehrbellin. Half waking and half asleep, Homburg is seated under an oak, twining a wreath. The elector, his wife, Princess Natalie, and others summoned by Count Hohenzollern step quietly from the castle and look down upon him. Curious to see what the prince will do in his sleep, the elector, who has hitherto refused to believe that the young soldier is a somnambulist, takes the wreath, twines a golden chain about it and hands it to Natalie. As Homburg rises, the elector steps back with the princess, who holds the wreath aloft; with outstretched arms the prince follows her, calling her his beloved and his betrothed. In an endeavor to seize the wreath, he grasps Natalie's glove just as all escape through a door which is quickly opened and closed by Hohenzollern. Hohenzollern now calls the prince by name and awakens him. Homburg sees the glove in his hand, has difficulty in recalling where he is, but realizes that he has been sleep-walking again. As he narrates his dream, he remembers the elector and the electress but declares he cannot recall to whom the ruler had handed the wreath.

The scene changes to the palace where the elector bids his officers write down the plan of battle as dictated by Marshal Dörfling. As the latter dictates to the group assembled about him, pages serve a breakfast to the electress, Natalie, and ladies of the court, on the other side of the stage. The aim of the battle, as set forth, is to annihilate the fleeing Swedes by preventing them from reaching the bridgehead which opens the way to further retreat across the river. The prince receives orders to station his cavalry opposite the enemy's right wing out of range of the cannons and is expressly commanded not to move from his position, however the battle may go, until, pressed by Hennings and Truchss, the enemy's left wing recoils upon the right. Then he is to drive the retreating Swedes into the swamp, where they are to be decimated. He is to wait, however, until the elector sends an officer to him with the express command to attack. While these commands are being dictated, the princess asks for her glove. The prince, whose attention has been riveted upon her, drops the glove together with his handkerchief, picks up the latter, but lets the former remain on the floor in plain view. When the elector discovers it, Homburg picks it up and presents it to Natalie. He stands there for a moment as if struck by a bolt of lightning, then walks back triumphantly to the circle of officers and pretends to write. Homburg's inattention has not been observed by the marshal, who is intent upon his reading. Before the officers disperse, the elector urges the impetuous prince to restrain himself and to remain calm in battle. Having deprived the elector recently of two victories, he is not to cause the loss of a third in which the whole realm is at stake. In a closing monologue the prince appeals to fortune to grant him victory. He regards the glove as an omen and pledge of success, and is confident that on this day he will overtake fickle fortune on the battlefield and win a full measure of happiness. As the battle begins in the distance, Homburg's comments indicate that he still knows virtually nothing about the plans for the defeat of the enemy. When the Swedes begin to yield, he impetuously commands Kottwitz to follow him in a charge. The colonel, however, cautions him to calm himself and reminds him that they are not to attack until they receive orders to do so. But the impatient prince taunts the colonel until the latter commands the bugler to sound the charge.

The scene changes to a village in which the electress has sought refuge. She is told that the victory has been won but that the elector was seen to fall with his white charger when Homburg's attack was halted by murderous fire. Infuriated at the elector's death, the prince charged so savagely that the Swedes were completely routed. Had they not escaped over the bridges, every foe would have been killed. It develops, however, that the elector has not been killed. His master of horse, Froben, had noticed that the white charger was the target for the enemy's bullets, exchanged horses with him on the pretext that the elector's steed needed further training to prevent him from shying under fire, and was killed almost immediately. Meanwhile the elector has set out for Berlin and ordered his staff to follow; a truce has been declared and peace may be in sight.

The scene shifts to Berlin, whither Homburg has accompanied the electress and Natalie. Here the elector declares that whoever led the cavalry and arbitrarily ordered the untimely attack has forfeited his life and shall be summoned before a court-martial. The hasty charge compelled the Swedes to retreat before the bridges had been destroyed and thereby prevented the complete success of his plans. Then the elector asks: Homburg did not lead the cavalry? To this question Truchss replies in the negative, adding that, as a result of a fall from his horse, the prince had been seriously injured. The elector declares that the day's victory has been a splendid one, but even if it were ten times greater, that would not excuse the man through whose instrumentality mere chance has given him the victory. Having more battles to wage, he must insist upon obedience to law. On the arrival of the prince, the elector learns that he led the attack, and places him under arrest.

The third act opens in a prison at Fehrbellin where Homburg is under arrest. His friend Hohenzollern informs him that at the command of the elector the death sentence has already been brought to him for his signature. The prince is dumfounded at the thought that the elector could possibly entertain an idea which would make the blackest deeds of tyranny seem white in comparison. When asked whether he has ever done anything to offend the proud spirit of the elector, Homburg replies that the very shadow of the ruler's head has been sacred to him. Finally, as Hohenzollern suggests that there are rumors of an alliance between Sweden and Brandenburg based upon negotiations for the marriage of Natalie, Homburg loses confidence and concludes that he is in disfavor because Natalie may have rejected the Swedish suitor out of love for him. He now believes he is lost and implores help from his friend who urges him to entreat the electress to plead his case.

The scene shifts to the room of the electress, who has just urged Natalie to make an appeal to her uncle when Homburg's troubled, insistent request to be admitted is announced. The fear of death has seized upon the prince. On his way, by the flickering light of torches, he has seen the grave which is being dug to receive his dead body; he who but today seemed at the very pinnacle of success and at the crest of life will tomorrow be decaying between the boards of a coffin. He is ready to accept any other punishment, even dishonorable discharge; after seeing his grave he desires nothing but life, no matter how ignoble it may be. In abject fear and despair Homburg declares he will renounce all claims to Natalie and that all his tenderness for her has become extinct; she is free, and the elector may give her in marriage to anyone he desires. The electress requests him to return to his prison. As he rises, Natalie seizes his hand and courageously bids him take another look at his grave; it is, says she, no darker than the grave he has faced a thousand times in battle. She promises to endeavor to move her uncle's heart to clemency. But if her uncle cannot change the verdict as determined by law, the prince, says she, will submit courageously to his fate, and he who was a victor a thousand times in life will be a victor in death as well. In a much calmer mood the prince departs.

At the beginning of the fourth act Natalie enters the elector's room, falls on her knees and urges him to pardon the prince. Her uncle counters by asking if she knows what her cousin's offense was. She argues that it grew out of his overzealous desire to add to the glory of the elector's name. To crown the prince as victor and then behead him would be all but inhuman, and yet, says Natalie, God created no man milder than her uncle. His reply is that if he were a tyrant, her words would melt the heart within him. But has he the right to set aside the sentence? She, however, assures him that the country will not be undermined by his yielding to the impulse of clemency, that martial law is to reign, but not to the exclusion of kindlier emotions; the state which he has founded will weather much more violent storms than this unbidden victory. When asked whether Homburg is of the same opinion and whether it is immaterial to her cousin whether law or caprice reigns, she answers that she has nothing but tears in reply. Amazed, he asks her what has happened. Natalie portrays the sorry spectacle presented by the prince who under cover of darkness came slinking to her aunt. She describes how he shuddered at the thought of death, how unheroic and crushed this gallant hero, celebrated by history, has become. Perplexed and momentarily overcome by this unexpected change in the prince, the elector impulsively exclaims that the prince shall be free, that he is to be pardoned. A moment later, the elector, who has throughout been desirous of finding some adequate, salutary, humane solution, has an inspiration worthy of a great, genial ruler. He tells Natalie that he has the profoundest respect for the feeling of the prince. If the latter considers the sentence unjust he shall be liberated. He writes a letter, gives it to Natalie, and requests her to take it to Homburg herself.

On her way to the prison Natalie is asked by Count Reuss to sign a petition drawn up by Kottwitz, respectfully requesting the elector to pardon the prince. Unfortunately Kottwitz cannot circulate the paper widely because he is stationed at some distance from the other regiments. Natalie, therefore, claims she has instructions from the elector to command the colonel to come to Fehrbellin. Having written an order to that effect, she seals it and hands it to the officer, but tells him not to transmit it to Kottwitz without further word from her.

Just prior to Natalie's coming, the prince returns to his prison. In a brief monologue he dwells with resignation and composure upon the transitoriness of life. Natalie enters and presents the letter in which the elector states that in arresting Homburg he thought he was doing his duty and believed he could count on the prince's approval of such an act. Nevertheless Homburg is to be freed if he considers that he has been wronged. On hearing the contents of the letter, Natalie turns pale, but as the prince looks at her questioningly, she feigns sudden joy and urges him to write. Alarmed by his calm reflectiveness, she reminds him of his yawning grave, but he tells her with a smile that the grave is not a panther ready to leap upon him from behind. Once more she endeavors to instill the fear of death by informing him that orders have already been issued for his execution by a firing squad on the morrow. But he assures her that he recognizes his guilt, that he cannot appear unworthy in the eyes of the elector, and that he will have no pardon at the cost of quarreling with one so worthy. Deeply touched and proud of the prince, Natalie embraces him, leaves, and instructs Reuss to carry her written order to Kottwitz. If Homburg follows the impulses of his heart she may be permitted to do likewise.

The fifth act opens in the palace. To the surprise of the elector, Kottwitz has meanwhile arrived at the head of his dragoons, and the entire general staff has assembled at the town hall. In a brief monologue the elector declares that he might be alarmed at such unauthorized steps if he were an oriental despot and if he knew his colonel less well. Instead of disturbing the quiet of the night by ordering Kottwitz back to Arnstein, he sends a messenger to inquire what is happening at the officers' meeting. Before the messenger returns, Marshal Dörfling rushes in, shouting rebellion. Unperturbed, the elector bids him be calm and reminds him that he is not fond of having people enter unannounced. Dörfling informs him of a petition which the officers are circulating, only to be told that the elector already knows about it and that his heart is with them if it is a move in the prince's favor. But when he is told that the officers intend to free Homburg by dint of violence if their petition is rejected, the elector becomes aroused although he pretends to disbelieve the statement. When Dörfling urges him to pardon the prince before the loyal admirers of the young hero take any unpleasant steps the elector declares he will first have to ask the approval of Homburg, who was not arrested by caprice and who cannot be freed arbitrarily.

A servant announces Kottwitz and other officers and presents Homburg's reply. After perusing it, the elector calls for the death sentence as well as the passport for the Swedish ambassador and then allows the officers to be admitted. Kottwitz presents the petition humbly in the name of the entire army. Before reading it, the elector ascertains that the colonel came to Fehrbellin at Natalie's command; he betrays no surprise but announces that Kottwitz's regiment is to do final honors to Homburg on the following day.

Then he reads the petition about which, as he is assured, the prince knows nothing. The colonel endeavors to justify Homburg's attack on the grounds that an unforeseen change in the situation warranted it. In reply, the elector first refutes this argument and subsequently asks how future victories can be expected if anyone may arbitrarily interfere with military plans. But in a speech of emotional fervor Kottwitz answers that it is not the letter of the law which is most effective in the heart of the soldier but the personality of the ruler and the devotion he inspires. The words of the old warrior are an eloquent injunction to the sovereign not to degrade his officers by making them mere tools devoid of spontaneity, love, and initiative:

Kottwitz.—
    My liege, the law, the highest and the best,
    That shall be honored in your leaders' hearts—
    Look, that is not the letter of your will!
    It is the fatherland, it is the crown,
    It is yourself, upon whose head it sits.
    I beg you now, what matters it to you
    What rule the foe fights by, as long as he
    With all his pennons bites the dust once more?
    The law that drubs him is the highest law!
    Would you transform your fervid soldiery
    Into a tool, as lifeless as the blade,
    That in your golden baldrick hangs inert?
    Oh, empty spirit, stranger to the stars,
    Who first gave forth such doctrine! Oh, the base,
    The purblind statecraft, which because of one
    Instance wherein the heart rode on to wrack,
    Forgets ten others, in the whirl of life,
    Wherein the heart alone has power to save!
    Come, in the battle do I spill in dust

My blood for wages, money, say, or fame?
Faith, not a bit! It's all too good for that!
Why! I've my satisfaction and my joy,
Free and apart, in quiet solitude,
Seeing your splendor and your excellence,
The fame and crescence of your mighty name!
That is the wage for which I sold my heart!
Grant that, because of this unplanned success,
You broke the staff across the Prince's head,
And I somewhere twixt hill and dale at dawn
Should, shepherd-wise, steal on a victory
Unplanned as this, with my good squadrons, eh?—
By God, I were a very knave, did I
Not merrily repeat the Prince's act!
And if you spake, the law book in your hand:
"Kottwitz, you've forfeited your head!" I'd say:
I knew it Sir! there, take it, there it is;
When with an oath I bound me, hide and hair,
Unto your crown, I left not out my head,
And I should give you nought but what was yours!

The elector makes no effort to match logical arguments against the eloquence and inexact analogy of his old colonel but sends for Homburg to answer for him. Meanwhile he reads a statement written by Hohenzollern, who endeavors to establish that the elector is himself responsible for Homburg's disobedience. Having stimulated the imagination of the somnambulistic prince in the opening scene, he is the cause of the latter's distraction, of his failure to hear orders, of his belief in a victory promised by heaven, and of his impetuous attack. But the elector carries this argument, which is based upon the peculiar concatenation of circumstances, a step further and turns the responsibility back upon Hohenzollern, who had called him to see the sleepwalker in the park. Homburg's coming is announced by an officer who accounts for the delayed arrival of the prince on the ground that, in passing, the young officer desired to view again the vault prepared for his grave. On reading the petition drawn up in his favor, Homburg asserts that he is desirous of suffering the death penalty in order to glorify the sacredness of martial law. What, says he, would one more military victory gained by him be worth in comparison with victory over the most destructive of foes, over defiant disobedience? He begs the elector to forgive him for having served him with overhasty zeal on the day of the battle. As a last favor he requests his sovereign to conclude no pact with the enemy but to write him a reply with bullets.

When Homburg has been led back to his prison Kottwitz coldly asks the elector if, in view of what has happened, they are dismissed. With severity the elector replies that the colonel will be told when he is dismissed. After looking fixedly for a moment at Kottwitz he sends the passport to the Swedish ambassador with the announcement that at Homburg's request warfare is to be resumed in three days. Then, after a pause, during which he glances at the death sentence, he asks the assembled officers whether in view of the three victories of which the prince has robbed him and in view of the school of experience of the past days they wish to run the risk of serving with Homburg anew. Old Kottwitz answers for them all by saying that the elector could stand on the very edge of an abyss and the prince would not move the point of his sword to rescue him unbidden. The elector tears up the sentence.

The scene reverts to that of the opening of the drama. As the blindfolded prince is led through the lower gate of the garden, a funeral march is heard in the distance. Homburg expects to be executed, has made his reckoning with life, and already regards the corporeal world as fading from view. As in the first scene, the elector appears on the ramp of the palace accompanied by the electress, Natalie, ladies of the court, and officers. He gives Natalie a laurel wreath with a golden chain entwined about it and leads her down the ramp accompanied by all. She places the crown on Homburg's brow, hangs the chain about his neck, and clasps his hand to her heart. Overwhelmed with emotion, he swoons away as all hail him. The drama ends with the cheer: Into the dust with every enemy of Brandenburg!

Broadly speaking, the general idea underlying the drama is that the individual is ennobled by sacrificial surrender of arbitrary personal desire in favor of the common good, and by intelligent voluntary acquiescence in laws that safeguard the best interests of the enlightened state. Although the elector and the unconverted Homburg represent two opposing conceptions of the relation of the individual to the state and to law, it cannot be said that the fundamental conflict is between the two men as representatives of clashing viewpoints. At bottom, the conflict is waged within the prince, who undergoes a resultant sweeping change, becomes convinced of the magnitude of his offense, and desires to expiate it as a tribute to the sanctity of constituted authority. At the same time there is the subtle implication that imposing the law in all its severity upon those who have no conception of the basis from which it draws its justification is no high ideal, but may become inhuman and demoralizing in its consequences. Moreover, the elector appears to come to a realization that genuine statesmanship must take cognizance of more than the letter of the law; practical and ethical considerations of profound significance are bound up with the reactions of per-

PRINZ FRIEDRICH VON HOMBURG

sonality toward the spirit that transcends the letter. Intangibles demand consideration, and the problem is a far more involved one than that of meting out justice in the abstract. For Kleist does not present a clear-cut issue that permits of a mathematically precise solution; there are imponderables which defy exact appraisal and which are portrayed with great objectivity. In part these arise from involved situations, and in part they grow out of the fact that Kleist did not create the elector and the prince as distinct types but rather as persons endowed with a variety of traits: they are complex individuals whose reactions are not of a simple, predictable order. As a result, interpretations of the ideas underlying this drama as they are evolved out of situation, character, and personality are bound to vary with the temperament and viewpoint of critics. At all events, the drama reflects a transition in Kleist, who has forsaken his early intense individualism and has come to a recognition of the right of his country to unqualified support in a time of crisis. Steadfast devotion and service to his fatherland he now regards as virtues. Nevertheless, through Natalie and Kottwitz the significant appeal is voiced that the state shall not become coldly rigid in exacting slavish obedience. Warm loyalty inspired by the enlightened, worthy head of the state is indicated as the means of winning enthusiastic compliance and support.

With commendable restraint and artistry Kleist refrained from the direct championing of his own ideas through a single spokesman. As a consequence, various interpretations have been placed upon his alleged intentions in this drama. Some have maintained that personal initiative is glorified over against the rigidity of the law, others have insisted that Kleist desired to emphasize the sacredness of law to the exclusion of all else, and still others have asserted that he points to a compromise between the two. The question has been obscured further by erroneous impressions of the victory in battle, for the idea has been advanced that the prince's attack resulted in a complete defeat of the enemy and that unforeseen circumstances had necessitated a change in the plan of battle, thereby justifying the prince's charge from a tactical standpoint. The obvious answer to this argument is that the hasty attack enabled the enemy to escape across the bridgehead and to avoid annihilation; moreover, the prince had specific orders not to move from the position assigned to him, no matter how the tide of battle might turn, until he received definite, personally transmitted orders to charge. And although Kottwitz presents this specious tactical argument in his defense of Homburg, the elector refutes him so convincingly that the colonel turns from such attempted logic to emotional persuasion. The fact remains that prior to his charge, Homburg refers in no way to the trend of battle as the reason for commanding the attack. Following upon a general triumphant cry of victory he impetuously orders Kottwitz to follow him, without making any comment whatever on the tactical situation.

The greatest difficulty in the interpretation of the drama centers about the motivation of the elector's conduct in the scene with Natalie as she pleads for Homburg. Since Kleist does not resort to the convenient device of allowing the elector to reveal his character, emotions, and motives in monologues and asides, it becomes necessary to read between the lines and to scrutinize with care every indication given. The question as to whether the elector would have carried out the death sentence in case Homburg had remained defiantly recalcitrant is beside the point.

He is not concerned with exacting his pound of flesh but with winning and upholding respect for law and authority as safeguards to the state. In all consistency, therefore, he cannot capriciously set himself above the law which he expects others to obey for the common good. With utter sincerity he tells the fieldmarshal that arbitrary caprice did not imprison the prince, nor can it free him. In ordering that whoever led the unauthorized charge be summoned before a court-martial and sentenced to death, he was doubtless under the impression that Homburg was not the offender. Nevertheless his firmness of character and seriousness of purpose leave no ground for assuming that he would have allowed personal reasons and affections to stand in the way of enforcing discipline, even had he known the prince to be guilty. In fact, nothing could have been more subversive to respect for military discipline than the making of an arbitrary exception in the case of his nephew. Nor is the elector forestalling the free exercise of authority by the court-martial in announcing the death penalty prior to the trial. For Homburg himself states that according to law the court was compelled to impose this sentence upon the offender. The essential point is that the elector subordinates himself to the best interests of his country and that he consequently feels compelled to uphold the authority of the law wherever it makes for the good of the fatherland, regardless of his personal preference. Kind and humane as he is, he will obviously welcome a happy solution of the problem, for he himself subsequently asserts that his heart is with those who contemplate a move on behalf of the prince. It is reasonable to assume that, from the outset, the elector stood ready to exercise his prerogative of pardoning, provided circumstances warranted this step—but only under such conditions. Valid reasons, based solely upon furthering the best interests of the state, are to be regarded as determining his course of action.

When Natalie intercedes for her cousin, the elector's first question is whether she knows the full significance of the offense. And since she underestimates its seriousness he asks if Homburg shares her viewpoint and if in the prince's opinion it is immaterial whether caprice or law reign in the fatherland. When Natalie tells him that he has crushed the heart of a hero, that the effect of the death sentence upon Homburg is such that he cares for nothing but his naked life, and that his whole country might perish before his very eyes without arousing the slightest emotion, the elector is, for the moment, utterly taken aback, confused, and upset in his expectations. He cannot believe her, cannot believe that Homburg is abjectly begging for mercy. He has expected manly composure in the young soldier, a subsiding of his spirit of defiance, and gradual recognition of the enormity of his disobedience as well as of the justice of the treatment accorded him. Stern disciplinary measures have seemed warranted as long as he is dealing with a defiant, recalcitrant offender whose refusal to honor law and authority serve as a dangerous example. If, on the contrary, as he learns with consternation, the young hero has lost all composure and self-control, if he has become crushed and cowardly in the face of the death penalty, then the carrying out of the sentence would be on a par with shooting down a whining dog. Why brutally enforce a law which degrades man by robbing him of all spirit? What good can come to the state from such an act of cold vengeance? With some such thoughts passing through his mind the elector tells Natalie impulsively that the prince is to have his liberty and be pardoned. And then, as he prepares to write the necessary orders, a last hope arises within him. It may be possible to rehabilitate this cowardly human hulk completely, to instill new spirit and courage into this pitiful creature and lead him to a sense of responsibility to the state by putting him to a test. He therefore writes that he had counted on the prince's approval of his arrest which was dictated by a sense of duty. If the prince is of the opinion that he has been wronged, he shall be freed.

The elector had expected that the prince would, of his own accord, come to a realization of the magnitude of his offense; this appeal to Homburg's sense of justice and honor, for which the elector has great respect, now becomes necessary in view of the young man's perturbed emotions. Such a step looks like a highly daring game on the part of the elector; it grows, however, out of his intimate knowledge of the prince's character and out of his confidence in the young man's moral fibre. Having decided to put Homburg to this test, he regards the outcome as certain. He is not toying with Natalie as he writes a letter to the prince but is resolved to restore the prince to full honor as the latter proves his worthiness. The elector might spare the life of a groveling coward out of a sense of the inappropriateness of shooting down one who has become so degraded; life in exile with the humiliation and opprobrium attached to it would have constituted the severest punishment. But a prince who rises to the test is worthy of full pardon and honor, and can be counted upon to serve the state unhesitatingly in the future. These two alternatives are suggested in turn by the elector's first involuntary exclamation that Homburg is to be free and by his subsequent genial decision, which is to restore more than mere freedom.

All threats to discipline and order, however, have not been silenced by the elector's successful appeal to Homburg, for Dörfling reports shortly after that the officers who have signed the petition intend to free the prince through an act of violence if the elector does not grant their request. The elector ignores Natalie's unauthorized summoning of her regiment from Arnstein to Fehrbellin; her motives, he knows, are not those of wilful disobedience. But the incipient spirit of defiance and insurrection on the part of his officers must be curbed. So he plays a daring game with them after he has read Homburg's reply and knows he can count on the prince's whole-souled recognition of authority. Only an excellent judge of human nature and particularly of the character of Kottwitz would carry a challenge as far as does the elector. After dismissing Homburg, who has, in the presence of the officers, declared his readiness to glorify law and discipline by a voluntary death, the elector still withholds from the officers his intention to pardon the prince's offense. He braves Kottwitz who coldly asks whether they are dismissed in view of what has happened—Kottwitz, who like Kleist, resented the thought of being degraded into a mere tool. The elector declares that war is to be resumed in three days and pauses to give his officers opportunity to state their refusal to serve him further without some compromise over the prince. Then, significantly enough, he does not ask whether, in view of the school of experience of the past days, they desire to continue serving under him, but rather whether they wish to risk anew serving with Homburg, of whose change of attitude they are aware.

The challenging game he plays with his officers in the fifth act, his toying with the somnambulistic prince in the opening scene, and the delayed, somewhat operatic revelation to Homburg of his full pardon accentuate a certain playful superiority in the elector. It is a mistake, however, to assume that the arrest of the prince and his subjection to the harrowing fear of an ignominious death at the hands of a firing squad proceed from this same desire to play with his subjects. Such conduct would be cruelly inhuman and in direct contradiction to Natalie's characterization of him as mild and gentle. Moreover, it would rob him of the majestic dignity with which the dramatist so successfully invested him. The elector postpones announcement to the officers of Homburg's pardon for disciplinary reasons and not out of a desire to toy with their emotions and to match his wits against theirs. At the same time the continued withholding of the announcement from Homburg himself is quite in keeping with Kleist's fondness for prolonged suspense; Strahl's late, theatrical proclamation of Käthchen as his real bride is another instance of this same tendency.

In the elector, Kleist portrayed steadfastness of purpose and stability of character—an ideal to which he himself vainly aspired. Only one other of his heroes, Robert Guiskard, is endowed with the same impressive majesty as is Friedrich Wilhelm of Brandenburg. With a sureness of touch, which is all the more artistic because of its simplicity, Kleist has succeeded in creating these two characters who convincingly dominate the entire situation and tower above all those around them. Kleist does not tell his readers and spectators through other personages that the elector is great, but portrays him so. And yet, even the steadfast elector, endowed as he is with warm, human emotions, is on his guard lest others might swerve him from his course of action and make him at variance with himself. It is not merely diplomacy but also the desire to escape anything which might trouble his judgment that makes him avoid all altercation and expression of opinion by Kottwitz and

Dörfling when he learns that it is the prince whom he has sentenced to death. Although placed in a situation in which his emotions might well trouble his judgment, the elector knows no vacillation. But, like Hermann, he is on the defensive against influences which might affect his firmness of purpose, although he is less impassioned and has an Olympian calm born of a less ardent temperament. Though rather strongly rationalistic, he is nevertheless not insusceptible to impulse and is endowed with human, sympathetic feeling, affection, and kindly humor. The elector's self-control, his restraint and calm judgment, stand out all the more sharply by dint of contrast with the capriciousness of Homburg, who is carried away by emotion and visionary ambitions. By virtue of his masterful personality, he stimulates his officers to their best endeavor. He is a towering, harmonious character who has learned absolute identification of self with duty and order; the welfare of the state is the source of his happiness and satisfaction.

Much of the excellence of the drama lies in subtle psychological motivation. As usual, Kleist does not hesitate to portray violently extreme manifestations of human nature. Homburg's abject fear of death is but another instance of Kleist's predilection for revealing the lengths to which unrestrained emotions may carry. Penthesilea had slain Achilles and joined her dogs in horribly mutilating the dead body of the man she passionately desired and by whom she believed herself spurned. Homburg, the intrepid hero of many a battle, is plunged into ignoble fear of death, renounces everything, and is ready to abandon Natalie to anyone, merely to save his life and eke out a miserable, ignominious existence. From the standpoint of classical idealism with its insistence upon dignity, harmony, restraint, and poise, Homburg's violent reaction to the threat of death is plainly unesthetic and hence intolerable. But the unsparing presentation of the prince's conduct is born of a very different conception of dramatic art in which verisimilitude, even under extreme conditions, is considered more significant than compliance with a formalistic, over-refined ideal of beauty. Kleist was more interested in the truthful reproduction of human conduct under the most trying conditions than in carving out composed, statuesque figures of marble. In Kleist's first drama, Sylvester Schroffenstein utters words which foreshadow the author's portrayal of Homburg:

> 'Tis true, a man
> May fall because he's strong. The withered tree
> Withstands the storm that lays the live oak low,
> Whose spreading branches are an easy prey
> To stormy winds. It is not meet that man
> Withstand all blows, and he who feels the hand
> Of God may sink to earth and groan in pain.
> The gladiator prides himself on his
> Stolidity. We men who do not fall
> For gold or show should rise again nor feel
> Ourselves disgraced thereby.

This statement is singularly applicable to the prince, a strong valiant hero who is plunged into ignominy but rises to greater heights after his fall. It is significant, moreover, that in response to the elector's challenge, Homburg's renewed fortitude and his firm desire to expiate are first revealed in the presence of Natalie, in whose eyes he might well have become odious by his previous conduct.

As in the case of Count vom Strahl, Kleist draws the veil from Homburg's soul and bares his inmost being by stripping all inhibitions from him in a somnambulistic state. The prince is a man of passionate feeling, desire, ambition, and volition; he is sensitive, egocentric, subjective, emotionally unstable, undisciplined, and unfortified by any conception of service to an ideal that transcends self. In these respects he is the antipode of the elector. As a dreamer, he is absorbed by his fanciful imaginings and desires to the extent that they do not lose their sway over him even in his waking hours. At the same time, as a valiant soldier, he is a man of action, even if his deeds are the result of impetuous promptings uncontrolled by reflection and reason. Homburg has Kleist's own capacity for self-absorption on which Christoph Martin Wieland commented. Under the spell of personal interests the prince is as deaf to everything about him as are Penthesilea and Achilles. Like them he lacks a sense of obligation to others. Even the elector's final injunction that he exercise restraint in the impending battle so as not to jeopardize a third and most strategic victory does not serve to impress him with his responsibility. Flushed with success in battle, he then envisages the fulfillment of all his dreams and ambitions until his arrest brings a rude jolt. At first he distrusts his senses when summoned to surrender his sword; on being acquainted by Hohenzollern with the reason for his arrest, he scoffs ironically at the elector's imitation of the stoical Roman who had his sons executed for conspiracy against the republic. Accustomed to noble generosity and love, he declares himself unable to admire so stern a pose.

The gradual change in Homburg, while in prison, from confidence in his prompt release to a panic-stricken fear of death is a masterful piece of psychological motivation. At first he assumes that Hohenzollern has come with the express purpose of announcing his liberation; when apprised that this is not the case, he remains coolly indifferent, for he is certain that the elector will soon send someone else on such a mission. He is surprised at the serious air of his friend even though he begins to realize that the elector, in ordering his arrest, is not playing the rôle of a Brutus but is complying with his sense of duty. With great confidence in the elector's affection, Homburg is convinced that his uncle will now obey the promptings of his heart and pardon him. The court-martial, he knows, has sentenced him to death, but under the law it has no other alternative. Under Hohenzollern's insistent questioning, the prince at length begins to have doubts and misgivings, which finally give way to fears when he hears that Dörfling, who carried the sentence to the ruler for his signature, is genuinely alarmed. Unable to comprehend the significance of his offense, which he avers consisted merely in decisively defeating the enemy two moments before the command was given, he, like Hohenzollern, is ready to attribute the most unworthy motives to the elector, whom he had just pronounced his loving, fatherly friend. Unable to reflect and to appraise the situation, he is a prey to changing emotion. From the heights of ambitions about to be fulfilled he has suddenly been dashed down to the prospects of disgrace and ignominious death. In this frantic state, the sight of his grave by fitful torchlight unnerves him completely. He becomes obsessed with a fear of death which holds him as firmly in its threatening grip as he has previously been absorbed by his ambitious dreams. Homburg seems to be capable of but one impression at a time; this single impression, magnified by a vivid imagination, obliterates everything else for the moment. Haunted as he is by the spectre of death, he loses all perspective, all poise and self-control. He craves nothing but naked life, for which he is ready to sacrifice even love and honor.

But Natalie's calm courage is not without effect upon Homburg; her appeal to his valorous defiance of death in battle, her promise to intercede in his behalf, and her unwonted manifestation of initiative reassure him somewhat. On his return to prison, his nervous tension and agitation have given way to resignation. Consequently the elector's appeal to his sense of honor, duty, and justice finds him in a calmer mood conducive to eliciting the desired response. Called upon to judge his own act with candor, the prince comes to a clear realization of the seriousness of his offense, of its disastrous effect upon discipline and its consequences to state and authority. Desirous of expiating his wrong, he insists upon going to his death in order that the sanctity of the law may be upheld and that defiant disregard of authority may be overcome by his example. He has become aware of the ennobling effect of dutiful service to the state when acquiesced in by the heart rather than imposed arbitrarily from without. Prior to the beginning of the action Homburg had been but an irresponsible youth and an impetuously courageous officer; now he has become imbued with a deep sense of responsibility to the state and has developed steadfastness and genuinely heroic qualities.

Nowhere has Kleist given a more intimate portrait of some of his own tendencies than in the characters of Penthesilea and Homburg. The prince, however, does not voice Kleistian sentiments that are far-fetched and out of keeping with his rôle as does the Amazon queen, who at times becomes the author's mouthpiece. Nor does Homburg reveal himself by his own words with the same obvious directness as Penthesilea repeatedly does. Kleist's method of presenting character has meanwhile become far more artistic, even though he does not shrink from exposing human frailty to the most glaring, searching light. In common with Penthesilea, Homburg has the instability of character that is subject to untempered, violent emotional reactions. He has much of the author's early egocentric individualism, ambition, and dislike for restraint. In *Penthesilea* Kleist portrayed the tragic disaster resulting from passionate yielding to subjective desire; in his last drama a tragic outcome is narrowly averted. The solution to which he points is voluntary, intelligent devotion of self to the enlightened service of a collective ideal which stabilizes and ennobles the individual. Homburg and his fellow officers, as well, have gained this insight into life as the result of the school of experience through which they have passed. In contrast with the instability and subjectivity of the prince is the steadfastness of the elector, which grows out of a sense of social duty that transcends individual desire. This firmness of character represents an ideal to Kleist who, ever since his youth, had sought to emancipate himself from the unworthy caprice of chance and circumstance by formulating some definite plan of life which might assure serenity even in adversity. In willing devotion to a collective ideal he now sees a force that raises man above the disturbing vicissitudes of a self-centered existence.

Among the secondary characters only Natalie and Kottwitz are of significance. Natalie is aroused to initiative and action when the man she loves is in danger. Then she rises to heights of calm courage and resourcefulness that are astounding even to the prince. Such determination is indeed surprising in one who but recently appeared so helpless on hearing of the alleged death of her uncle and protector. She sends Homburg back to his prison in a state of mind conducive to a suitable reception of the elector's challenging letter, pleads his case admirably before her uncle, and, on her own initiative, orders Kottwitz's regiment to move to Fehrbellin, where the colonel can promote Homburg's cause more effectively. She makes an unselfish plea for the prince, bears him no ill will for his humiliating renunciation of her, aids in his rehabilitation, and manifests that feminine devotion which Kleist regarded as an ideal of womanhood. Natalie is not an episodical character as is Thekla, in Schiller's *Wallenstein*, with whom she has often been compared, but is intimately linked up with the central action.

Kottwitz is a gouty, doughty old warrior, a strange combination of impetuous courage and of shy deference to the elector. His eloquent speech championing initiative in the soldier and dealing a blow at the cold letter of the law is reminiscent of Kleist, who as a young officer had chafed under the necessity of blindly carrying out orders regardless of his views or their merit. The old colonel's warm loyalty to his sovereign is refreshing in its sincerity. The other officers are types. Among them, Hohenzollern stands out as the prince's confidant who fills the double function of presenting the exposition and of aiding in the characterization of Homburg.

Structurally, *Prinz Friedrich von Homburg* is the most regular of Kleist's dramas. After *Penthesilea* and *Der zerbrochene Krug* he abandoned the drama without division into acts as unsuited to the requirements of the stage. Each of the five acts of his last drama is a well-rounded unit in the compact structure of the whole. The somewhat operatic close ushers in once more the background of the opening scene, whose playful mood had pointed toward a happy outcome of the action. Kleist's strongly developed sense of musical form is manifest in reverting to the opening motif at the close of his composition. The fanciful beginning and end add a lighter, poetic touch to the stern presentation of a problem which under the hand of other dramatists might easily have found too rationalistic a treatment. The drama is highly unified in action and interest, the development of events is rapid and unbroken, and there are no episodes to detract from the central unity. Kleist's sense of form is nowhere more decidedly in evidence. The condensed exposition of significant preceding events is given in less than thirty lines at the opening of the drama and produces an effect of military terseness and precision. In compact unity and skillful technique Kleist here achieved a degree of excellence unsurpassed in any of his other dramas. Moreover, he succeeded in creating suspense by more natural and less obvious means than he frequently does elsewhere. Nevertheless, the tendency toward prolonging suspense is still manifested by the elector's rôle in the last act.

Kleist does not studiously avoid monologues and asides. Of the five monologues, four are spoken by Homburg, and the remaining one by the elector. As usual, Kleist avoids the long monologue in which Schiller allows his characters to reveal themselves, their motives, inward struggles, and emotions. Nor does he employ the reasoned monologue of Hebbel, in which a character sums up the entire situation and draws the inevitable conclusion which inexorably determines his future course of conduct. Two of the prince's monologues express his exultation at the happy prospect of success. A third is a reflection on the transitoriness of life as he returns to his prison; in the last one, as he fancies he is to be executed, he envisages immortality. The elector's single monologue gives a splendid picture of his assurance of Kottwitz's loyal devotion. Each monologue grows directly out of and reflects a certain phase of the action; it is not a sententious, rhetorical divagation on mere generalities suggested by vague analogy.

Although the scenic background and the stage setting are indicated with some care, Kleist is much less concerned with such details here than in the spectacular drama, *Käthchen von Heilbronn*. On the other hand, the wealth of stage directions intended to serve as guides to the actors is indicative of Kleist's growing desire to succeed on the stage of his time. In spite of the fancifulness of the opening and closing scenes, the careful, detailed psychological motivation inclines far more toward later nineteenth-century realism than toward abstractly idealistic classicism or fantastical, lyrical romanticism.

The iambic pentameter of *Prinz Friedrich von Homburg* differs from that of his other dramas only in its comparative regularity. Although more inclined to restraint, Kleist still takes liberties by introducing trochees, anapests, and lines of varied length. The highly appropriate diction covers a wide range in doing justice to the variety of emotions, moods, characters, scenes, and action portrayed. Although much more harmonious and moderate, the diction has lost none of its characteristic vigor and vividness. Exclamations, interrogations, repetitions, broken lines, pauses, and occasional long, involved periods produce a pulsating rhythm throbbing with life and emotion. Much of the strong emphasis of Kleist's lines is due to his frequent practice of placing the most significant element of a sentence in bold relief at its very beginning. As elsewhere, numerous concrete details add a realistic, plastic touch to descriptions which might otherwise be vague or lacking in individuality. Without presenting the battle scene on the stage and without resorting to the long descriptive accounts so common in *Penthesilea*, Kleist evokes a stirring picture of the battle. Amplified figures of speech and imagery are more moderate and in better taste, yet forceful and effective. There is none of the rhetorical striving for exaggerated effect which is so obvious in *Das Käthchen von Heilbronn*, nor do characters use language out of keeping with their person or with the situation. As in *Die Hermannsschlacht* Kleist demonstrates a growing ability to achieve vigor in style and diction through naturalness rather than by strained hyperbole and violent artifice. Emotion still carries him away at times as in the long speech pronounced by Kottwitz in defense of the prince's act of insubordination, but the colonel's words ring true because they spontaneously reflect a point of view so characteristic of Kleist at one stage of his development. The varied dialogue moves rapidly and pulsates with life but has less of the hacked jerkiness which threatened to become a mannerism in earlier dramas. Greater moderation and harmony have been attained throughout, without sacrifice of power, emphasis, and individuality.

In spite of its maturer artistry the drama long remained in obscurity. Kleist's plan of dedicating it to Queen Luise of Prussia was frustrated by her untimely death. He then decided to dedicate it to Princess Marie Anna von Hessen-Homburg, a sister-in-law of the Prussian king. Failure to induce Reimer, the publisher of *Das Käthchen von Heilbronn*, to print the drama, necessitated presenting the princess with a dedicatory copy in manuscript. This manuscript, now preserved in the library of Heidelberg University, is the only one extant and is not in the author's handwriting. The drama was first published posthumously in 1821 by Ludwig Tieck, who made minor changes in the text to suit his own preference. The first performance, an adaptation entitled *Die Schlacht bei Fehrbellin*, was given in Vienna on October 3, 1821. Poorly played, it was greeted with laughter and hisses. Although staged soon after in Breslau, Frankfurt am Main, and Dresden, the drama had difficulty in gaining recognition. Not until about sixty years after the author's death did it begin to find wider appreciation on the stage.

One great obstacle to its success lay in Homburg's frantic fear of death. In 1822, Heinrich Heine wrote with his customary ironical mockery that the drama was not to be played in Berlin because, as he had heard, a certain noble lady was of the opinion that her ancestor cut rather a sorry figure in it. It is of interest to note that this noble lady was none other than the princess to whom the author had dedicated his work. Kleist fared no better at the hands of Vienna censorship. Here, in 1822, Archduke Charles prohibited further performances of the drama at the court theater and in all Austria as well, on the ground that the manner in which the prince manifested his attachment for life might exert a demoralizing influence on the army. Singularly enough, Kleist had hailed this same Archduke Charles as the deliverer of Germany from Napoleonic oppression and had celebrated him in a poem written after the battle of Aspern as the "victor over the invincible."

Among German dramatic geniuses who were enthusiastic in their praise of the drama Richard Wagner and Friedrich Hebbel deserve mention. The former referred to it as Kleist's wonderful *Prinz von Homburg*, and pronounced it a most excellent stage drama. He regarded the ability of actors to interest the German theater-going public in its faithful presentation from beginning to end as a telling criterion of their histrionic art. Hebbel, who considered the drama a tragedy, asserted that it was one of the most original creations of the German spirit, for the reason that by the mere threat of death it achieves what death alone accomplishes in all other tragedies, namely the moral clarification and transfiguration of the hero.

CHAPTER TEN

CONCLUSION

NO GERMAN dramatist of note has been considered quite so enigmatic as Heinrich von Kleist. Attempt after attempt has been made to fix him in a definite category and to explain and interpret him and his works from a single viewpoint. The very diversity of these analyses points toward the unsatisfactoriness of such an undertaking. A strictly rationalistic approach to him at any period of his life inevitably results in failure because he was at no time temperamentally a thoroughgoing rationalist. Even in the period prior to his disillusionment by Kantian philosophy Kleist was by no means the rationalist that he temporarily fancied himself and for which he has so frequently been taken. The very enthusiasm, fervor, and ardor with which he approached the philosophy of enlightenment betokens a profoundly emotional nature and precludes the possibility of the sway of cold, mathematical, impersonal, logical abstraction. This passing enthusiasm for a rationalistic conception of life and of the universe sprang largely from his youthful desire for happiness and from his ethical idealism. Aware only too early of the contradictoriness of life, of the waywardness of fortune, and of the instability born of his highly emotional, imaginative temperament, Kleist vainly searched for a stabilizing force without which human existence seemed too uncertain and too terrifying. Stimulated by his readings, the youth began a veritable worship of the life of reason based upon a carefully wrought plan for his future development. Desirous of being serenely happy, Kleist regarded the triumphant sway of reason as the best protection from the insecurity and changefulness of existence and consequently as the safest guarantee of contentment.

The optimistic period in which Kleist firmly believed that happiness can be attained under the guidance of reason is the one which gave rise to most of his extant letters. Their comparative bulk and their impressive insistence on a single point of view have misled many critics into an overemphasis of his alleged rationalistic propensities. Logically minded and desirous of achieving unity, they have frequently yielded to the temptation of reasoning away all contradictory aspects of his nature and writings. In their endeavor to harmonize, they have lost sight of imponderables and of the complexities underlying a personality of profoundly emotional temper. The desire to reduce all reactions and manifestations of the individual to a single formula has caused rationally minded scholars to overlook the fact that sensitively organized beings defy such processes of simplification, which do violence to them by stripping them of much of their individuality. Kleist is too complex to permit of classification as a classicist, a romanticist, or even as a romanticist with certain reservations. And the attempt to account for certain peculiarities in Kleist and his characters by such superficial designations as abnormal, pathologic, morbid, and neurotic, merely obscures and distorts. The fact is that his personality, like that of some of his characters, defies rationalistic analysis because it is essentially emotional.

Among the limitations of the human mind must be included its inability to analyze and comprehend emotion. Conduct which defies logical interpretation and seems to fly in the very face of reason is frequently pronounced unreasonable, quixotic, capricious, or whimsical. Yet such designation does not serve to define or explain the nature, causation, and origin of unreasoned conduct. Since many human acts are imponderable, unreasoned, and unpredictable, and since many run counter to all logical expectations, why should not a dramatist portray such aspects of human life by the side of others? Why not widen the scope of dramatic literature by presenting imponderables as such? Why not stage quixotic acts and caprices as such? If these aspects of man's behavior are an undeniable part of life, why not depart from hoary, logical tradition as well as from dramatic and theatrical convention and simply stage occasional unreasoned acts of emotional personages without attempting complete, exhaustive, logical motivation and explanation of that which defies analysis? This is what Kleist has repeatedly done; he has portrayed the contradictoriness and the inconsistency in human conduct which he observed in himself as well as in others. In such presentation he made no attempt to avoid extremes. In fact, emotional instability seemed all the more impressive and none the less true to life because of its eruptive, violent excesses.

Under the influence of a rationalistic tradition, careful dramatists prior to Kleist had meticulously motivated the acts of characters who themselves were the conceptions of a rationalistic mind. Their actions had to be logical, in keeping with their nature, and hence predictable. Lessing, for example, held that on the stage the public is to learn what every man of a given character will do under given circumstances.

And in keeping with such a viewpoint heroes and heroines were so portrayed that their acts were the inevitable, consistent outcome of their reasoned nature. The ideal dramatic problem as based upon character was one of mathematical exactness in which two and two were bound to make four. This well-nigh sacred convention manifested itself clearly in the monologue in which the dramatist demonstrated to the audience the exactness of his skillful calculations. The old stilted monologue reflected the conviction that acts must not only be in harmony with character but must be clearly intelligible as such. The serious business of drama was to create personages of a definite stripe and to present their deeds as the obviously natural consequence of their nature. And to make doubly sure that no one should fail to comprehend, the hero explained in monologues what he was doing, and why he was doing it, and that his conduct was just what one had a right to expect of him.

Now one interesting aspect of life is its uncertainty and its unpredictability. And it is unpredictability in the reactions and acts of persons which, within certain limits, lends them fascination. In fact, it is just this element, based upon emotion and subjective preference, which tends to differentiate the individual from the type. The difficulty lies in presenting a character of this unusual nature in such a manner that his conduct may not seem strained, absurd, or freakish. Consequently the dramatist is not freed from the necessity of careful characterization. It must be borne in mind that even people whose conduct almost invariably seems based on careful analysis of situations occasionally fly impulsively in the face of all logic and make a choice based entirely upon subjective preference. Obviously enough, the individual whose nature is fundamentally emotional is given to acts which, because they defy analysis, seem unreasonable and capricious to his logically minded fellows. What type of dramatist is likely to create characters of this kind? In all probability, the poet of just such temperament will express these eruptive, volcanic tendencies in the persons he creates. And in the case of Heinrich von Kleist we have to do with a man whose conduct was based to a remarkable degree upon feeling, emotion, and intuition. The objection may be raised that impulsive, capricious acts require no motivation in character and that consequently it would have been quite unnecessary for Kleist to portray personages as carefully as he did. But it must not be overlooked that it is only an occasional unreasoned act which makes its appearance in personages like Penthesilea, Strahl, Thusnelda, and Homburg. And even here Kleist sometimes gives a clue as to what may be expected. Of himself he once said that the only constant thing about him was his inconstancy. Similarly, in the case of Penthesilea he prepares the reader or spectator for the incommensurable and imponderable element in her nature through the words of Prothoe who asserts that the queen's soul is incalculable.

Kleist well realized how inconsistent he was inclined to be and how illogical his conduct seemed to others. Endowed, like Homburg, with a vivid imagination, inordinate ambition, and powerful, violent emotion, he was doomed to ups and downs; periods of exultation and high expectancy alternated with deep despair. He was fully aware that unbridled emotion might lead to catastrophe and tragedy; it was this realization that lent terror to life and filled him repeatedly with a nervous, haunting fear and with nameless dread. In such moments he longed for death and yet trembled at the thought of annihilation. Consequently he aimed in one way or another to fortify himself against shocks to his emotions from the vicissitudes of life. His youthful rationalistic plan of life grew out of his instinctive realization of the need for some dominant motive coming from without, which might transcend his existence and fortify him against adversity. When, owing to the inadequacy of its foundations, his early philosophy of life based upon the idea of human perfectibility crumbled, life seemed a hopeless maze, devoid of any stabilizing force. Human existence appeared devoid of sense and the world a madhouse peopled by bewildered, helpless humanity. His first drama was born of such a pessimistic outlook.

If reason fails to function when man is blinded by towering passions, if its conclusions are not to be trusted, then some other stabilizing force must be sought in a seemingly indifferent or even malevolent world. And once more begins a search—a frantic, despondent search—for an anchor in a storm-tossed existence. Naturally enough, this quest is reflected in Kleist's dramas. His characters struggle for poise; they are fearful of anything which may confuse them and undermine their calm. It is strange that Goethe, who strove to attain an Olympian serenity and who carefully endeavored to keep disturbing influences out of his life, should have misjudged Kleist's characters, who, though buffeted about, strive to gain and maintain poise. Kleist was not, as Goethe asserted, everywhere intent upon undermining the stability arising from trusting to feeling and intuition. Although the fortitude of his heroes and heroines is sorely tried, he is much more concerned with ascertaining some means of stabilizing them than with undermining their security. They reflect the storminess of life as he himself experienced it. Painfully reminded of his own youthful struggles, Goethe sensed a Wertherian morbidity in the young dramatist, shrank from the turbulent emotions portrayed in his works, and was unable to judge him with detachment. Consequently he misunderstood Kleist's intention in portraying the rude tests to which mankind is exposed.

It is a commonplace that the emotional element is outstanding in many of Kleist's dramatic personages. He had lost confidence in reason as a reliable guide to thought and action. Knowledge, as such, lost its charm for him when he arrived at the conclusion that it held no absolute truths of universal validity. Characteristically enough, he looked to the opposite pole for salvation and pinned his faith to feeling and intuitive judgment. Deeds, he now maintained, were superior to knowledge, and since the heart prompted spontaneous acts, its voice was to be heeded. He concluded that, because of its tendency to weigh and balance, reason merely made for indecision, and thereby paralyzed initiative. Great creative deeds seemed born of impulse, of trusting to the heart and yielding to its dictates. Hence there arises Kleist's insistence upon obeying the first impulse of one's heart and upon following one's intuitive feeling through which God points to what is right. And since unity and harmony result from absolute reliance upon innate feeling, Kleist's characters endeavor to avoid anything which may render them at variance with themselves. They sense danger in the opposition of the mind to the heart, in doubt, and in the conflict of emotions. Moreover, even tremendously intense emotions may surge back and forth, thereby perturbing the individual. With nothing outside himself to transcend subjective desire, man may become a prey to the instability of changing emotions, no matter how powerful their momentary sway may be. And just this is true of Kleist's characters; unless fortified by some other agency they come to grief in moments of doubt, stress, and strain. Tragedy and catastrophe exist where confusion prevails. These may be averted and security and poise may be obtained by placing one's self in the service of an ideal which transcends the individual. Such a conception of life makes for serenity even under the most untoward circumstances. Having arrived at this conclusion, Kleist turned from tragedy to drama of a more optimistic, conciliatory nature in which man is able to regain composure even after having been severely tried and temporarily worsted in the struggle of life. The most important single motif running through Kleist's dramatic works lies in the effort of his characters to maintain or regain serenity in the face of adversity.

In *Die Familie Schroffenstein* human reason proves inadequate to prevent disaster because madly raging passion obscures it, renders its exercise impossible, and leads to illogical acts of eruptive violence. Blinded by suspicion, jealousy, hatred, and the desire for revenge, man is unable to make an active stand against the destruction growing out of these baser passions. Here man is like a plaything tossed hither and thither by powerful but turbulent and turgid emotions. Yet even in this gloomy tragedy there is a ray of light. In the minds and hearts of Agnes and Ottokar, unselfish, sacrificing love makes for momentary tranquillity, harmony, and peace even though the lovers are beset by murder. The unwavering devotion which Kleist demands of love manifests itself in Ottokar, who gives his life in the hope of saving Agnes. But his efforts are made futile by the inability of others to stifle the vengeful hatred that clouds their reason. Passion, vengeance and murder triumph, but the emotion of self-sacrificing love enjoys a brief moment of happiness even in the face of death.

In *Robert Guiskard* the hero has a definite goal as contrasted with the aimlessness which is so marked in Kleist's first tragedy. Guiskard wages a courageous battle with forces which block his way to the successful achievement of his plans of gigantic conquest; here there is concerted action, struggle, and combat, all of which were substantially lacking in *Die Familie Schroffenstein*. This represents progress in dramatic concepts and values. Relying upon himself alone, the hero copes valiantly with superhuman odds by asserting a will which hitherto has triumphed over all obstacles. Here Kleist portrays an attempt to secure mastery and stability in a hostile world by the assertion of the human will. Yet the crowning achievement of a great adventurous career remains unrealized because man's will does not suffice to triumph over bodily infirmity. The outcome of this tragic conflict is failure, and is born of a continued pessimistic conception of life. Yet struggle there is, and heroic struggle; Guiskard succumbs while grandly asserting himself.

In *Die Familie Schroffenstein* reason was darkened by base passions, was unable to cope with them, and left man without any stabilizing force to ward off disaster. In *Robert Guiskard* the human will failed to overcome the frailties of the flesh, and once more man was a victim to the vicissitudes of life. In the former, aimlessness; in the latter, a purposeful aim which was defeated. In *Penthesilea* the motive force which impels the heroine is powerful emotion undisciplined by reason or will. Here Kleist portrays the violent extremes to which outraged sensibilities may lead. The queen forgets all obligations to the Amazon tribe, becomes oblivious to the laws of her state, is swept into a fury of temporary insanity and rends and tears the body of her lover who, she fancies, has spurned and humiliated her. Powerful, primitive emotions; but, devoid of stability, they run riot and drive the heroine to a mad act of violence. But in this tensely emotional nature of Penthesilea lies the power of self-annihilation as well. On realizing that she has slain Achilles, she needs no weapon to end her life; her emotions suffice. Kleist, who repeatedly thought of death as the sole escape from an intolerable existence, must frequently have yearned for the strength of emotion of Penthesilea which enabled her to triumph over matter by ending her life without the need of murderous weapons. Out of the depth of her feelings she summons death.

In three tragedies Kleist presented the failure of reason, will, and instinctive obedience to feeling to serve as man's guides or to enable him to triumph over adversity. His other dramas reflect a different conception of life. He writes one comedy fraught with serious elements, one out-and-out comedy, a romantic fairy drama with a holiday mood, and a brace of dramas in which a mature, optimistic view of life predominates. Alkmene is fortified by a profound conviction of the fundamental innocence of her intent; Eve's sacrificial love for Ruprecht and the consciousness of her innocence enable her to endure misrepresentation, slander, abuse, and accusations challenging her honor. But in Käthchen utter devotion and self-sacrificing love celebrate their greatest triumphs as the source of serenity and happiness. Living, as she does, for love and its ultimate realization, she has no doubts and no uneasiness. Unlike Penthesilea, she is a naïve, untroubled child of nature, under no compulsion to be anything other than herself. Her one concern is to be in the presence of the man she loves; having no designs, she remains untroubled at heart, even when repulsed. No reflection undermines the harmony of her being, no doubts arise, and no other emotion wars with her love, which is deep enough to fortify her in her faith in the ultimate goodness of things.

Finally, in his two patriotic dramas, Kleist set forth the stability which may be gained by devotion to a great cause. Hermann's intense patriotism and thirst for freedom lend him a singleness of purpose that triumphs over the waywardness of feeling; he knows no vacillation because individual desire and self-aggrandizement have been submerged in the service of a transcending ideal. Likewise, the Great Elector is calm and self-contained because he subordinates himself to the welfare of the fatherland. By placing themselves in the service of an ideal, Hermann and the elector have risen above the petty, disturbing incidents of human existence and live in a higher sphere. In these two personages Kleist portrayed the harmony and poise which were denied him in his struggles to rise above confusion and chaos. His final "plan of life" points to the whole-souled service of an ideal which absorbs the full depth and strength of man's emotions, determination, and energies. The ultimate tragedy of Kleist's career lies in the fact that conditions in his country made active surrender to a program of this kind impossible at the very time when he longed to embrace such an opportunity. Denied this opportunity for service, he was forced to present it merely as a compensatory ideal; he found nothing else to make existence tolerable, and ended his life. Had the war of liberation come earlier, Kleist could have translated his ideal into action. And so one reason for his untimely, tragic end lies in the fact that he was denied the privilege of serving his country actively at the most critical moment of his life.

In view of the significance he attaches to emotion, the question arises as to Kleist's relation to the romanticist's insistence on feeling. Kleist's emphasis is not upon vapid emotional states as such nor upon the hazy expression of a vague mood that longs for a narcotic atmosphere into which it may be dissipated. He regards feeling as the powerful, energizing, impelling factor in human conduct and not as a vapid state of self-intoxication in which the individual is merged into a dreamy, cosmic whole. He treats emotion as the fundamental, dynamic quality of the individual; the best, most reliable judgments are intuitive; and feelings, rather than the iron logic of the situation, are the best guides to action. He delights in the portrayal of eruptive emotions which at times burst forth into acts of extreme violence. This predilection for emotion leading to deeds differentiates Kleist from the sentimental, more listless treatment of emotion by certain romanticists.

Kleist's sense of form in drama differs from the lyrical undisciplined drama of romanticism. Yet with all his discipline in matters of dramatic form and structure he is a pronounced individualist in the liberties he takes with all formalistic elements. And he is a realist in his refusal to sidestep extreme manifestations of human conduct. In his presentations of emotional excesses he is unconcerned with the resulting violence of behavior. Unhesitatingly he sacrifices esthetic qualities in favor of vraisemblance. The individualization of his more sharply defined personages removes them from the classicistic tendency to typify. Moreover, his presentations of emotional outbursts of a volcanic nature are foreign to the measured calm and repose of classicism. Although his characters strive for poise, their path is likely to lead through excruciating anguish. His curtailment of the monologue as undramatic, his particularization of character, and his emphasis upon the psychological element in the motivation of conduct are realistic tendencies. On the whole, Kleist may be regarded as a bridge leading from classicism and romanticism to modern psychological realism.

Whoever sees beauty and artistry only in classical repose, in Olympian calm, in restraint and moderation, in the even cadence of smooth rhythm, in regularity and harmony, will fail to appreciate Heinrich von Kleist as a dramatist. His uneven periods, irregular, choppy meter, broken lines and jerky, abrupt tempo are an expression of the nervous torment of his life, of sweeping, cataclysmic change, of demoniacal unrest, and of pent-up emotion which finally bursts forth uncontrollably. But whoever is interested in the manifold manifestations of surging, throbbing, straining life, and considers that they, too, deserve to be reproduced in art, will find in Kleist a significant widening of the boundaries of the drama of his time.

BIBLIOGRAPHY AND NOTES

Although he has been sparing of notes, the author has appended a working bibliography. In the very nature of the case he is indebted to the numerous critical biographies as well as to various more specialized and briefer studies.

GENERAL BIBLIOGRAPHY

CHAPTER ONE

Heinrich von Kleists Werke. Im Verein mit Georg Minde-Pouet und Reinhold Steig herausgegeben von Erich Schmidt. Leipzig und Wien. Bibliographisches Institut, 1904-1905. References are to volume and page of this edition.

Bab, Julius: *Preussen und der deutsche Geist. Heinrich von Kleist.* Konstanz. 1915.

―――――: *Heinrich von Kleist und seine Bühnenwerke.* Berlin. 1922.

Behme, Hermann: *Heinrich von Kleist und C. M. Wieland.* Heidelberg. 1914.

Bertram, Ernst: *Heinrich von Kleist. Eine Rede.* Bonn. 1925.

Berwin, Beate: *Heinrich von Kleist.* Stuttgart, Berlin, Leipzig. 1926.

Biedermann, Flodoard v.: *Heinrich von Kleists Gespräche, Nachrichten und Überlieferungen aus seinem Umgange.* Leipzig. 1912.

Bischoff, Heinrich: "Der Satzbau bei Heinrich von Kleist," *Zeitschrift für den deutschen Unterricht,* XIII (1899), 713-20.

―――――: "Lessings Laokoon und Heinrich von Kleist," *Zeitschrift für den deutschen Unterricht,* XII (1898), 348-52.

Blankenagel, John C.: "Heinrich von Kleist's Pursuit of Happiness," *University of Wisconsin Studies in Language and Literature,* XXII (1925), 25-46.

―――――: "Heinrich von Kleist and Wieland," *Journal of English and Germanic Philology,* XXV (1926), 54-65.

———: "Wertherian Tendencies in Heinrich von Kleist," *Journal of English and Germanic Philology*, XXVIII (1929), 86-110.
Bonafous, Raymond: *Henri de Kleist. Sa Vie et ses Oeuvres.* Paris. 1894.
Brahm, Otto: *Das Leben Heinrichs von Kleist.* 4-°. Berlin. 1911.
Braig, Friedrich: *Heinrich von Kleist.* München. 1925.
Bruns, Friedrich: "Die Motivierung aus dem Unbewussten bei Heinrich von Kleist," *University of Wisconsin Studies in Language and Literature*, XXII (1925), 47-77.
Bülow, Eduard v.: *Heinrich von Kleists Leben und Briefe.* Berlin. 1848.
Bulthaupt, Heinrich: *Dramaturgie des Schauspiels.* 12-°. Oldenburg. 1908. I, 481-555.
Cassirer, Ernst: *Heinrich von Kleist und die kantische Philosophie.* Berlin. 1919.
Corssen, Meta: *Kleists und Shakespeares dramatische Sprache.* Lüneburg. 1919.
———: "Kleists und Shakespeares dramatische Gestalten," *Jahrbuch der deutschen Shakespeare-Gesellschaft*, LVIII (1922), 46-67.
Croce, Benedetto: *Poesie und Nichtpoesie.* Übertragen von Julius Schlosser. Zürich, Wien, Leipzig. 1925. pp. 93-101.
Eloesser, Arthur: *Heinrich von Kleist. Eine Studie.* Berlin. 1905.
Federn, Karl: "Kleist und Goethe," *Preussische Jahrbücher*, CXCVIII (1924), 80-85.
Fischer, Max: *Heinrich von Kleist. Der Dichter des Preussentums.* Stuttgart, Berlin. 1916.
Fischer, Ottokar: "Mimische Studien zu Heinrich von Kleist," *Euphorion*, XV (1908), 488-510; 716-25; XVI (1909), 62-92; 412-25; 747-71.
Friedmann, Sigismondo: *Il drama tedesco del nostro secolo. I Enrico di Kleist.* Milano. 1893.—*Das deutsche Drama des neunzehnten Jahrhunderts in seinen Hauptvertretern.* Autorisierte Übersetzung von Ludwig Weber. Erster Band. Leipzig. 1900. pp. 3-86.
Fries, Albert: "Miszellen zu Heinrich von Kleist," *Studien zur vergleichenden Literaturgeschichte*, IV (1904), 232-47.
———: "Zu Heinrich von Kleists Stil," *Studien zur vergleichenden Literaturgeschichte*, IV (1904), 440-65.
———: *Stilistische und vergleichende Forschungen zu Heinrich von Kleist mit Proben angewandter Ästhetik.* Berlin. 1906.
Füller, Franziska: *Das psychologische Problem der Frau in Kleists Dramen und Novellen.* Leipzig. 1924.

Füser, Heinrich: *Der reimlose fünffüssige Jambus bei Heinrich von Kleist*. Seesen a. Harz. 1911.
Gaudig, Hugo: *Heinrich von Kleist. Shakespeare. Lessings Hamburgische Dramaturgie*. 2-°. Leipzig, Berlin. 1918.
Gundolf, Friedrich: *Heinrich von Kleist*. Berlin. 1922.
Hart, Julius: *Das Kleist-Buch*. Berlin. 1912.
Hellmann, Hanna: *Heinrich von Kleist. Darstellung des Problems*. Heidelberg. 1911.
Hermann, Helene: "Studien zu Heinrich von Kleist," *Zeitschrift für Ästhetik und Allgemeine Kunstgeschichte*, XVIII (1924-25), 273-304.
Herzog, Wilhelm: "Paris in Kleists Briefen und in Tiecks William Lovell," *Euphorion*, XV (1908), 713-16.
―――――: *Heinrich von Kleist. Sein Leben und sein Werk*. München. 1911.
―――――: "Kleist und Goethe," *Westermanns Monatshefte*, CVI, 2 (1909), 865-70.
Hoffmann, Paul: "Zu den Briefen Heinrichs von Kleist," *Studien zur vergleichenden Literaturgeschichte*, III (1903), 332-66.
―――――: *Kleist in Paris*. Berlin. 1924.
―――――: *Heinrich von Kleist und Wilhelm Reuter*. Berlin. 1927.
Holzgraefe, W.: *Schillersche Einflüsse bei Heinrich von Kleist*. Progr. Cuxhaven. 1902.
Kayka, Ernst: *Kleist und die Romantik*. Berlin. 1906.
Koerner, Josef: *Recht und Pflicht. Eine Studie über Kleists Michael Kohlhaas und Prinz Friedrich von Homburg*. Leipzig, Berlin. 1926.
Krynska, Helene: *Der sprachliche Ausdruck der Affekte in Kleists dramatischen Werken*. Bernau. 1909.
Kühn, Walter: *Heinrich von Kleist und das deutsche Theater*. München. 1912.
Lex, Michael: *Die Idee im Drama bei Goethe, Schiller, Grillparzer, Kleist*. München. 1904.
Lloyd, Francis, and Newton, William: *Prussia's Representative Man*. London. 1875.
Lublinski, S.: *Literatur und Gesellschaft im neunzehnten Jahrhundert*. Berlin 1899. I, 119-52.
Lütteken, Anton: *Die Dresdener Romantik und Heinrich von Kleist*. Borna-Leipzig. 1917.
Mauerhof, Emil: *Schiller und Heinrich von Kleist*. 2-°. Zürich. 1898.
Meyer-Benfey, Heinrich: *Das Drama Heinrich von Kleists*. Göttingen. Vol. I, 1911. Vol. II, 1913.
―――――: *Kleists Leben und Werke*. Göttingen. 1911.

———: *Kleist*. Leipzig, Berlin. 1923.
Minde-Pouet, Georg: *Heinrich von Kleist. Seine Sprache und sein Stil*. Weimar. 1897.
———: "Neue Briefe Heinrich von Kleists," *Deutsche Rundschau*. Oktober 1914. pp. 112-126.
———: "Ein neuer Kleist-Brief," *Berliner Tageblatt*. Nr. 1, Jan. 1, 1924.
———: *Kleists letzte Stunden*. Teil I. *Das Aktenmaterial. Schriften der Kleist-Gesellschaft*. Berlin. 1925.
Minor, Jakob: "Studien zu Heinrich von Kleist," *Euphorion*. 1894. I, 564-90.
Morris, Max: *Heinrich von Kleists Reise nach Würzburg*. Berlin. 1899.
Muschg, Walter: *Kleist*. Zürich. 1923.
Muth, K.: "Heinrich von Kleist kein Problem," *Hochland*. 1911-1912. IX, Jg. I, 190-207.
Nadler, Josef: *Die Berliner Romantik*. Berlin. 1921. pp. 150-52; 168-70; 175-90; 218-20.
Petersen, Julius: "Heinrich von Kleist und Torquato Tasso. Eine Studie über literarischen Einfluss," *Zeitschrift für den deutschen Unterricht*, XXXI (1917), 273-89; 337-59.
Petsch, Robert: "Heinrich von Kleist als tragischer Dichter," *Germanisch-Romanische Monatsschrift*, I (1909), 529-50.
Pniower, Otto: *Dichtungen und Dichter. Essays und Studien*. Berlin. 1912. pp. 215-37.
Prellwitz, Gertrude: "Heinrich von Kleist und Goethe," *Jahrbuch der Goethe-Gesellschaft*, VIII (1921), 88-94.
Rahmer, S.: *Das Kleistproblem*. Berlin. 1903.
———: *Heinrich von Kleist als Mensch und Dichter*. Berlin. 1909.
Roetteken, Hubert: *Heinrich von Kleist*. Leipzig. 1907.
Rouge, I.: *Heinrich von Kleist. Les cent chefs-d'oeuvre étrangers. Notice et traductions*. Paris. 1921.
Sadger, Isidor: *Heinrich von Kleist. Eine pathographisch-psychologische Studie*. Wiesbaden. 1910.
Sauer, August: *Kleists Todeslitanei*. Prag. 1907.
Schlosser, Heinrich: "Heinrich von Kleist und die Musik," *Die Musik*, II (1911), 195-203.
Schmidt, Erich: *Charakteristiken* I. Berlin. 1886. pp. 350-80.
Schneider, Hermann: *Studien zu Heinrich von Kleist*. Berlin. 1915.
Scholl, John W.: "Kleist at Boulogne-sur-Mer," *Publications of the Modern Language Association*, XXIX (1914), 359-87.
Schulze, Berthold: *Neue Studien über Heinrich von Kleist*. Heidelberg. 1904.

―――: "Über Heinrich von Kleists Universitätslehrer Wünsch," *Pädagogisches Archiv*, XLVIII (1906), 705-16.
―――: "Heinrich von Kleists Verhältnis zu Fichte und Arndt," *Preussische Jahrbücher*, CXL (1910), 481-97.
Schütze, Martin: *Studies in German Romanticism.* Chicago. 1907.
Servaes, Franz: *Heinrich von Kleist.* Leipzig, Berlin, Wien. 1902.
―――: *Heinrich von Kleists tragischer Untergang.* Berlin-Lichterfelde. 1922.
Silz, Walter: "Rational and Emotional Elements in Heinrich von Kleist," *Modern Language Notes*, XXXVII (1922), 321-27.
―――: *Heinrich von Kleist's Conception of the Tragic.* Göttingen. 1923.
―――: *Early German Romanticism. Its Founders and Heinrich von Kleist.* Cambridge, Mass. 1929.
Stefansky, Georg: "Ein neuer Weg zu Heinrich von Kleist," *Euphorion*, XXIII (1921), 639-94.
Steig, Reinhold: *Heinrich von Kleists Berliner Kämpfe.* Berlin. 1901.
―――: *Neue Kunde zu Heinrich von Kleist.* Berlin. 1902.
Taillandier, Saint-René: "Poètes Modernes de l' Allemagne. Henri de Kleist—Sa Vie et ses Oeuvres," *La Revue des Deux Mondes*, June 1, 1859, pp. 604-40.
Teller, Frida: "Neue Studien zu Heinrich von Kleist," *Euphorion*, XX (1913), 681-727.
Treitschke, Heinrich von: "Heinrich von Kleist," *Preussische Jahrbücher*, II (1858), 599-623.
―――: *Historische und politische Aufsätze.* 5-e. Leipzig. 1886. I, 75-112.
Unger, Rudolf: *Herder, Novalis und Kleist. Studien über die Entwicklung des Todesproblems.* Frankfurt-am-Main. 1922.
Wachter, Hans: *Zu Heinrich von Kleists Gedächtnis.* Steglitz. 1914.
Wagner, Albert M.: *Goethe, Kleist, Hebbel und das religiöse Problem ihrer dramatischen Dichtung.* Leipzig, Hamburg. 1911.
Walzel, Oskar: *Heinrich von Kleists Kunst.* Bonn. 1928.
Weissenfels, Richard: *Über französische und antike Elemente im Stil Heinrich von Kleists.* Braunschweig. 1888.
Wethly, Gustaf: *Heinrich von Kleist, der Dramatiker.* Strassburg. 1911.
Wilbrandt, Adolf: *Heinrich von Kleist.* Nördlingen. 1863.
Willige, Wilhelm: *Klassische Gestaltung und romantischer Einfluss in den Dramen Heinrichs von Kleist.* Heidelberg. 1915.
Witkop, Philipp: *Heinrich von Kleist.* Leipzig. 1922.
Wukadinovic, Spiridon: *Kleist-Studien.* Stuttgart. Berlin. 1904.

252 BIBLIOGRAPHY AND NOTES

Zillmann, Friedrich: *Heinrich von Kleist als Mensch und Künstler. Zwei Aufsätze.* Berlin—Halensee. 1920.
Zimpel, Helene: "Heinrich von Kleist und die Romantik," *Nord und Süd*, LXXVII (1896), 369-91.
———: "Heinrich von Kleist und die Frau," *Nord und Süd*, XCII (1900), 306-26.
———: "Kleist der Dionysische," *Nord und Süd*, CVIII (1904), 187-214.
Zolling, Theophil: *Heinrich von Kleist in der Schweiz.* Stuttgart. 1882.
Zweig, Stefan: *Der Kampf mit dem Dämon. Hölderlin, Kleist, Nietzsche.* Leipzig. 1925.

For detailed bibliographies by Professor Georg Minde-Pouet and for numerous studies on Kleist see the *Jahrbuch der Kleist-Gesellschaft* from 1921 to the present.

NOTES AND SPECIAL BIBLIOGRAPHIES

CHAPTER TWO

Die Familie Schroffenstein

NOTES

1. Heinrich Meyer-Benfey: *Kleist*, p. 30. See General Bibliography.
2. IV, 148-50. "Brief eines Dichters an einen andern," *Abendblatt*, Jan. 5, 1811.
3. Heinrich von Kleist: *Die Familie Ghonorez.* Schriften der Kleist-Gesellschaft. Berlin. 1927. p. 128.

BIBLIOGRAPHY

Brahm, Otto: "Heinrich von Kleists Familie Thierrez-Ghonorez-Schroffenstein. Nach handschriftlichem Material," *Vossische Zeitung*. 1883. Sonntagsbeilage. Nos. 10, 11.
Conrad, H.: "Heinrich von Kleists Familie Ghonorez," *Preussische Jahrbücher*, XC (1897), 242-79.
Howe, George M.: "The possible source of Kleist's Familie Schroffenstein," *Modern Language Notes*, XXXVIII (1923), 148-53.
Kilian, E.: "Kleists Schroffensteiner in echter Fassung," *Studien zur vergleichenden Literaturgeschichte*, III (1903), 367-71.
Schillmann, A. R.: *Heinrich von Kleist, seine Jugend und die Familie*

Schroffenstein, nebst einem noch ungedruckten Stück aus dem Katechismus der Deutschen. Frankfurt a.d. Oder. 1863.
Schneider, Hermann: *Studien zu Heinrich von Kleist*, pp. 24-80. See General Bibliography.
Scholl, John W.: "The Cave Scene in Die Familie Schroffenstein," *Modern Philology*, XVIII (1921), 136-43.
Wolff, Eugen: *Die Familie Ghonorez*, herausgegeben und eingeleitet. Halle a. S.: 1902.—*Bibliothek der Gesamtliteratur des In-und Auslandes.* No. 1634.
Wolff, E.: "Inwieweit rührt Die Familie Schroffenstein von Kleist her?" *Zeitschrift fur Bücherfreunde.* 1898-1900. II, III, IV.

CHAPTER THREE

Robert Guiskard

NOTES

1. Jakob Minor, "Studien zu Heinrich von Kleist,"*Euphorion*, I (1894), 565.
2. Paul Hoffmann, Review of Fries, Albert: *Stilistische und vergleichende Forschungen zu Heinrich von Kleist mit Proben angewandter Ästhetik*, in *Studien zur vergleichenden Literaturgeschichte*, VII (1907), 377.
3. Hugo Gaudig, *Heinrich von Kleist*, pp. 104 f. See General Bibliography.

BIBLIOGRAPHY

Brahm, Otto: "Heinrich von Kleist und sein Dramenfragment Robert Guiskard," *Deutsche Rundschau*, XXXIX (1884), 52-66.
Fischer, Ottokar: *Kleists Guiskardproblem.* Dortmund. 1912.
Kaper, Ernst: *Heinrich v. Kleist. Robert Guiskard.* Kopenhagen. 1908.
Minor, Jakob: "Studien zu Heinrich von Kleist," *Euphorion*, I (1894), 564-81.
Rössler, Konstantin: "Robert Guiskard," *Preussische Jahrbücher*, LXV (1890), 485 ff.
Teller, Frida: "Neue Studien zu Heinrich von Kleist," *Euphorion*, XX (1913), 681 ff.
Wukadinovic, Spiridon: *Kleist-Studien*, pp. 55-134. See General Bibliography.
Zillman, Friedrich: *Heinrich von Kleist als Mensch und Künstler*, pp. 34-75. See General Bibliography.

CHAPTER FOUR

Amphitryon

NOTES

1. Heinrich Füser, *Der reimlose fünffüssige Jambus bei Heinrich von Kleist*, p. 90. *See* General Bibliography.

BIBLIOGRAPHY

Edelmann, Ernst: "Kleists Amphitryon und sein Verhältnis zu Molière," *Neue Jahrbücher für Altertum und Pädagogik*, XLIX (1922), 310-12.
Hellmann, Hanna: "Kleists Amphitryon," *Euphorion*, XXV (1924), 241-51.
Kayka, Ernst: "Heinrich v. Kleists Amphitryon," *Zeitschrift für vergleichende Literaturgeschichte*, N. F. XVI (1905), 62-78.
Minor, Jakob: "Studien zu Heinrich von Kleist," *Euphorion*, I (1894), 589-90.
Reinhardstöttner, Carl von: *Plautus. Spätere Bearbeitungen plautinischer Lustspiele*. Leipzig. 1886. pp. 115-229.
Ruland, Wilhelm: *Kleists Amphitryon*. Berlin. 1897.
Sauer, August: "Zu Kleists Amphitryon," *Euphorion*, XX (1913), 93-104.
Schlodtmann, Paula: "Kleist und Molière," *Die Grenzboten*, LXIII, 2 (1904), 269-80.
Toldo, Pietro: "Amphitryon," *Zeitschrift des Vereins für Volkskunde*, XV (1905), 367-73.
Wolff, Max: *Molière. Der Dichter und sein Werk*. 2-°. München. 1923.

CHAPTER FIVE

Der zerbrochene Krug

NOTES

1. Karl Siegen, *Der zerbrochene Krug. Lustspiel in einem Aufzuge von H. v. Kleist. Festschrift zu des Dichters Säkularfeier. Neu für die Bühne bearbeitet* etc. (Leipzig, 1876), p. ix.
2. Theophil Zolling, *Heinrich von Kleist in der Schweiz*, pp. 36 n., 39 n. *See* General Bibliography.
3. Raymond Bonafous, *Henri de Kleist*, p. 329. *See* General Bibliography.
4. Eduard Genast, *Aus dem Tagebuche eines alten Schauspielers* (Leipzig, 1862), I, 169 f.

BIBLIOGRAPHY AND NOTES

5. Heinrich Meyer-Benfey, *Das Drama Heinrich von Kleists*, I, 399.
6. *Heinrich von Kleist's hinterlassene Schriften* (Herausgegeben von L. Tieck. Berlin. 1821), p. xliv.
7. Friedrich Hebbel, *Sämtliche Werke* (ed. R. M. Werner, Berlin, 1903), XI, 350 f.
8. Gustav Buchtenkirch, *Kleists Lustspiel Der zerbrochene Krug auf der Bühne.* Heidelberg. 1914.

BIBLIOGRAPHY

Birk, Karl: *Heinrich von Kleist: Der zerbrochene Krug. Ein Beitrag zur Inszenierung des Lustspieles.* Prag. 1910.
Michael, Friedrich: "Goethes Amtmann und Kleists Dorfrichter," *Jahrbuch der Kleist-Gesellschaft.* 1922. pp. 75-84.
Schneider, Hermann: *Studien zu Heinrich von Kleist*, pp. 81-97. See General Bibliography.
Semler, Christian: "Der Dorfrichter Adam in dem Zerbrochenen Krug von Heinrich von Kleist," *Zeitschrift für den deutschen Unterricht* VII (1893), 374-84.
Siegen, Karl: *Heinrich von Kleist und Der zerbrochene Krug.* Sondershausen. 1879.
von Gordon, Wolff: *Die dramatische Handlung in Sophokles' König Oidipus und Kleists Der zerbrochene Krug.* Halle. 1926.
Walzel, Oskar: *Der zerbrochene Krug. Ein Lustspiel.* Leipzig. 1904. *Meisterwerke der deutschen Bühne.* Vol. 32.
Wolff, Eugen: *Heinrich von Kleist: Der zerbrochene Krug. Kritische Ausgabe nach der Handschrift mit Erläuterungen.* Minden i. W. 1898.

CHAPTER SIX

Penthesilea

NOTES

1. Heinrich Meyer-Benfey, *Das Drama Heinrich von Kleists*, I, 542 f.
2. Heinrich Wittig, *Das innere Erlebnis in Heinrich von Kleists Penthesilea.* Berlin. 1912.
3. V, 275. 4. V, 291. 5. V, 300. 6. V, 300 f.
7. V, 301. 8. V, 346.
9. Georg Minde-Pouet, *Heinrich von Kleist. Seine Sprache und sein Stil*, pp. 231 ff. See General Bibliography.
10. V, 245.
11. Paul Lindau, *Penthesilea. Ein Trauerspiel von Heinrich von*

BIBLIOGRAPHY AND NOTES

      Kleist. In vier Aufzügen für die Bühne eingerichtet. (Leipzig, 1911). *Reclams Universalbibliothek.* Vol. 5325, p. 105.
12. Heinrich Füser, *Der reimlose fünffüssige Jambus bei Heinrich von Kleist,* p. 100. *See* General Bibliography.
13. Theophil Zolling, *Heinrich von Kleists sämtliche Werke. Deutsche National Literatur,* Vol. 149, 2. pp. 276 f.
14. Paul Lindau, "Penthesilea. Nach der Aufführung," *Die Gegenwart,* IX (1876), 298-302.
15. Raymond Bonafous, *Henri de Kleist,* p. 219, note 2. *See* General Bibliography.
16. *Ibid.,* p. 237.
17. Heinrich Meyer-Benfey, *op. cit.,* I, 501.

BIBLIOGRAPHY

Bab, Julius: *Das Drama der Liebe.* Stuttgart, Berlin und Leipzig: Deutsche Verlags-Anstalt. 1924. pp. 92-114.
Berger, Alfred von: *Studien und Kritiken.* Wien. 1896. *Kleists Penthesilea.* pp. 156-66.
Fischer, Ottokar: "Mimische Studien zu Heinrich von Kleist," *Euphorion,* XV (1908), pp. 488 ff.
Fries, C.: "Zu Kleists Penthesilea," *Zeitschrift für den deutschen Unterricht,* XXV (1911), 178 f.
Hellmann, Hanna: "Kleists Penthesilea und Klopstocks Hermann und die Fürsten," *Zeitschrift für den deutschen Unterricht,* XXXIII (1919), 469-73.
Herzog, Wilhelm: "Penthesilea," *Die Schaubühne,* VI, 2 (1910), pp. 768-77.
Kanter, Fritz: *Der bildliche Ausdruck in Kleists Penthesilea.* Borna-Leipzig. 1913.
Klein, Hans: *Die antiken Amazonensagen in der deutschen Literatur.* Leipzig: 1919. pp. 37-107.
Kluckhohn, Paul: "Penthesilea," *Germanisch-Romanische Monatsschrift,* VI (1914), 276-88.
Niejahr, Johannes: "Heinrich von Kleists Penthesilea," *Vierteljahrsschrift für Literaturgeschichte,* VI (1893), 506-53.
―――――: "Kleists Penthesilea und die psychologische Richtung in der modernen literarhistorischen Forschung," *Euphorion,* III (1896), 653-92.
Petsch, Robert: "Zu Kleists Penthesilea," *Euphorion,* XIII (1906), 561-62.
Roetteken, Hubert: "Kleists Penthesilea," *Zeitschrift für vergleichende Literaturgeschichte,* N. F. VII (1894), 28-48.
―――――: "Nochmals Penthesilea," *Zeitschrift für vergleichende Literaturgeschichte,* N. F. VIII (1895), 24-50.

BIBLIOGRAPHY AND NOTES

———: "Einige Bemerkungen zur Methode der Literaturgeschichte. Mit besonderer Berücksichtigung der Penthesilea," *Euphorion*, IV (1897), 718-55.
Schulze, Berthold: *Kleists Penthesilea oder von der lebendigen Form der Dichtung*. Leipzig. Berlin. 1912.
Teller, Frida: "Neue Studien zu Heinrich von Kleist," *Euphorion*, XX (1913), 720-27.
Weissenfels, Richard: "Vergleichende Studien zu Heinrich von Kleist. I, Der Tod der Penthesilea," *Zeitschrift für vergleichende Literaturgeschichte*, I (1887), 273-94.
Wukadinovic, Spiridon: *Kleist-Studien*, pp. 60 ff. *See* General Bibliography.

CHAPTER SEVEN

Das Käthchen von Heilbronn

NOTES

1. V, 380 f.   2. V, 248.   3. IV, 133 ff.
4. Friedrich Röbbeling, *Kleists Käthchen von Heilbronn* (Halle, a. S. 1913), pp. 81 f.
   Friedrich Braig, *Heinrich von Kleist*, pp. 283 ff. *See* General Bibliography.
5. Spiridon Wukadinovic, *Kleist Studien*, pp. 150 f. *See* General Bibliography.
6. Heinrich Meyer-Benfey, *Das Drama Heinrich von Kleists*, II, 143 ff.
7. Friedrich Röbbeling, *op. cit.*, pp. 35 f.
8. Reinhold Stolze, *Kleists Käthchen von Heilbronn auf der deutschen Bühne* (Berlin. 1923), p. 14.
9. Theophil Zolling, *Heinrich von Kleists sämtliche Werke. Deutsche National Literatur*. Vol. 150, 3. pp. xii f.
10. Reinhold Stolze, *op. cit.*
11. Heinrich Meyer-Benfey, "Sind bei Kleists Käthchen von Heilbronn verschiedene Pläne anzunehmen?" *Bühne und Welt*, N. F. II (1902), 188-93.

BIBLIOGRAPHY

du Prel, Carl: *Käthchen von Heilbronn als Somnambule*. *Allgemeine Zeitung*. München. 18. Nov. 1890. No. 320.
Hebbel, Friedrich: *Gedanken beim Wiederlesen des Käthchens von Heilbronn von Heinrich Kleist*. *Sämtliche Werke*. XI, 86-90.
Lechner, Wilhelm: *Gotthilf Heinrich Schuberts Einfluss auf Kleist, Justinus Kerner und E. T. A. Hoffmann. Beiträge zur deutschen Romantik*. Borna-Leipzig. 1911.

258 BIBLIOGRAPHY AND NOTES

Lyon, Charles E.: "The Phöbus Fragment of Kleist's Käthchen von Heilbronn," *Journal of English and Germanic Philology*, XIV (1915), 35-55.
Merkel, Franz Rudolf: *Der Naturphilosoph Gotthilf Heinrich Schubert und die deutsche Romantik*. München. 1913.
Morris, Max: *Heinrich von Kleists Reise nach Würzburg*, pp. 34-43.
Petsch, Robert: "Das Käthchen von Heilbronn," *Germanisch-Romanische Monatsschrift*, VI (1914), 389-405.
Wukadinovic, Spiridon: "Über Kleists Käthchen von Heilbronn," *Euphorion*. 1895. Erstes Ergänzungsheft. pp. 14-36.

CHAPTER EIGHT

Die Hermannsschlacht

NOTES

1. IV, 30 ff. 2. IV, 35. 3. IV, 38 f. 4. IV, 30 n. 5. IV, 81 f. 6. IV, 100 ff. 7. IV, 115 ff. 8. IV, 120.
9. Hanna Hellmann, "Kleists Hermannsschlacht und Das erste Buch Samuelis," *Zeitschrift für Deutschkunde*, XXXVIII (1924), 99-105.
10. II, 462 f.
11. *Heinrich von Kleists hinterlassene Schriften* (Herausgegeben von L. Tieck. Berlin. 1821), p. lv.
12. Heinrich Füser, *Der reimlose fünffüssige Jambus bei Heinrich von Kleist*, p. 112. See General Bibliography.
13. Otto Fraude, *Heinrich von Kleists Hermannsschlacht auf der deutschen Bühne* (Kiel, 1919), p. 90.

BIBLIOGRAPHY

Fischer, Max: *Heinrich von Kleist. Der Dichter des Preussentums* See General Bibliography.
Fries, Albert: "Miszellen zu Heinrich von Kleist," *Studien zur vergleichenden Literaturgeschichte*, IV (1904), 246 f.
Gereke, P.: *Heinrich von Kleists Hermannsschlacht, erläutert und gewürdigt für höhere Lehranstalten*. Leipzig. 1905.
Kaibel, Franz: "Dichter und Patriotismus," *Jahrbuch der deutschen Shakespeare Gesellschaft*, Berlin, LII (1916), 42-47.
Kühnemann, Eugen: *Vom Weltreich des deutschen Geistes*. München. 1914. pp. 407-20.
Mathias, Theodor: "Die Grundlagen zu Heinrichs von Kleist Hermannsschlacht," *Deutscher Frühling*, I (1907), 134-37.
Niejahr, Johannes: "Heinrich v. Kleists Prinz von Homburg

und Hermannsschlacht," *Vierteljahrsschrift für Literaturgeschichte*, VI (1893). 409-29

Ortner, Heinrich: *Bemerkungen zu Heinrich v. Kleists Hermannsschlacht. Programm zum Jahresbericht des K. neuen Gymnasiums zu Regensburg.* 1894.

Schulze, Berthold: "Heinrich von Kleists Verhältnis zu Fichte und Arndt," *Preussische Jahrbücher*, CXL (1910), 481-97.

Sprengel, Johann Georg: *Das Staatsbewusstsein in der deutschen Literatur seit Heinrich von Kleist. Zeitschrift für den deutschen Unterricht.* 1918. 12. Ergänzungsheft. pp. 11-26.

Steffen, E.: "Ein deutsches Drama: Kleists Hermannsschlacht," *Zeitschrift für den deutschen Unterricht*, XIX (1905), 545-71; 618-40.

Teller, Frida: "Neue Studien zu Heinrich von Kleist. II. Klopstock und Kleist," *Euphorion*, XX (1913), 709 ff.

CHAPTER NINE

Prinz Friedrich von Homburg

BIBLIOGRAPHY

Blankenagel, John C.: "Schiller's Wallenstein and Kleist's Prinz Friedrich von Homburg," *The Germanic Review*, II (1927), 1-11.

Bucherer, Fritz: "Ein antikes Motiv in Kleists Prinz Friedrich von Homburg," *Neue Jahrbücher für das klassische Altertum, Geschichte und deutsche Literatur und für Pädagogik*, XXXV (1915), 477-80.

Carré, Jean-Marie: "Der Somnambulismus in Kleists Prinz von Homburg," *Zeitschrift für den deutschen Unterricht*, XXV (1911), 513-19.

Duschinsky, W.: "Über die Quellen von Kleists Prinzen von Homburg," *Zeitschrift für die Oesterreichischen Gymnasien*, LII (1901), 197-218.

Edelmann, Ernst: "Das sittliche Gesetz in Kleists Prinz von Homburg," *Zeitschrift für Deutschkunde*, XXXV (1920), 471-75.

Engert, Horst: "Persönlichkeit und Gemeinschaft in Kleists Drama Prinz Friedrich von Homburg," *Jahrbuch der Kleist-Gesellschaft für 1925 u. 1926.* pp. 1-16.

Erdmannsdörfer, B.: "Zu Kleists Prinzen von Homburg," *Preussische Jahrbücher*, XXXIV (1874), 205-10.

Farinelli, Arturo: "Heinrich von Kleists Der Prinz von Homburg," *Journal of English and Germanic Philology*, XXI (1922), 621-44.

Fittbogen, Gottfried: "Heinrich von Kleists vaterländische Dichtung," *Deutsche Rundschau*, July and August, 1917. pp. 87-101; 223-46.
Gaudig, Hugo: *Heinrich von Kleist*, pp. 286-351. See General Bibliography.
Gilow, Hermann: *Die Grundgedanken in Heinrich von Kleists Prinz Friedrich von Homburg*. Berlin. 1893.
———: "Das Homburgbild im Kronprinzlichen Palais in Berlin und Kleists Prinz von Homburg," *Westermanns Monatshefte*, June, 1908, 379-85.
———: "Kretschmars Homburg—Gemälde vom Jahre 1800 und Kleists Drama," *Euphorion*, XV (1908), 171-72.
———: "Heinrich von Kleists Prinz Friedrich von Homburg," 1821-1921; "Ein geschichtlich-kritischer Rückblick," *Jahrbuch der Kleist-Gesellschaft für 1921*, pp. 22-50.
Grünwald, E.: "Zu Kleists Prinz Friedrich von Homburg," *Zeitschrift für den deutschen Unterricht*, XII (1898), 669-73.
Heimann, Moritz: "Zum Prinzen von Homburg," *Die Schaubühne*, X, 2 (1914), 223-27.
Hellmann, Hanna: "Kleists Prinz von Homburg und Shakespeares Mass für Mass," *Germanisch-Romanische Monatsschrift*, XI (1923), 288-296.
Herrmann, Helene: "Studien zu Heinrich von Kleist, II. Gedanken zum Prinzen von Homburg," *Zeitschrift für Ästhetik und Allgemeine Kunstwissenschaft*, XVIII (1924), 287-304.
Howard, W. G.: "A Representative Man," *Publications of the Modern Language Association*, XXXVII (1922), pp. lxi-lxxxvi.
Ibershoff, C.H.: "A Note on Kleist's Prinz von Homburg," *Journal of English and Germanic Philology*, XXI (1922), 670-74.
Jungfer, J.: *Der Prinz von Homburg nach archivalischen und anderen Quellen*. Berlin. 1890.
Kümmel, Prof. Dr.: "Aus deutschen Schuldramen," *Zeitschrift für den deutschen Unterricht*, XXVI (1912), 326-32.
Lüdemann, Dr.: "Der Kurfürst in Kleists Prinz Friedrich von Homburg," *Zeitschrift für den deutschen Unterricht*, XXIII (1909), 319-23.
Luther, Bernhard: "Heinrich von Kleists Patriotismus und Staatsidee," *Neue Jahrbücher für das klassische Altertum Geschichte und deutsche Literatur und für Pädagogik*, XXXVII (1916), 518-38.
———: "Kleists Prinz von Homburg und Adam Müllers Elemente der Staatskunst," *Zeitschrift für den deutschen Unterricht*, XXX (1916), 171-83.

Niejahr, Johannes: "Heinrich von Kleists Prinz von Homburg und Hermannsschlacht," *Vierteljahrsschrift für Literaturgeschichte*, VI (1893), 409-29.

———: "Ein Livianisches Motiv in Kleists Prinz von Homburg," *Euphorion*, IV (1897), 61-66.

Pniower, Otto: *Dichtungen und Dichter*, pp. 215-37. See General Bibliography.

Rötteken, Hubert: "Bemerkungen zum Prinzen von Homburg," *Zeitschrift für den deutschen Unterricht*, IV (1890), 441-50.

Schöntag, F.: "Die Tat des Prinzen von Homburg, ihre Beurteilung durch den Kurfürsten und die aus der Dichtung sich ergebende Lösung der grundsätzlichen Frage," *Zeitschrift für den deutschen Unterricht*, XII (1898), 567-89.

Schultheiss, Hermann: "Heinrich von Kleist als patriotischer Dichter," *Zeitschrift für den deutschen Unterricht*, XXIV (1910), 790-806.

Schulze, Berthold: "Der Kurfürst in Kleists Prinzen von Homburg," *Zeitschrift für den deutschen Unterricht*, XIV (1900), 448-60.

Schultze-Jahde, Karl: "Zur Interpretation von Kleists Schauspiel Prinz Friedrich von Homburg," *Jahrbuch der Kleist-Gesellschaft für 1927 u. 1928*, pp. 105-48.

Schwiefert, Fritz: "Prinz Friedrich von Homburg," *Die Schaubühne*, X, 2 (1914), 178-82.

Seiler, Friedrich: *Die Behandlung des sittlichen Problems in Schillers Kampf mit dem Drachen, der Erzählung bei Livius VIII, 7, Kleists Prinz von Homburg und Sophokles' Antigone*. Eisenberg. 1890.

Sprengel, Johann Georg: "Das Staatsbewusstsein in der deutschen Dichtung seit Heinrich von Kleist," *Zeitschrift für den deutschen Unterricht*, 1918. 12. Ergänzungsheft. pp. 11-26.

Unruh, Ferdinand: "Die Umstimmung des Kurfürsten in Heinrich von Kleists Schauspiel Der Prinz von Homburg," *Zeitschrift für den deutschen Unterricht*, X (1896), 813-23.

Varrentrapp, Konrad: "Der Prinz von Homburg in Geschichte und Dichtung," *Preussische Jahrbücher*, XLV (1880), 335-58.

Wagner, Kurt: "Die Umstimmung des Kurfürsten in Kleists Prinzen von Homburg," *Zeitschrift für den deutschen Unterricht*, XXVI (1912), 108-12.

Wendriner, Lothar: "Zum Verständnis von Kleists Drama Prinz Friedrich von Homburg," *Neue Jahrbücher für das klassische Altertum, Geschichte und deutsche Literatur und für Pädagogik*, XXXIII (1914), 570-80.

Wukadinovic, Spiridon: *Kleist-Studien*, pp. 173-92. See General Bibliography.

Addendum

In an article entitled "Unbekannte Erst- und Frühaufführungen Kleistscher Dramen," *Jahrbuch der Kleist-Gesellschaft 1929 und 1930*, p. 14, Robert Baravalle calls attention to a presentation of *Die Familie Schroffenstein* at Graz on January 9, 1804. The article appeared too late to permit of changes in this volume. The statement that but two of Kleist's dramas were staged publicly during his lifetime needs to be amended.

September 30, 1931

J. C. B.